JOHN CLIVE
AND
NICOLAS HEAD

ARK

VIKING

ACKNOWLEDGEMENTS

I should like to thank John Downing of the *Daily Express* for his invaluable information and technical advice. Also, Nigel and Valerie Woodford of Richmond Film Services. Nadine Lawrence, who helped me with the translations from the Ship's Log. And finally, my brother Michael, who solved the title problem.

JC

VIKING

Penguin Books Ltd, Harmondsworth, Middlesex, England
Viking Penguin Inc., 40 West 23rd Street, New York, New York 10010, U.S.A.
Penguin Books Australia Ltd, Ringwood, Victoria, Australia
Penguin Books Canada Ltd, 2801 John Street, Markham, Ontario, Canada L3R 1B4
Penguin Books (N.Z.) Ltd, 182–190 Wairau Road, Auckland 10, New Zealand

First published 1985

Typeset in VIP Palatino

Typeset, printed and bound in Great Britain by
Hazell Watson & Viney Limited,
Member of the BPCC Group,
Aylesbury, Bucks

British Library Cataloguing in Publication Data

Clive, John, 1938-
   Ark.
   1. Beirut (Lebanon)—History   2. Lebanon
   —History—Civil War, 1975- —Personal
   narratives
   I. Title   II. Head, Nicolas
   956.92   DS89.B4
   ISBN 0-670-80399-5

PROLOGUE

The old man walked slowly. He was bent almost double. The gradient in the tunnel was steep and the bucket of water he carried heavy. He transferred it with some effort to his other hand to give his aching arm relief. The air was thick and foul, though Samra hardly noticed it any more. It just slowed him down, making him breathe more quickly. His body had adjusted.

The tunnel was poorly lit – bare electric light bulbs were scattered haphazardly along its length. Some had worn out and not been replaced, deepening the gloom so that it was almost impossible to see.

Not that Samra needed the light. He had trudged this way a thousand times before and knew exactly where he was by the feel of the surface through the wornout shoes on his feet.

Now he could see the guard at the end of the tunnel, a vague, shadowy figure, outlined by the faint light behind him. His olive-green combat uniform was invisible down here, but the sub-machine-gun he held loosely in his hands was real enough. Samra stopped beside him and held out his bucket of water for inspection. The guard examined it briefly, then waved him forward into the huge, cavernous area that had been his prison for six years.

Condensation dripped from the slimy walls and the air was fetid with the body smells and urine of the 300 men locked within its dungeon-like interior. Most lay stretched out on cots that lined the walls, too weak to move. Some sat mutely, staring into space. Cut off from the sun, living perpetually in darkness or artificial light, their minds had slowly withdrawn, blanked out the horror to which their bodies were being subjected.

Samra doled out the water into metal cups, fixed by long chains to the beds. Some seized it avidly, drinking quickly; others paid him little heed. He paused by one cot. He could see the tube leading from the syringe inserted into the man's arm. It led up from the bed, over a stand and dripped his life blood away into a plasma bottle.

The man gradually became aware of Samra's presence near the foot of his bed. He turned his head, a weak flash of recognition in his eyes. He raised his free hand to his lips to indicate his need for water. Samra glanced back to where the guard was standing close to the tunnel entrance. He was not watching.

Samra moved in closer to the side of the bed and sat down, leaning over to dip the metal cup into the bucket. He lifted it up, full, and put his hand beneath the man's head to raise it. He stopped; the eyes were still open, but already glazing. Samra glanced quickly up to the blood bottle. The tube no longer dripped, the heart no longer beat. His friend was dead.

Samra turned and looked down at his face. It shone sallowly, sweat still gleaming on the pale, drained features. He felt a surge of pain and anger; it surprised him – he thought that all emotions had long since been squeezed away. He threw the metal cup on to the stone floor. It bounced several times before being jerked to a halt by the chain. The sound echoed hollowly up to the high, impenetrable ceiling above.

Samra gently pulled the needle from the dead man's arm; blood seeped from it. Disgusted, he flung it away and the blood splattered the floor. He fell to his knees beside the bed, clasping his hands tightly together, closing his eyes, rocking himself from side to side, trying to find an escape from the nightmare around him. The guard strode from his position and lifted Samra's wasted body with brutal ease, one hand grabbing the front of his threadbare jacket. He raised the weapon in his other hand, threatening to club him with it. Samra held up his arms desperately to ward off the blow. 'It's no good – he's dead. You will get no more blood from him . . .'

The guard paused, looking down at the man on the bed. He

released his hold on Samra and leaned over the body. The eyes stared fixedly up through him, as though seeing into his soul. The guard shivered in spite of the sticky, fetid heat, threw the filthy blanket over the dead man's face and turned away, back to his place by the tunnel.

Samra stood for a moment, his head bowed, utterly weak and empty. He slumped down on to the side of the bed and slowly drew back the blanket. He looked at his friend's dead face and tried to identify the strange feeling within him; then he knew . . . it was envy. He put the palm of his hand over the eyes and drew them shut. 'You are free now,' he whispered . . . 'you are free.'

A tear slid down his parchment face, mingling with his sweat . . . Samra was thirty-eight years old.

CHAPTER

ONE

The men wore olive-green bush jackets and shorts. One, somewhat incongruously, carried a briefcase. They paused at the checkpoint and spoke quietly to the official. He raised the weighted pole and they passed through and on down the featureless road towards the quay.

They moved slowly. The heat haze shimmered off the white, dusty concrete. On either side stretched barren ground strewn with debris from the recently completed marina building that stood, raw and squat, brooding quietly by itself, waiting for occupants to give it life.

The hard, bumpy road turned sharply right. They rounded the empty building and emerged on to the quayside. Some of the yachts had been hoisted out of the water and on to the dock to await repairs. Shorn of their sails and stripped of their paint, only the graceful lines of their hulls remained to indicate their beauty. The three men passed by, sweating in the heat, their eyes flicking from side to side, looking for something.

A dog watched their approach balefully. As they came closer his lips rolled back into a snarl, his coat ruffled up in anger. He leapt from behind an upturned box as they drew level, hackles up, barking furiously. The men stopped momentarily, then the long lead snapped taut, holding the animal at bay. They continued without comment. The dog, once they had passed, slunk back to his place behind the box and settled down, duty done, waiting for someone else to surprise.

The concrete road pointed like an ugly grey finger out into the blue waters of the marina. Schooners, yachts, motor vessels slumbered on either side, waiting for their owners to emerge and face the heat of a Cyprus morning. It was quiet, even peaceful – the only sounds were the water slapping against the quay and the hulls and the occasional creak of moorings as they strained against moving water.

The men moved watchfully along the quay, walking further out into the marina. A cockroach, dazed by the sun, did not hear their approach until it was too late and was halted in mid dash as one of the men trod on it deliberately. Rousseau abhorred beetles and killed them without compunction.

A faint breeze ruffled the surface of the marina, carrying with it the voice of a child imitating a machine-gun. The men paused, looking ahead to where the boy was playing. The vessel was larger than most in the marina. Her long wooden hull was at anchor, beam on to the quay. She was narrow, painted all white, and shone brightly in the sunlight. Only the burnished brass fittings and brown teak deck offset the single colour. The name, painted in blue, that decorated the side of the superstructure was *Sea Victory*. The three men had found what they were looking for. They glanced quickly at each other and moved towards the vessel.

Charlie saw them first. He was playing on the upper deck behind his father, who was using a hose and a long-handled brush to swab down the deck. The boy glanced quickly at his father's back, then raced as fast as he could to the bridge. He crouched down behind the superstructure so that he could not be seen from the quay below and waited excitedly.

The men were looking up at his father, who was still immersed in his work. Then, as they drew level, Charlie leapt up and levelled his toy machine-gun and pretended to fire at them, the yammering noise he made echoing loudly off the water.

Just for an instant one of them crouched, wheeling to face the sound. Then he smiled and waved to the boy, relaxing. 'You almost got me that time.'

Charlie laughed delightedly and rushed back to his father waving the gun. 'I got them,' he shouted. 'I got them.'

Tom Forester turned, leant on the brush and wiped the sweat from his face with the back of his hand. 'Got who?' he said.

Charlie pointed over the side at the quay. 'Three men, down there.'

Forester sighed, then shook his head exasperatedly and crossed to the rail, leaning on it, looking down at the small group. They had stopped and were staring up at him. Rousseau raised an arm to shield his eyes from the glare of the sun, which was directly behind the man and the boy. Charlie joined his father and leant on the rail beside him, adopting the same pose.

Forester noted the olive-green bush jackets. They were new, and none of the men had been on the island long enough to have acquired a tan. But there was a professional look about them, as though they were part of a team, used to working with each other.

'I'm looking for the owner of this vessel.'

The English was good, but the accent was unmistakably French. Forester appraised them quietly. They did not look like tourists – there was the briefcase – yet they were not business-men either.

'I'm the owner. What do you want?'

The man who had spoken to him glanced briefly at his companions and something was said that Forester could not hear, then he turned back to the boat again. 'Is it possible to come aboard? There's something we'd like to discuss.'

Forester glanced at the unfinished deck behind him, still awash with water, but that could wait. 'Sure, come aboard. Up that gangplank there.' He pointed. 'I'll join you in the stern.'

He moved away from the rail and squatted down, turning off the hose. Charlie gazed down at it enviously. 'Can I do it, Daddy?'

Forester glanced up at his four-year-old. He could see the mischief dancing in his eyes. 'No, it's a tricky business, swab-bing decks, and you'll have enough of that before you're much older.'

The disappointment spread immediately across the boy's face. Forester stood up and took his hand. 'You can come down with me and meet these men – I think they come from France.'

The disappointment disappeared instantly. 'Is that far?'

'Oh yes, that's a long, long way.' Forester wiped his wet hand

11

on his trousers and started to clamber down the companionway. 'Come on, let's find out.'

Charlie followed him enthusiastically.

As Forester reached the bottom step he turned and faced the men who were standing in the stern. Rousseau indicated his two companions. 'This is Armand.'

The smaller man smiled nervously. He was dark, Latin and sweating slightly. 'Bonjour.'

'And this is Jack Kemp.'

Kemp was tall, with lank brown hair hanging down over his forehead. 'Hello,' he said briefly and left it at that. The accent was North American. Later, Forester would discover he was Canadian. There was something about Kemp's eyes that was vaguely disconcerting. They were fathomless, as though he were looking past him.

Forester ruffled his son's hair. 'I'm Tom Forester, and this is Charlie.'

Philippe Rousseau indicated the boy. 'He is your son?'

Charlie nestled into his father's side, holding on to one of his legs. He gazed up at the Frenchman. 'You're dead. I shot you with my gun.' He waved his toy weapon to confirm his claim.

Rousseau stared seriously at the small boy. 'Yes, you did, and it hurt a lot. We must play again sometime, when I know where you are hiding.'

Water suddenly dripped down from the deck above and splashed on to his head. Rousseau jumped. Charlie laughed uproariously, pointing at the offending drip. Forester tried not to smile. 'I'm sorry, it's leaked through. I was swabbing the deck above.'

Rousseau, having recovered from the surprise, looked at the boy and rubbed the water vigorously into his hair. 'It's good. I needed to cool down after that walk.'

Charlie tugged at his father's arm. 'Can I do it, Daddy . . . please!'

Forester shook his head. 'No, we have to talk now, you go and play.'

Charlie grimaced, then thought of something. 'I'll go and keep a look-out for any more men.' He ran from the stern, through the saloon and disappeared forward.

Armand watched him go with obvious relief. 'Is there some-where we can go?'

Forester glanced at him, slightly irritated by his manner. 'Through here.' He gestured towards the saloon. There was a small bar at the end; Forester went behind it and busied himself preparing a drink. The two Frenchmen sat on stools facing him, while Kemp paced up and down, checking the view through the saloon windows.

'Is there anything you'd like . . . a beer, brandy sour?'

Rousseau eyed the drink Forester was making. 'Is that a brandy sour?' Forester nodded. 'Then I'll have the same.'

Forester glanced at Armand enquiringly. The Frenchman shook his head impatiently. 'No, not for me.' He sat uneasily on the bar stool.

There was a tension about him that worried Forester. He topped up both glasses with ice and an extra one for Kemp, then handed one to Rousseau. 'Cheers . . .'

The Frenchman raised his glass and repeated the toast, taking a long drink. He gazed at what was left appreciatively. 'This is good . . .'

Forester nodded. 'It takes the edge off the thirst.'

Armand could take the socializing no more. He stood up suddenly and walked across to one of the saloon windows. He gazed moodily out to the entrance of the marina and across the bay beyond.

Kemp stared at him for a moment, then turned to the Englishman. 'This vessel . . . would you be prepared to consider a charter?' He waited for a response.

Forester took another swallow from his glass. 'I might . . . we are a charter yacht. What have you got in mind?'

Rousseau was watching him carefully. 'We've got to get into Beirut – the airport has closed down. Would you be willing to risk it?'

Forester took a half-smoked cigar from his shirt pocket and stuck it in his mouth. He lit it with a match and drew in some smoke. 'How urgently?'

'Tonight.'

If Forester was surprised he didn't show it. He puffed gently on his cigar.

Rousseau sipped his drink. 'There are four of us altogether.'

Kemp leaned on the bar, staring hard at Forester. 'We need an answer, we've gotta be there by tomorrow.'

Forester studied them through the smokescreen he had created. 'Why?'

Rousseau smiled. 'We're a television news crew. We work for an independent news agency in Paris, and the news is in Beirut this week.'

This time Forester was surprised. 'Television! . . .'

'That's right. Jack's on camera, Armand sound, and I present it.'

'And the other person?'

'A photographer. She works for a number of newspapers – *France-Soir*, *Paris Match*, that sort of thing.'

Forester tried not to show his relief. 'Good, I thought perhaps you were trying to smuggle in arms.'

Rousseau finished his drink. 'Some people think we are more dangerous than bullets.' He looked at his empty glass. 'Can I have another?'

Forester picked up the large flagon from the freezer and poured out some more. 'I think I'd sooner face a camera than a loaded rifle.'

Armand turned sharply from the window. 'Will you or won't you take us to Beirut?' he demanded.

Forester stared at him contemplatively. The Frenchman was pale and sweating, the tension all too apparent. And now he knew why: Armand was frightened. He replaced the flagon in the ice box, then faced him. 'I might,' he said quietly. 'Then again, I might not.' He eyed Armand through another cloud of cigar smoke.

Rousseau spoke quickly, fearing an explosion from his jumpy partner. 'What do you mean?'

Forester stuck the cigar back in his mouth. 'Lebanon's a mess . . . Beirut's even worse. The Israelis have it locked in by sea as well as land . . . I could lose the yacht, everything.'

Armand turned away in disgust. Kemp sat down on one of the stools, ignoring him. 'Don't take too much notice, Captain. Guns scare the hell out of him – until he turns on his tape recorder. Then he's the best sound man in the business.'

14

Armand did not respond. He continued to sulk, his back to them.

It was Rousseau's turn: 'You are the only vessel big enough to make this trip.'

It wasn't true. Plenty of the smaller craft could have made it, but Forester didn't enlighten him.

'According to my information this boat —'

'Yacht,' Forester interrupted laconically.

Rousseau paused, then continued, 'This *yacht* has been on the slip at Haifa and the Israelis are well aware of its presence, and who owns it. They're not going to mistake you for a gun-runner.'

That was true – he had kept his nose clean. This part of the Middle East was too dangerous to take chances with. Please one side and you offend the other. Retribution could be swift and deadly, and he wasn't on his own any more – there was Charlie and Annabel. He smiled thinly. 'My, you have been doing your homework.'

Rousseau nodded. 'That's right, I have.' He stared hard at the Englishman. 'So . . . while there is a risk, I believe it's acceptable.' He glanced at Kemp. 'So do the others. You have a better chance of getting into Beirut than anybody else. Whatever your normal fee is, we'll double it.'

Armand turned round to watch him apprehensively, waiting for the decision.

Forester chewed thoughtfully on the cigar, making a few quick calculations. To cover expenses and make a reasonable profit, say about £5,000. Doubling it made it attractive, but there was more to be squeezed from this. They were all just a mite too anxious. Maybe they had tried some of the other boats in the marina and failed. He shook his head doubtfully. 'It's not on. This yacht and the chartering I do round the island in the summer is worth a total of more than a couple of hundred thousand. Why should I risk it all for ten thousand pounds? I'd be taking you into a war zone – I'd never be able to get insurance.' He stubbed out his cigar. 'I'm sorry, gentlemen, you'll have to find someone else.'

Armand was still sweating. He spoke hesitantly. 'There is no one else.'

Forester grinned. 'I know.'

Kemp studied him quietly for a moment, then rose from the bar stool. 'What do you want, Forester – what's your price?'

This was the moment he had been waiting for. Now he knew exactly how far he could pitch it. But this wasn't the time to rush his fences. He let them sweat some more while he slowly refilled his glass from the flagon. Then he looked up. 'Make it fifteen thousand and I'll see if I can raise a volunteer crew.'

Armand glared indignantly at Rousseau. The other Frenchman raised his hand to silence the protest. 'If we sail tonight . . . And if you get us into Beirut, it's a deal.'

Forester picked up his glass. 'Not directly into Beirut – it's not possible. But a few miles up the coast – a place called Jounieh. It's a small holiday resort and a marina. I think we can get in there.'

Kemp picked up his glass for the first time. 'I'll drink to that.'

Rousseau smiled. 'To Jounieh?'

Forester raised his. 'And back.'

Charlie leapt into the saloon and fired his machine-gun at Rousseau. 'Bang, bang, bang,' he yelled, 'you're dead. I've killed you.'

Rousseau didn't move.

Forester glanced at his watch. Annabel would be back soon, but there might still be time. He clambered down the companionway, then through the cabins into the stern. He heard a metal object clatter against the casing as it was dropped. The curse that followed was quiet, controlled. Then silence as Rhys, his engineer, searched among the labyrinth of pipes and equipment to find the offending object. Forester wondered if he got any real relief – he knew what his own reaction would have been.

He peered down through the hatch into the gloom of the engine room. The heat was stifling. It rose in waves, mixed sickeningly with the smell of diesel oil. There was no ventilation. He called down loudly. He didn't want to descend into that steaming interior. Curiously, it never seemed to affect Rhys. If anything, the New Zealander seemed to enjoy the discomfort.

Forester heard footsteps on the metal deck below, then Rhys's face appeared in the hatch. He wiped the sweat from his eyes –

spreading more oil over his face – and grinned up at Forester, teeth gleaming from his blackened face. 'What is it?'

'Could you come up? I want to talk to you.'

'Sure.'

He climbed the short flight of steps as Forester started back the way he had come. Forester called back over his shoulder, 'Do you want to come into the saloon?'

'Why not? I could use a drink.'

After Rhys had settled down with a glass in his hand, Forester put it to him. He held back nothing – without the New Zealander there would be no charter. Rhys listened quietly, occasionally wiping his hard, rough hands on an oily rag, frowning with concentration but making no comment.

Forester stopped. 'Well, what do you think?'

Rhys stared at the deck, thinking about the options. 'It's bad – the Israelis will blockade all the ports. They'll be waiting for the PLO to try and break out.'

'We won't be carrying anybody out; we just take the television crew in.'

'How can you be sure of that? We don't know what we're going to find once we get in there. They might try to take this over. She's a good vessel, and it wouldn't be the first time.'

Forester knew he was right – but for the moment all he wanted was to get there. 'That's the risk we take. I think we can handle it. The Israelis know us. All we carry are a few civilians – nothing else.'

Rhys nodded. 'That's true. There's a chance all right. Pity about Jim – we could have used him on a trip like this.' Unwittingly, Rhys showed he was already planning ahead for the voyage – he had accepted it. There was an instinctive commitment.

'That was my fault,' Forester said. 'Didn't think we'd need him for a couple of months.'

Rhys remembered something. 'There's Henshaw.'

Forester thought about him. The Australian had a boat in the marina and a finger in a lot of pies. He was an oddball. He knew a lot of people, but few knew much about him. Still, he was a good seaman. 'OK, talk to Henshaw. That makes three of us. Think we can handle it?'

Rhys picked up his drink and tossed it back in one gulp. 'Sure, why not? Better than steaming round this island four days a week, getting nowhere.'

Forester smiled, picking up his glass. 'I'll drink to that.'

He heard the Morgan come gunning down the quay – then Charlie's excited voice calling from the upper deck. Annabel was back.

Forester rose from behind the bar. 'OK, that's settled. You'd better go below while I have a word with you-know-who.'

Rhys stood up quickly, edging his way out of the saloon. 'Right, I'll leave that to you, boss.'

Forester nodded wryly. The only time the New Zealander called him boss was when he knew there was trouble about. And Annabel was going to be trouble. 'You do that,' he said.

Rhys scuttled down below. The thought of breaking an Israeli blockade or risking a PLO take-over did not alarm him; Annabel did. He was happy to dump the problem and tend to his engines. Down there at least he wouldn't be able to hear it.

Forester fortified himself with another drink and waited. He heard her climbing up the gangplank – then calling out in her usual way, 'Hello-o-o, I'm back.'

'In here,' he said.

She came into the saloon in a rush, dropping a mass of shopping on one of the bench seats. Forester eyed her quietly, trying to gauge her mood. Annabel was a tall, blonde, long-legged girl who had had a pretty potent effect on the local male Cypriot population – especially the Customs and Excise. She seemed to take an almost malicious delight in charming them out of their officious attitudes, and twisting them round her little finger. This made her extremely useful to have around. And she still surprised him, which delighted him. However, the price-tag was a mind and a spirit of her own, and he knew his task was not going to be easy.

She brushed back her hair from her forehead. 'Oh God, it's so *hot*.' She pointed at the glass in his hand. 'Give me one of those quick, before I die of thirst.'

He poured out another one and handed it to her. 'What did you get?'

She glanced quickly at him. Tom didn't usually concern

himself with her shopping. 'Oh, food mostly – but I did manage to pick up a nice one-piece bathing costume that was on offer in a sale.'

Tom smiled. 'Where is it?'

Once again she looked at him, puzzled by his interest. 'Do you really want to see it?'

'Sure,' he said benignly.

Pleased by his curiosity, she plunged into one of the plastic bags, fished around and pulled out a pink bathing costume. She held it up against her body. 'What do you think?'

He sipped reflectively at his drink. 'I like it. You'll look great in it, though I'd sooner see you take it off.' He grinned lasciviously.

She waved it at him in mock disgust. 'Shut up. Charlie might hear you.' She came and sat on a stool opposite him, swallowing some of the drink thirstily. 'Mmmm, that's good.'

A long blonde hair was sticking to her face. He leaned over across the bar and pushed it to one side. She looked deep into his eyes. They were troubled. He turned away, the impassive mask slipping back over his face. 'What's wrong?' she asked. She had lived with him long enough to know that she would have to trigger whatever it was.

He stared out of the window, his back to her. 'I've been offered a job.'

She shrugged her shoulders. 'So?'

'It's a long-haul, deep-sea charter.' He turned and faced her. 'Into Lebanon . . .'

She stared at him incredulously. 'Lebanon!'

'That's right.'

She shook her head disbelievingly. 'Have you heard the news lately?'

He felt a little knot of anger inside him, but he kept his voice level. 'Yes – I know what the problems are. But the people who want me to take them in are all in the media. Newspapers, television . . . nothing stupid, all strictly above board.'

She stood up abruptly. 'What difference does that make? A bullet doesn't ask what profession you're in.'

He knew now there was no way of avoiding it – not that there'd ever been much chance with Annabel. 'It's a legitimate charter into Jounieh. We've been there before. If the Israeli gunboats stop us, they know the yacht, they know me. And if they come aboard they'll know who we're carrying. They don't want to risk a lot of bad publicity by stopping a neutral vessel going about its business.'

Annabel paced up and down in front of the bar, then stopped in front of him. 'So it's all right for me to come.'

Forester took a deep breath; she had surprised him again. 'No, it's not. You'll have to stay here and look after Charlie.'

She threw back her head and laughed. 'That's what you think! Ivy can look after him while we're away. I'm coming with you.'

He stared at her unblinkingly. Although she had seen that look before, it still sent icy shivers down her spine. His eyes were basilisk, predatory. 'No,' he said quietly, 'you're not. It could be dangerous – I can't risk it, not the both of us.'

She bit her lip, determined not to cry. 'But it's all right for you to risk your life. What about me, what about Charlie, or doesn't that matter to you?'

He couldn't stand it when she cried. He steeled himself not to respond. The least bit of compassion in his voice now and he knew the tears would come. He came round from behind the bar and placed his hands on her shoulders. 'Listen. They are offering me fifteen thousand pounds for this one trip. I just go in and come out. With that kind of money we can forget about this season. We can get *Sea Victory* across to the West Indies before the winter comes. God knows we've talked about it a million times, but it's never been possible before; now it is. You see that, don't you?' He held her close, pressing his body into hers.

It made sense. At least, as far as he was concerned – she could see that. And she could also feel the excitement in him, an almost animal-like quiver, his body tense against hers as if waiting to spring. It had always been a part of his make-up, the dangerous element that had drawn her in the first place. She knew he wanted this challenge, and she had never tried to stifle it before – it satisfied something in her, too.

But now there was Charlie – they were not on their own any more. Her stomach turned over at the thought of leaving him. He was only four, a miniature replica of Tom, and she loved them both dearly. But she knew she was going to have to make a choice.

She pushed him away, putting some distance between them. She stared up into his eyes. 'All right – I know what this means to you. As long as it's only for this one trip. But there's a condition: I come too.'

He started to protest. She cut him off. 'No. I've never been more certain of anything in my life. You will need me on this trip. If they're paying that kind of money, someone's got to look after them, feed them. You and Rhys will have your hands full taking *Sea Victory* through that blockade, watching the radar scanner. You'll have no time for domestic chores. Ivy will look after Charlie – she's good with him, it's no problem.' She paused, and swallowed the lump in her throat. 'Besides, if you are out there taking risks, I want to be there too . . .' She gripped his arms tightly. 'I couldn't stand the waiting, Tom.'

She stood before him so straight, her shoulders square, like a soldier's, yet blinking back the tears. He was sunk, and he knew it. He took her in his arms and stroked her hair, talking softly. 'All right, twit. If you're determined to finish up as a cabin steward, who am I to stop you?'

Annabel held on to him, listening to him, trying to draw on the strength she felt in his body. She was safe with him and she blanked out little Charlie. She couldn't think about her son at this moment.

CHAPTER

TWO

André Khalil parked the Citroën in the underground car park close to his apartment block. It would be safe from shell or bomb blast there. He had already made sure the tank was full and he had a couple of spare cans in case they should prove necessary. He walked quickly up the steps and approached the revolving door that led into the main hall. As the doors began to swing he saw the PLO soldier standing by the entrance to the lift. He didn't pause; the soldier was watching him and it might arouse suspicion. Tension was high in Beirut and fingers on triggers were light – it did not take much to become a target, and Khalil intended to survive.

He walked unhurriedly towards the lift. Mr Frangieh, the manager of the luxury block, was standing close to the hall porter's desk. He was sweating, and not just with the heat. André nodded affably to him and moved to press the button for the lift. The soldier barred his progress, holding up his sub-machine-gun across André's body. There was no mistaking his purpose and Khalil stepped back, glancing towards the manager. The soldier jabbed him with the weapon. 'Who are you?' he demanded.

Khalil betrayed none of the hot surging fear he felt inside. 'I live here.'

The soldier studied him expressionlessly. 'What floor?'

Khalil looked around at the manager, who hadn't moved. The soldier jabbed him again, harder. 'Tell me.'

'Seventeenth,' he blurted out, rubbing his ribs where the barrel had struck him. 'Apartment 1712.'

The soldier suddenly grabbed him by the arm and shoved him face first against the wall, kicking his legs apart and running his hands over his clothing.

Khalil didn't protest – he was too frightened. He didn't know what he'd said to provoke the soldier – it had to be something to do with his apartment. He suddenly felt quite sick. His sister Leila was there. Was she all right? What had happened?

The soldier found nothing. He turned to the manager and gestured him to come over. Mr Frangieh approached the soldier apprehensively, trying not to look at Khalil.

'This man, he lives here?'

The manager chewed his lip nervously. 'That's right,' he said reluctantly. 'He shares an apartment on the seventeenth floor.'

'Who with?'

The manager kept his eyes averted from Khalil to show that he was not involved with him in any way. 'His sister,' he answered.

The revolving door began to spin sharply and three more soldiers came into the lobby, each of them carrying parts of a dismembered weapon. The soldier who was questioning the manager immediately lost interest and moved towards them. Khalil stepped into the open door of the lift and pressed the button for the seventeenth floor. The soldier turned and saw the door closing. He leapt across and jammed the barrel of the sub-machine-gun between the doors before they slammed shut.

Khalil froze. The barrel pointed directly at his chest. The doors slid open again automatically and the soldier eyed him sardonically, but said nothing. He held the doors open until the other three had carried the heavy parts of the weapon into the lift, then he jerked his thumb at Mr Frangieh who obsequiously came inside and stood by the control panel.

By now the lift was jammed tight with men and equipment. Khalil could see that the weapon was some kind of rocket-launcher, but he had no knowledge of armaments. The manager's hand hovered over the floor indicator buttons and he looked at the soldier questioningly, waiting for his instructions. The soldier glanced at Khalil, than jammed the barrel of his gun on to the button indicating the seventeenth floor.

The doors slid shut and the lift began to ascend. The first

23

soldier continued to stare at Khalil, not taking his eyes off him once in the long, sweaty ride up to the seventeenth floor.

Khalil was fearful for his sister, his head buzzing with terrifying possibilities. The PLO soldier had reacted dangerously when he had told him the floor number, but he hadn't known who occupied 1712 . . . The lift continued upwards, the light flicking through each floor as they ascended swiftly. Khalil could smell the manager's fear – it was distinct and sour.

At last the doors slid open and the militiamen stepped out on to the landing, carrying the weapon. Khalil followed, but the manager stayed poised over the control panel waiting to go back down. The first soldier grabbed his arm and hauled him out, pointing to the room at the end of the passage. 'Open it.'

Mr Frangieh shakily led the way towards the apartment and Khalil stood still, waiting to see what he had to do. Halfway down the passage the soldier turned and waved his gun, indicating to Khalil that he could proceed to his apartment.

Relieved, Khalil acknowledged the gesture and walked in the opposite direction to 1712. He inserted the key in the lock, turned it and opened the door. He glanced down the passage. The soldiers carrying the rocket-launcher were entering the last apartment; the other man was watching him. Khalil pushed his way through the door and shut it quietly behind him. He leaned against it. He could hear the blood pounding in his head. The feeling of relief was overwhelming.

Leila was moving around in the kitchen preparing a meal. Everything in the apartment seemed normal. The soldiers' suspicions must have been aroused simply because he was going to the same floor as the one they intended to occupy.

Khalil tried to compose himself – there was no point in alarming his sister. He wiped the sweat from his brow and called out, keeping his voice as normal as possible. 'Leila . . . I'm back!'

'In here,' she answered.

He took off his jacket and dropped it on a chair, then walked through into the kitchen. She turned from the cooker and smiled at him, lifting her face for him to kiss her on the cheek. She was slightly flushed from the cooking. Like him, Leila had brown eyes and dark shiny hair which she wore short, brushed back

24

from her forehead. She was three years younger than André and they had lived together much more closely since the death of their parents in the civil war six years earlier.

André kissed her quickly on the cheek and removed his tie. 'That smells good. What is it?'

She watched him walk across the room; intuitively she sensed the tension in him, but put it down to the war and the continued encirclement of the city by the Israelis.

André picked up a newspaper. It was an old one. 'Where's today's?'

Leila checked the meat on the spit. 'In the living room.'

André walked through the archway into the main room and found the paper on an armchair. He picked it up and began to thumb through the pages quickly.

Leila watched him from the kitchen. 'How bad is it, André?'

He looked up, hearing the concern in her voice. 'Oh, it's bad all right. The city is practically dead. I got here in less than fifteen minutes . . . Did you listen to the radio?'

'No, it's too depressing. I switched it off.'

André had found what he was looking for in the shipping columns. Arrivals and departures from the port of Jounieh. He looked up. Leila had asked him a question.

'What?'

'I said, are you going out tonight?'

'No, we must stay here and stick together from now on – I don't want you to go out either.'

Leila didn't answer him. She turned back to the cooker and automatically adjusted the heat under the vegetables.

They had often discussed the possibility of leaving Beirut. They had connections in France, mainly through the bank, and André knew people in England where he had been educated. André had always insisted that they were perfectly safe provided they took precautions. The bank where he worked had stayed open in spite of the battles raging round the city until three days ago. She wondered what had been said at the meeting today – she knew that several of the French staff had already left before the airport closed. Now there was only the sea.

She heard a faint whistling noise – it sounded like the whistle on a kettle when it boiled. But there was no kettle . . . It grew

25

louder and she turned to look at her brother. He had stood up and was facing her; he could hear it too. It grew in intensity and suddenly André knew what it was.

He screamed at Leila to lie down. She looked at him blankly, unable to hear him and too frightened to move. Then the shell struck the apartment block and the shock wave threw Leila against the wall, then to the floor. Masonry collapsed about her, debris missed her by inches and dust covered her in a fine white powder. She lay still.

At first she could hear nothing, her ears deafened by the concussion. Slowly, sounds began to reach her: water was spilling from the end of a pipe where once the tap had been. Incredibly, the pans still sat on the cooker, though the spit under the grill was not moving.

She blinked, trying to recover her senses, and remembered her brother. She tried to move, but an upturned table lay across her legs. She reached out and pushed it away. It slid harshly on the floor and more dust and debris fell from above. She glanced up. There was a huge hole gaping in the ceiling above her and a man's arm hung limply through it. Blood dripped from the hand, falling beside her. Leila grimaced with fear and disgust and pushed the table clear of her legs. Her clothing was torn by the blast, but she seemed to be unhurt.

She looked to where the archway had been. The whole wall had disappeared and a flashing red light filtered through the pall of dust in the other room. At first she could not identify it, then she realized it was the name of the apartment block that was illuminated at night. Part of the outside wall had disintegrated under the impact of the shell and all that remained was the strobe lighting.

Leila pulled herself groggily to her feet and picked her way through the wreckage of her kitchen. She reached the area where André had been standing and looked around fearfully. The flashing light illuminated the remains of the room intermittently. What little she could see was destroyed, unrecognizable. She tried to call out, but her throat was dry with dust and she choked, coughing to clear it. She tried again. 'André . . . André.'

There was no sound, apart from the constant dribble of

concrete dust through the cracks in the building's structure. In despair Leila called again. She heard something. It was close to the inside wall that backed on to the passage. Leila felt her way across the room, blundering noisily into broken furniture that was strewn haphazardly amongst the wreckage. She reached the wall. At first she could see nothing, then, as the dust slowly settled, she saw a bloody hand emerging from the rubble piled into the corner. The fingers had been partially blown away by the blast and only the stumps remained. She could see the white of the bones.

Leila covered her mouth with her hand to prevent herself from screaming. She stood frozen with fear and horror. Her brother's hand moved and Leila cried out, flinging herself forward on to the rubble, tearing it away from André's body, shouting his name constantly. The sound of her own voice somehow gave her strength.

She cleared the rubble from his face and wiped the dirt and dust from his eyes. He was alive. Leila cried out in relief and clasped him to her, rocking him in her arms like a baby, brushing the dust from him. She felt him move and flung the remainder of the rubble from his body.

As he regained consciousness he felt her hands on him, holding him tightly, protectively. Her voice was close and he reached for her. Then the pain in his hand as it touched her made him cry out in agony.

'Don't move,' she said, 'don't move . . .'

He could hear the desperation in her voice and he lay still trying to focus his eyes on her, but it was dark. He realized the lights must have gone. 'Leila, where are you? Hold my good hand and help me up, we must get out of here.'

Leila grasped it, holding his hand to her face. He could feel the wetness of her tears. 'Don't cry, Leila, we'll be OK.'

He raised himself slowly. His hand hurt agonizingly, but otherwise he seemed to be all right. He could feel her beside him, and he tried to turn and face her, but his legs wouldn't move – they were trapped. 'God, it's so dark, Leila, I can't see you.'

As he spoke the lighting from the sign came on briefly and Leila saw his face clearly for the first time. His eyes were wide open, staring at her. But they didn't see anything, they were dead. He was blind. Leila choked back a scream and it took all of her willpower not to turn away from him, to turn and run.

He sensed her horror immediately. 'What is it? Leila, what's wrong?'

She didn't answer – she knelt, frozen before him. His good hand waved desperately in front of her, trying to find her.

'For Christ's sake, Leila, speak to me. Where are you?'

Leila took a long juddering breath and reached out, grasping him, pulling him to her, holding him gently in her arms, calming his terror. 'I'm here, darling, I'm here.'

CHAPTER

THREE

The man was dressed in a well-cut lightweight suit. He walked casually along the quay, looking from one side to the other, checking the names on the hulls of the vessels. He was in his late twenties, of medium build, with dark hair, cut short, and he moved loosely, hands in pockets, pausing occasionally to admire one of the boats.

He came to *Sea Victory* and gazed up at her name on the superstructure. There was no one on any of the decks. He strolled along the quay to the stern and walked up the sloping gangplank. He paused before stepping down on to the deck and called out, 'Hello. Anyone about?' He waited, but nobody appeared from below and he crossed to the saloon, peering inside. That too was empty, as was the small bar at the end.

He stood, puzzled, for a moment, wondering what to do, then glanced up the companionway that led to the upper deck and the bridge. He climbed up, his white, rubber-soled shoes making no sound on the steps. He lifted his head above the deck and looked around. Still no one. He pulled himself up and moved forward to the door that led into the wheelhouse. It was open and he poked his head around it.

Forester was leaning over the chart table examining the Lebanese coastline through a large magnifying glass. The man tapped on the door and Forester turned quickly. The man grinned, slightly embarrassed. 'Sorry to disturb you.'

The accent was American. Forester stared at him without expression, taking in the suit, the shoes and the tie slightly loosened in the heat.

The man gestured towards the stern. 'I did call out, but nobody answered.' He paused as Forester did not respond, then continued, 'I'm looking for the owner.'

Tom spoke for the first time. 'You've found him. What can I do for you?'

The man put his hand in his inside pocket and pulled out a leather wallet, then selected a card from it and handed it to Forester. 'My name is Kass, David Kass. I heard you might be sailing for the Lebanon.'

Forester examined the card. It was printed on good paper. Kass was a doctor – the address, New York. He glanced at the American. 'Where did you hear that?'

'My hotel, there are some television people staying there.'

Forester weighed this up. He'd informed Rousseau that the trip was definitely on, but he wasn't sure he wanted them to broadcast the fact. The fewer people who knew about this the better. 'What hotel are you staying at?'

Kass smiled at Forester's caution. 'The Four Lanterns on the seafront.'

Forester picked up the chart he had been studying and rolled it up. 'And suppose I was?' The stiff paper rustled loudly in the confines of the wheelhouse.

Kass gazed levelly at Forester. 'I want to go.'

There was an intensity about his reply that Forester found interesting. In spite of his directness, there was an uncertainty about the American, something hidden just beneath the surface. He slipped the chart into its cardboard tube and placed it on the rack above the table. 'Look, I'll be absolutely straight with you.' He turned and faced him. 'If I go to the Lebanon it will be no pleasure cruise – not a normal charter. There's a full-scale war going on and I can't afford to risk passengers who might just be on a sightseeing trip. Why do you want to go, Mr Kass?'

The American eyed him steadily, trying to decide how best to explain. He'd thought about this on the long hot walk down to the quay – he still didn't know. 'It's difficult – I don't know quite how to put it.'

Forester waited unhelpfully for him to continue and Kass gestured irritably. 'Look, I've got some time, a month from my practice in New York. As you can see, I'm a doctor. I thought . . .'

He paused, aware of the naive implications of what he was trying to say. 'Jesus, I know it sounds corny, but you said it yourself. There's a war going on and I know how stretched the medical services are in Beirut . . .' He shrugged his shoulders. 'I thought they might be able to use some help.'

Forester stared at him for a moment. There was no doubting his sincerity. He turned away and gazed out of the broad windows across the bay. The sun sparkled off the blue sea, a yacht beat lazily before the offshore breeze and it was hard to believe that there was a war going on less than 150 miles away. But he'd seen the grim pictures of the wounded on television, just as the doctor had. The bombing and shelling was so intense it was difficult to know how the civilians could survive – they would certainly need help, and there was no guarantee that *Sea Victory* would not come under fire. It might be extremely useful to have a doctor on board. He faced the American. 'Are you sure about this?'

Kass smiled deprecatingly and shook his head. 'No . . . I don't really know why I'm standing here.'

Forester warmed to him. 'I'm beginning to feel the same way myself.'

There was a moment of silence between them, a sense of understanding. They grinned at each other foolishly.

Kass held up his hands. 'OK, so what happens now?'

'If we go, it'll be tonight. I'll let you know in good time, then you'll have to decide.'

Kass nodded. 'Right.' He turned and crossed to the door, pausing there to face Forester. 'Thanks, Captain.'

The Englishman waved a dismissive hand. 'My name's Forester, Tom Forester. Only the crew call me Captain, and not always that, but I'll definitely call you Doctor . . . I've got this problem with my back.' He rubbed it, affecting a pain.

Kass smiled. 'I'll see you.'

'Maybe.'

The American stood in the doorway. 'You can bet on it. Besides,' he added, 'I've got to fix that back.' He grinned and left.

Forester stared at the empty door for a moment, his face blank, wondering if he had done the right thing. He stepped over to the door and watched Kass walking briskly up the quay, back to the checkpoint. Kass was probably a Jew. It was the Israelis who were encircling Beirut. The irony did not escape him.

Forester was satisfied. The meeting with Gemino had gone well. The Italian ran the best shipping agency in Cyprus, and he had looked after *Sea Victory* since their arrival three years before. He could trust Tony Gemino. He believed him when he said that he had made no request for war insurance.

The sun beat back off the concrete road that led to the quay. It didn't bother Forester – he was used to it. But war insurance did. It bothered him quite a lot.

Where had it come from? Who had arranged it if not his shipping agent? And why? That's what really bugged him – why?

Forester rounded the last corner before the quay, then stopped. 'What the hell . . .?' he muttered.

The area round the dockside was a hive of disorganized activity. An articulated oil tanker dominated the scene, pulled in close to *Sea Victory*, its huge wheels dangerously near the edge of the dock. Lines snaked from it into the vessel, slowly filling *Sea Victory*'s tanks. Parked just behind the tanker was Annabel's small, open-topped Morgan, piled high with goods which she and a rotund Cypriot were slowly unloading with the enthusiastic, if unhelpful, support of Charlie. Forester recognized Lee Henshaw standing with Rhys, who was supervising the fuel changeover. Surrounding all this activity was a crowd of onlookers staring curiously at the yacht, as if they didn't expect to see it again. The news had already got around. So much for secrecy.

The tethered dog was lying morosely in his usual spot. He didn't give Tom his usual frenzied greeting – he was exhausted from trying to deal with the crowd. The dog looked at him sadly as he passed, not even a raised lip or a growl. Forester felt almost sorry for him.

Annabel was loading boxes of canned goods into the perspiring Cypriot's arms. She smiled a greeting and indicated the unfortunate man. 'Hello, darling. Grab a box, will you, and give us a hand? You know Mr Koliandri, don't you? He's very kindly come along from the supermarket to help.'

Forester nodded affably and grabbed one of the boxes from the top of the pile teetering in the Cypriot's arms. 'Hello.'

Mr Koliandri grimaced. It was meant to be a smile. 'How do you do,' he said politely, poking his head from behind the boxes. 'I'm er . . . the er, manager of the supermarket. I'm not entirely used to this, you understand.'

Forester removed another box that looked in danger of toppling. Mr Koliandri continued, 'Your wife seemed to need some help . . . She is er . . .' He paused, looking for the right word. 'She is a very powerful woman.'

Annabel, who was still unloading behind him, silently flexed her arm, feeling her bicep, making a pretence of strength.

Forester tried desperately to repress a smile. Charlie laughed delightedly, imitating his mother. Forester took another box from the manager and gave it to his son. 'Take this,' he said authoritatively, 'and put it on the stern.'

Charlie staggered away manfully. Forester smiled at Mr Koliandri. 'Yes,' he said brightly, 'she can be a little . . . formidable.' He glanced at Annabel, who made a face, then continued hurriedly, 'It's very kind of you to help . . . Can you manage that now?'

Annabel appeared in front of the bemused Mr Koliandri and wiped the sweat from his brow with a hanky. 'Of course he can, can't you, Mr Koliandri?' She indicated the pile still in his arms. 'If you'd be kind enough to put that on the stern, please? But watch your step on the gangplank.' She smiled charmingly. He nodded, still confused, but overwhelmed by Annabel's apparent concern.

They watched him totter along the quay towards the gangplank. Forester made a move to go after him, but Annabel took his arm. 'He'll be all right.'

He stared at her disbelievingly . . . 'God, woman, you're a tyrant!'

'Nonsense. Look, he's OK.'

They watched the overweight Mr Koliandri cross the gangplank unsteadily, then set the supplies down with evident relief.

Forester sighed. 'You'd better send him home before he has a heart attack.'

Annabel picked up a large box and proceeded towards the boat. 'What, dear Mr Koliandri? Never! He's got eleven children.'

'No wonder he looks exhausted.' He followed her, carrying more boxes.

Rhys waved to him from the bridge. 'Could you come up here a minute?'

Forester dumped the boxes on the stern and smiled encouragingly at Mr Koliandri, who nodded forlornly and walked reluctantly back to the car with Annabel. He climbed the companionway and hauled himself on to the upper deck.

Rhys was in the wheelhouse, keeping an eye on the fuel gauges. Lee Henshaw was with him. Rhys introduced him and they shook hands. 'He's agreed to crew with us this trip,' Rhys said.

Forester eyed the tall, bearded Australian speculatively. 'I've seen you around, haven't I?'

'That's right. I've got a small boat over there.' He gestured to the other side of the marina.

Rhys glanced from one to the other. He sensed an underlying prickliness in Forester's reaction. 'He's a qualified engineer, Tom.'

Forester nodded. 'Good, we might need that if you fall overboard.' He looked directly at Henshaw. 'You know what you're getting into, don't you? This will be no bloody picnic. Those Israeli gunboats will have the ports sown up tighter than a Scotsman's wallet.'

Henshaw scratched his head reflectively. 'Never did like picnics much, anyway . . . too many bloody flies in Australia.' A smile spread slowly across his face.

Forester unfroze a little. 'Welcome aboard – seems we finally got ourselves a crew.'

A car horn blared from the quayside; the background chatter of the crowd went up a decibel or two. Forester strode over to the rails and looked down on the scene below. Rhys and Henshaw joined him.

Two cars had pulled up on the already crowded quay and were trying, unsuccessfully, to force their way through the milling onlookers to get into a position alongside *Sea Victory*. Philippe Rousseau, in the first car, was getting increasingly annoyed. He was hot and uncomfortable, and although all the windows were open it was still stifling inside. Getting the cars and all their equipment together had been a frustratingly long business, aggravated by the bureaucratic delays of an official at the marina gates. The news photographer on the back seat hadn't helped. She was cold and aloof. There was an ambivalence about her that the Frenchman found disconcerting. Nazira Yammine worried him.

Now the cars were surrounded by this crowd, blocking the last fifty metres to the vessel. What was worse, they smiled benignly every time his driver sounded the horn.

Behind him, in the other car, were Jack Kemp and Armand. Armand watched anxiously as the crowd pressed in, halting the car completely. He was beginning to feel claustrophobic. The Canadian was, as always, carrying his video camera. It was clear the Frenchman was getting agitated. He sighed, and dug him in the ribs. 'Come on, let's shoot some of this . . .'

Armand stared at him incredulously. 'What?'

'Let's roll some tape. It's better than being cooped up in here, and we might get some good background footage.'

Armand was flabbergasted. But he liked Kemp, trusted him, and knew the Canadian was right: there was footage here. The prelude to their departure; the voyage and the anticipatory crowd, sensing the danger of *Sea Victory*'s attempt to break the blockade . . .

He capitulated. 'All right, let's see what we can get.' He already felt better.

Kemp was glad to get out of the car. His legs were almost round his neck in the back seat, and the crowd might be interesting. He opened the door and climbed out stiffly, stretching himself.

Armand tapped the Cypriot driver on the shoulder. 'Don't move until I get my things from the back.'

The driver gazed morosely at the throng solidly blocking his path. There was no way he was going to be able to move in or out until the ship sailed. 'OK,' he said resignedly, 'I won't.'

Armand got out and opened the boot. The curious eyes of the

35

crowd watched every move. They'd already seen the video camera, and the heavy BVU Sony recorder and gun microphone increased their respect. Some of the men pushed back the crowd to give him room. They beamed at him, hoping to get in shot. The media magic was casting its usual spell.

The first car blared its horn uselessly and tried to inch forward once again – it was hopeless. Rousseau's patience finally snapped. He flung open the door, leapt from the car and began yelling at the crowd in French. This caused further amusement. He started to push people aside and gradually managed to clear some sort of a path for the vehicles. Kemp and Armand recorded their presenter's little drama for posterity, and Rousseau turned sharply to get back into his car before the gap closed again. He caught one of the crowd square in the chest with his shoulder.

The man staggered back, not realizing how close he was to the edge of the dock. As he began to lose his balance, his arms windmilled unavailingly. A ludicrous expression of surprise and despair crossed his face before he disappeared from Rousseau's shocked gaze. A moment later there was the sound of a huge splash.

The Frenchman rushed to the side of the dock and Jack Kemp moved in quickly to cover the shot as the onlookers crowded forward to see what had happened. They waited silently, fascinated by the widening ripples. When the unfortunate man finally surfaced a gasp of excitement swept through them. The man splashed about noisily in the dirty water, screaming something in Cypriot that neither Rousseau or Kemp could understand. No one in the crowd made the slightest attempt to help him – though he was clearly in distress.

It was Annabel who finally managed to push her way through the crowd and fling down a lifebelt that she had grabbed from its emergency position on the quay. It spun down to the surface and, as if drawn by an invisible thread, struck the man a resounding blow on the head. Once more he disappeared below the surface, and once more everyone waited breathlessly to see if he would come back up again.

A hand slowly emerged from the mucky water and grabbed at the floating lifebelt. The man hauled himself up until his head and shoulders were comfortably inside it, then looked up at the crowd above him and saw the cameraman. He spat out some of the water and brushed his wet hair back from his face, realizing he had a very interested audience. He smiled broadly and waved. The crowd cheered – it was a good show.

Forester, on the bridge, shook his head resignedly. 'How in God's name am I going to get this sorted out by tonight.'

The question was rhetorical. Neither Henshaw nor Rhys bothered to answer.

CHAPTER
FOUR

The Director stared at the decoded telex that had just been placed on his desk. He was pleased; the operative had done well in so short a time. He dialled a number on his direct line, switching on the scrambler, and glanced at his watch. It was just after ten a.m., and his contact should be in his office. He heard the ringing tone and it was picked up almost immediately. 'Yes.'

'Good morning, sir.'

'Oh . . . good morning, Hank. What can I do for you?' The politician's automatic and polite question was reflex.

The Director smiled to himself. 'Regarding our discussion the other day . . .'

'Yes?'

'I've set a few things in motion. We found a vessel, almost a hundred and twenty tons. It's normally used on a charter basis in the coastal waters around Cyprus.'

'Is it one of ours?'

'No. An Englishman runs it with his wife.'

'British?'

'Yes.'

'And it's a civilian craft?'

'That's right, sir.'

'Good.'

'The couple live on board with their son, and there is a small crew — skipper and deckhand. It's nicely appointed without being luxurious.'

'Sounds ideal.'

'There are several points in its favour. It's been operating in that area

for about three years now and it has spent time in Haifa being refitted, so the Israelis will be familiar with it.'

'They may have already checked it out.'

'I was coming to that, sir.'

He heard the politician chuckle. 'Sorry, Hank.'

'That's all right, sir – it's nice to know we're on the same wavelength.'

'Go ahead.'

'Well, without making the Israelis aware of my interest, I've checked them out, and they have cleared the vessel.' The Director waited while the politician absorbed that; he sensed his satisfaction.

'It all fits . . . you've done well, Hank.'

'Thank you, sir . . .' It was time to guard his flanks a little. 'There are elements here that we cannot control, of course. Number one, it's got to get through the Israeli blockade. We can't help them, otherwise we blow our interest.'

'Yes, of course – what are their chances?'

'About fifty-fifty, I'd say. But the problem would be the same with any civilian vessel trying to get into Lebanon, and this vessel has a better chance than anything else in those waters.'

'What's it doing now?'

'It's been chartered to take some television people into Jounieh.'

'Where's that?'

'Just a few miles north of Beirut – perfect for our purposes. We're in pretty good shape. But it is absolutely crucial that no one, apart from our operative on board, be aware of the role this vessel may play eventually.'

'That's no problem this end, it's all completely under wraps. What about your man, can you count on him?'

'I didn't say anything about a man. I said we had an operative on board.'

The politician smiled. 'Sorry, Hank – but you're not saying it's a woman, are you?'

'I'm not saying it is or it isn't, sir . . . but in answer to your question, the operative is one of the best we have.'

'OK, point taken. What happens if the vessel makes it safely to this place . . . er, Jounieh?'

'That's where you come in, sir. We have to make use of it openly, for *diplomatic services. And it would be better if others were able to use it also.'*

'In order to give us cover?'

'Exactly, sir.'

There was a silence — then came another question. 'Do we have anyone operating in Jounieh?'

'No, sir — but someone has.'

'What do you mean?'

'We've picked up high-frequency radio signals from the town, but we can't locate the source yet.'

'But you're on to it?'

'We are now, sir . . .'

'OK, Hank, that seems to cover it. It's good work. I'll take care of things this end — but keep me fully informed.'

'I'll do that, sir.'

'Right . . . oh, one thing, Hank?'

'Sir?'

'What's the name of the vessel?'

'Sea Victory, sir.'

CHAPTER

FIVE

The apartment was silent except for the slight click, then the fizzing noise as the neon sign worked intermittently, casting a red glow over the shattered room. No one had responded to her cries for help – it seemed everyone had fled. Leila did not know how badly damaged the block was, but it did not take much imagination to realize that at any moment this whole floor could collapse into the street, seventeen storeys below.

She tried again to lift the heavy upholstered armchair from André's legs, but it wouldn't budge. It had protected him to some extent from the falling masonry, but now it was trapped beneath a wooden beam that had fallen from the ceiling and it had resisted all her efforts to dislodge it.

André sensed her rising panic. The weight on his legs hadn't altered – he pulled once more, trying to free them, but they didn't move at all and he could get no leverage with only one good hand. He lay back on the floor, limp from the effort, the darkness around him complete, the pain from his mangled hand making him feel sick. He lay absolutely still, choking down the scream that rose in his throat. Unless he kept control of himself he would die here and so might Leila. That thought calmed him down. He reached up and touched her with his good hand. 'It's no good, Leila, you will have to go and get some help.'

She leaned down over him, trying not to cry, lifting his head into her lap. 'No, I can't go – anything might happen. You need me here.'

'Leila . . .' He tried to keep a reasonable tone in his voice. 'If you don't get someone we shall be here all night, and there is no guarantee that anyone will come in the morning.'

She knew he was right, but she could not bear the thought of leaving him alone, knowing he was blinded. She had wrapped his hand in a torn-up tablecloth and despite the calmness in his voice she knew he must be in agony. She ran her fingers through his hair, brushing it away from his sweaty face. She knew she would have to go. Even if the situation in the shambles of the apartment did not deteriorate, he needed medical attention as quickly as possible.

She waited for the light to flick on again, then looked quickly round the apartment. She saw what she wanted. She laid his head gently down. 'I'll only be a moment,' she whispered.

She reached across to the armchair that trapped her brother's leg and removed the heavy seat cushion. She placed it under his head, making him as comfortable as possible. There was nothing else she could do.

She lay down beside him, holding him close, feeling his chest rising and falling quickly as he breathed. 'I'm going now – I shall try to bring someone back . . . Will you be all right?'

'Listen,' he said urgently. 'Just get someone up here, don't worry about me, I'm fine now.'

Leila clung to him for a moment, then kissed his face. 'I'll be as quick as I can.'

He tensed. 'No! Go slowly, carefully. The building could be badly damaged.'

She held his hand to her lips, then slipped away, crawling through the rubble towards the door that led into the hallway. The light flicked on. There was no pattern about it. Sometimes the gaps were short, sometimes the darkness seemed interminable.

The vestibule had been protected by the kitchen wall and she was able to stand up. The door to the apartment hung drunkenly from its hinges, pushed outwards by the blast. She paused in the gaping doorway, looking back into the darkened apartment. She called out, 'André?'

He shifted his position as much as he could and raised his head. 'It's all right, you go now . . . fetch help.'

'I'll be back, André, whatever happens.'

He did not answer and she waited no longer. Some of the doors to the other apartments had been left open by the hasty departures. In the poor light that occasionally reflected from the neon sign, she could see that they had suffered little damage. The shell had struck directly into their side of the building. She moved slowly, feeling her way along the wall until she came to the double doors that led to the emergency staircase. They creaked noisily in the dark, echoing down the uncarpeted stairs. She felt her way to the balustrade and began to descend, keeping one hand on the metal rail.

Leila did not know how far down she had gone when she first saw the pale glow of a light below her. She had counted about six or seven levels, but could not be sure. The light seemed to be moving and she stopped, uncertain as to what it was. She called out, 'Hello . . .'

The light halted, her voice still echoing back from the well of the staircase. Then a man's voice responded. 'Who is it?'

She recognized it instantly. It was Mr Frangieh, the manager who fussed over the block. 'It's me, Leila Khalil. Can you come, please? I need help.'

Her voice sounded faint and frightened, mocking her as it bounced off the walls. Then Mr Frangieh's voice, officious as ever and slightly effeminate. 'Stay where you are, Miss Khalil. I'm coming, be with you in a moment.'

Leila sat down quickly on the concrete stairs as her legs seemed to give way. Dear Mr Frangieh, only he would venture up to see how badly damaged his beloved apartment block had been. The relief from fear was pure and physical. She clasped her head in her hands and determined not to cry. They could do it now; with Mr Frangieh's help they would be able to release André and get him out of the apartment. She could hear the manager complaining to himself as he wearily climbed the emergency stairs. The light grew stronger as he ascended towards her.

Leila heard the sound of a shell whistling its way towards its target and she flinched, waiting for the impact. The building trembled slightly, though the shell had exploded some distance away. She wondered how safe the apartment block was after

43

the damage it had suffered, whether it might collapse and come tumbling down on her; but there was no alternative. At least here in the manager's rooms they were on the ground floor, but they could not venture out during the hours of darkness.

All night the shelling and the occasional burst of automatic fire had continued, making it impossible for her to sleep. She had dressed the injuries to her brother's hand as best she could with iodine and bandages. Mr Frangieh had provided her with pain killers from an emergency first aid kit, and eventually André had fallen into an uneasy sleep. Getting him out of the wreckage of their apartment and down the seventeen flights of stairs had been a nightmare that had seemed unending, but somehow she and the manager had struggled their way safely down and into his apartment.

Leila had wrapped herself in a blanket and spent the night on an armchair beside André, refusing the offer of a bed. She wanted to be there when he woke up.

Over and over the same thoughts had gone through her head. She had to get André into a hospital, but the manager had refused point blank to let her go out after dark during the curfew, and she knew he was right. Leila glanced at the door to the bedroom where Mr Frangieh was sleeping. She had never much cared for the sweaty little man, but he was their only source of help. Their apartment had been in danger of total collapse and, although badly frightened, he had managed to move the beam and the heavy armchair from André's legs and carry him out. She would not forget Mr Frangieh.

She looked at her watch again. The luminous dial glowed in the darkness of the room. It was coming up to five a.m. Soon it would be light. Leila threw off the blanket and walked quickly across the carpeted floor to the window. She opened the curtain fractionally, just enough for her to see outside. The sky in the east behind Mount Lebanon was already glowing pink, casting a long shadow over the city. In the vague half-light the street looked normal enough, except that it was utterly deserted. She knew it would not remain so for long.

André groaned and she turned and walked quickly back to him, kneeling down beside the sofa, peering down at his pale face. He moved restlessly, then suddenly his eyes opened, staring up at her unseeingly. All night long she had prayed that when he woke his sight might be restored, but it had not happened. Unless he got first-class medical treatment her brother would remain blind. His unseeing, staring eyes frightened her. She felt tears running down her cheeks and wiped them quickly away in case they fell on his face. He must not know her fear.

André knew his eyes were open, yet he did not seem to be awake. It was his recurring nightmare – half-awake, half-asleep, wanting to push back the suffocating sheets from around his head, yet totally unable to move, finding it increasingly difficult to breathe. He concentrated, taking a deep breath, then with an enormous effort of willpower he raised his arm. His injured hand hit something and the pain was unbearable. He cried out, wide awake now, yet still unable to see. He heard his sister's voice and felt her hands holding his arm, preventing it from moving. Suddenly he remembered. The bone-crushing impact of the explosion, the feeling of being lifted by some immense force and flung against the wall . . . then nothing.

He sat up, feeling Leila's arms around him. He clung to her, smelling the white powder of the broken ceiling that still clung to her clothes. It was all stark and clear in his mind now. It was real, it had happened: the pain in his hand, the awful dark void that surrounded him.

He could hear Leila whispering to him, comforting him. He cleared his throat, staring at where he knew she was. 'What happened, Leila. Where are we?'

She held him at arm's length. There was a calmness about him, a steadiness in his voice that surprised her. 'We are in the manager's apartment – he is still asleep. We brought you down; our place is destroyed.'

The endless descent came crowding back into his mind. His feeling of utter helplessness as they half-carried him down, the pain in his hand that filled his darkness.

Leila saw him flinch as though he were warding off a blow. 'It's all right now, André, we are safe here. The soldiers have gone and soon it will be light enough for me to take you to the hospital.'

His empty eyes widened. 'No, I don't want to go.'

'But you must, your hand needs treatment and –' She stopped.

'And my eyes,' he said bitterly.

Leila suddenly felt angry. 'Yes, your eyes, they must do something.'

He shook his head. 'It's no good, Leila, there is nothing they will be able to do here.'

Suddenly she was crying. His despair triggered off the anguish and pain she had bottled up all night while she stayed awake, desperately trying to reason a way out. Now he was rejecting her plan and she could hold the tears back no longer.

He reached out and pulled her to him, finding a strength in himself he did not know existed. He touched her face gently, wiping the tears away, cupping it in the palm of his good hand. 'Listen to me, Leila. They will keep me there and we cannot stay in Beirut any longer. There will be hundreds of people crowding the hospital with far worse injuries than mine.' The tears had dried; she was listening now. 'If I am to get my sight back we have to get to Europe – we have money there, friends. Do you understand?'

Leila knew there was truth in what he said, but she was not entirely convinced, nor could she see how they were going to escape. 'What about your hand?'

He was silent for a moment.

'That's all right now. It doesn't hurt so much . . .'

She knew he was lying, how much it cost him to say that. She was close to tears once more. 'Oh, André . . .'

He sensed her breaking point immediately. His voice hardened. 'Get us to Jounieh, Leila. Use the car. You must tell no one, do you understand?'

She drew back, recognizing his authority as her older brother. 'I'll say nothing, don't worry.'

He listened to her voice – it was OK now, she had control of herself. 'We'll be all right, Leila. We can do this together, I know we can. Remember when we were children, all the places we explored together and we were never lost. I always got you home, remember?' He took her hand again. 'Well, now it's your turn, you must be my eyes. Think of it as one of our games,

Leila. Take us to Jounieh. We can find a boat there.' He squeezed her hand tightly. 'Do as I say.'

Mr Frangieh held on to André's arm while Leila opened the back door of the Citroën. Then, carefully, they sat him down in the seat and closed the door after him. Leila turned to the manager and held out her hand. 'Thank you, Mr Frangieh,' she said, knowing the words were not enough to convey her gratitude. 'We would never have got out...' She stopped, remembering the horror of their apartment.

He touched her bare arm comfortingly. His hand was hot and sweaty, but she didn't mind any more. It was a part of Mr Frangieh, as much a part as his nervousness and apprehension, yet she owed him more than she could ever repay.

'I still think you are making a mistake,' he said. He gestured towards André. 'You should let me take him to the hospital. Maybe they can do something for his eyes.'

Leila would have liked to believe him, but she suspected her brother was right. The explosions had stopped for the moment, but already she could hear small-arms fire coming from the eastern side of the city. The Israeli advance into Lebanon and their imminent encirclement of Beirut had done nothing to stop the internal war between Muslim and Christian.

She smiled at him. 'That is kind of you, Mr Frangieh, but I must try to do as my brother wants. He believes we can board a ship in Jounieh.'

Mr Frangieh nodded his head understandingly. 'Of course you must do as you think best. If you can't get through, come back here. I will do what I can.'

Leila moved to get into the driving seat.

'Wait,' he said. He leaned down and picked up the brown paper bag he had carried from his apartment. 'There is a flask here and some sandwiches.' He handed them to her and waved aside her thanks. 'One more thing...' He lowered his voice so that her brother could not hear. 'The roads may be dangerous – don't say anything to him' – he indicated André – 'but you will need this.' He slipped a small pistol from his pocket and before she could refuse it he had placed it in the brown bag with the sandwiches. He opened the door for her and gazed at her directly. 'Please,' he said quietly. 'I'll feel happier if you have it.'

Leila bit her lip, then leaned forward and kissed him on the cheek. Mr Frangieh blinked and she slid quickly into the driving seat, placing the brown bag on the seat beside her. The manager shut the door.

Leila started the engine and waited for the Citroën to rise up on its hydraulic suspension. Mr Frangieh stood quietly beside the car. He seemed reluctant to let them go. She realized suddenly that he must be a very solitary man. He lived alone in his ground-floor apartment and, like everybody else who lived in the block, she seldom exchanged more than a few words with him. This moment of danger for them all had somehow forged a bond between them. She leaned out of the window and looked up at him. 'Come with us,' she said impulsively. 'Who knows what will happen here?'

He shook his head sadly. 'I cannot.' He gestured towards the apartment block. 'Who would look after my building? The Israelis, they may come . . .' He shrugged eloquently. 'But they believe in business, they would not want to destroy it – there is no reason.' He smiled regretfully. 'But I am grateful that you asked. We shall see each other again, I hope.'

André leaned forward from the back seat. 'We must go now.' He tried to keep the impatience from his voice.

Leila smiled. 'Goodbye, Mr Frangieh.' She pushed down the clutch and let in the gear. The car moved forward.

'Goodbye,' she heard him say. She glanced in the rear-view mirror. He was still standing in the same place. She put out her hand and waved to him, then they turned the corner into the road and he was gone.

The small-arms fire grew in intensity as she approached the main thoroughfare that led to the coast road. As she came to the intersection the volume of traffic suddenly increased and they were surrounded on all sides by vehicles heading northwards out of the city. It seemed as if people and possessions were jammed into anything that would move. Many of the cars looked dangerously overloaded, the roof racks piled high with furnishings and goods, strapped and roped together. Lorries had loads and people in the back that forced the rear hard down on to their springs, making them look strangely comical as they moved forward, bonnets high in the air.

There was nothing comical about the militiamen who lounged on the corners, sub-machine-guns held ready, a stark grimness of purpose about them as they waited.

A car, horn blaring, came fast up behind her. Leila moved over to give it room to overtake. Inside were more uniformed men, while a Phalangist soldier clung to the runningboard, gun at the ready. The car in front did not move aside quickly enough and the soldier fired three rounds into the air. There was room for him to pass in an instant.

André leaned forward and touched his sister's shoulder. 'What was it?'

'Nothing, just a militiaman anxious to get by.'

He sat back in his seat and felt the small comforting bulge in his pocket. The uncut stones would be good currency, whatever the situation. He'd planned his move well ahead and there was bound to be shipping they could board in Jounieh. If only they had left a day earlier. If only that shell had hit somewhere else . . . if only. He wanted to weep and scream his anger at the fates who had decided he was to be their target, but again he was restrained by the need to keep control – if he was to survive there was no alternative.

The long line of traffic finally ground to a halt. Leila could see it winding up the hill ahead of her where a convoy of army trucks had stopped, temporarily blocking the road as troops unloaded equipment. The heat haze shimmered over the distant vehicles, making it difficult to see clearly what was happening, but it was obvious the traffic would not be moving for some time. She glanced back the way they had come: the traffic was solid and building behind her.

'Why have we stopped?' His voice was sharp and edgy. She told him. He sat quietly, keeping in his mind's eye the route they had to travel. From Beirut to Jounieh along the coast road was only about nine miles, but he could not be sure if they had reached the road yet. A sound crept into his consciousness. He sat bolt upright in the back seat, fear turning his insides to water. The faint whistling sound grew quickly, deepening into a throaty roar and he realized it was not a shell, but a jet engine.

The F16 Fighting Falcon swooped low over the line of stationary traffic, its shadow flashing across the city. Leila watched in frozen horror as the two rockets detached themselves from under the wings of the diving plane and bulleted towards the army convoy, leaving a trail of grey smoke behind them. They buried themselves soundlessly into the lorries, tossing them into the air like broken toys, instantly turned into balls of fire. Soldiers were frantically trying to escape the inferno, tiny figures running in a mirage-like landscape. Then the sound of the explosion engulfed her. She heard people screaming and some began to flee from their cars, seeking cover either side of the road. André was grabbing her shoulder and shouting into her ear. She tried to yell back above the noise as the jet swooped gracefully in the cloudless blue sky and came back in again, directly above and in line with the road.

It dived, bearing down the road, seemingly just above the traffic, directly towards her. Leila could see every detail of the underside of the aircraft. People all along the road in front of her were running from their cars, but she just stared at the deadly shape, mesmerized, unable to make a move, hardly aware of her brother's hand digging deeply into her flesh. His voice was drowned in the rush of sound from the jet crashing through the air towards them.

She waited, expecting to see the fiery red flashes from under its wings, or the ricochet of cannon fire from the tarmac, but nothing happened. The pilot did not open fire on the fleeing Lebanese. His purpose was to block the road as best he could and try to stop any PLO from escaping. His task accomplished, this was a final flourish to sow more panic and delay.

The jet flashed above the Citroën, the sound wash quickly abating as it disappeared behind them. Leila could feel André's hand now clawing at her. She tore it loose and glanced behind her, slipping the car into reverse until she had enough space to turn. The Citroën hit the verge separating the two-way flow of traffic, the hydraulic suspension taking most of the impact. Then it bounced down on to the other side and Leila raced the car down the empty carriageway, heading back the way they had come.

She yelled to her brother in the back, 'Are you all right?'

He nursed his injured hand, holding it up to his chest. 'I heard the explosions and the jet. What happened?'

'It was an Israeli plane; there was a convoy ahead of us . . .' She didn't finish the sentence – there was no need. The highway ahead was clear and she kept her foot hard down on the accelerator. 'You remember the road up into the mountains through Broummana?'

'Yes.'

Leila came to a fork in the road and bore off to the left. 'If we continue northwards we can come back down from the mountains and rejoin the coast road at Antelias.'

He knew the road. It was a bad one, especially in these conditions. It looped high into the mountains behind Beirut to the east and the north and would add at least another twenty-five miles to their journey. But he did not try to dissuade her. He was in her hands and if the route to the coast road was blocked, he could think of no other solution. Israeli jets were after troop concentrations, and civilians who got in the way were bound to be hurt. Better to be moving than holed up waiting to get out. Somehow, the mere fact that they were travelling seemed to ease the pain of his injured hand – perhaps it just took his mind off it. Whatever the reason, he was grateful.

The car gradually ascended from the northern suburbs of the city. The road became narrow and dusty as they left the buildings behind. With the rising sun directly in her eyes and still low enough to dazzle, Leila had to concentrate hard as they twisted round the side of the mountain. From time to time she heard the sound of distant explosions and the whine of jets crisscrossing the city below, pulverizing targets with rocket and bomb attacks.

André remained quiet and impassive in the back, but she knew her brother, and knew how much he was suffering. As soon as they reached the first clear view of the city she stopped the car. He leaned forward at once, tense and worried.

'What is it? What's wrong?'

She pulled the flask and the sandwiches from the brown paper bag Mr Frangieh had given her, leaving the pistol inside.

'Nothing,' she said reassuringly. 'Would you like something to drink?'

He relaxed. 'What have you got?'

Leila unscrewed the cap and held the flask to her nose. 'Coffee.'

He wanted to refuse – the delay worried him – but then the delicious smell wafted through from the front and he changed his mind. 'Yes, I'll have some.'

Leila filled the top of the flask and handed it to him. 'Be careful, it's hot.' She placed his fingers on the plastic handle and he blew on it to cool it down. 'I've got some sandwiches here as well.'

André shook his head. 'No, I'm not hungry.'

He listened to the distant sounds of gunfire drifting up from the city below. Leila rolled down her window, looking out towards the airport. Without thinking, she began to describe the scene to him as she chewed a sandwich.

'There's nothing taking off or landing at the airport. I can see some planes still standing in front of the buildings – one of them is badly damaged, looks as if it's been on fire.'

André, too, accepted the changed circumstances automatically, listening intently to what she had to say. 'Probably a rocket attack,' he commented.

Leila looked up. 'There are still aircraft about, but they seem to be much higher now. I can see the vapour trails.'

André nodded. 'The PLO are supposed to have Sam missiles which can home in on the heat of their engines.' He paused as another explosion drifted up to them. 'Can you see what's happening in the city?'

Leila watched the mushrooming cloud of smoke rising from behind some tall buildings. 'Looks like a bomb . . . can't see what it hit, but it's bad.' She stopped, remembering the horror of the blast from the shell that had blinded André. She couldn't look any more. 'Have you finished the coffee?'

He sensed her change of mood and guessed the reason for it. He drank half the coffee and gave the rest back to her. 'You finish it off.'

Leila gulped it down. It was hot and sweet, just like Mr Frangieh, she thought. If only he could have come with them.

She hoped he would be all right. She screwed the top back on to the flask, stuffed it back into the bag and started the engine. 'OK?' she called.

'OK,' André said quietly.

They continued, climbing higher all the time. They passed through Mansouriye without incident. It was utterly normal, the village undamaged, and Leila was relieved to see no signs of any military activity. Two miles after the village she forked left at a junction, taking the road to Air Saade, heading northwards once more. The road climbed higher, becoming increasingly rugged as the terrain grew more spectacular. The air cooled as they ascended. Leila remembered similar days when, as a child, she had come with her parents into these mountains, fighting in the back of the car with André until her father's tone had warned them both to stop. The ground to the left of the road suddenly dropped clear away and in the distance she could see St George's Bay glittering in the sun. The sounds of conflict had faded completely. Only the reassuring hum of the engine pervaded the solitude and peace of the mountains. It was hard to believe the war was so close.

They came to Air Saade. As in the previous village, she could detect nothing out of the ordinary. Leila was happy to pass on, sometimes talking to André between the long silences.

The road began to climb sharply, twisting back on itself as it looped up the side of the mountain. She eased the Citroën slowly round a tight bend, up a steep incline, and saw two men standing in the road.

They were wearing a uniform of sorts, their combat greens torn and covered in the white dust from the road. They both carried sub-machine-guns, pointed directly at the Citroën. She stopped the car, but did not turn off the ignition. One of the militiamen came round to her, while the other stood a few feet in front of the bonnet.

André knew something was wrong. He listened intently. The man's boots crunched on the road and stopped by the front door of the car beside Leila.

The militiaman examined the woman, then the injured man in the back. They appeared to be unarmed, but he took no chances. The woman was beautiful, her thin summer dress clinging damply to her in the heat of the car. 'Where are you going?' he asked.

'To Jounieh.'

He exchanged a look with the other soldier. 'You are well away from the main road. You should have gone straight along the coast.'

'I couldn't, it was blocked. The Israelis were bombing so I came up here. My brother is injured. We can get back on the coast road at Bikfaya.'

The militiaman studied her quietly. He'd got some information and he had no reason to doubt her. He waved the sub-machine-gun. 'You and your brother will get out now. We have to examine the vehicle.'

Leila had no intention of getting out. If they took the car, she and André were finished. She protested, her hand feeling for the brown paper bag beside her. 'But you can't! My brother is badly wounded – he cannot even see.'

The other soldier walked around the side of the car peering in at the man in the back. André sat perfectly still, cocking his head to one side as he tried to hear everything. The heavy boots crunched on the road as the soldier checked the inside of the car for weapons.

Leila appealed once more to the man holding the gun on her. 'Please don't make us get out. Surely you can see we are carrying nothing.'

The man jerked his gun impatiently. 'Get out, both of you. We want the car.'

Leila realized then that she had only one chance. She glanced in the mirror. The other soldier was leaning down over the rear of the Citroën, trying to open the boot. She made as if to pull the handbrake on and took the pistol from the brown paper bag, covering it with her arm. She fired at point-blank range into the soldier. His face distorted as the bullet tore through his throat, splattering his blood over the car. She lifted her foot from the brake pedal as she fired, allowing the car to roll back down the steep incline. She heard the other soldier scream and felt the horrible soft bump as the car wheels ran over his body. She jammed on the brakes before the car could get out of control and slammed her foot on to the accelerator, pushing the car into first gear. The front wheels whirled in the dust, then took hold, pulling the vehicle forward. Leila twisted the wheel sharply, avoiding the body lying in the road, and quickly they picked up speed.

She flung the pistol down on the seat and concentrated on her driving, trying not to see the blood on the windscreen. She felt André's hand on her shoulder, strong and reassuring.

'Are you all right?' he said quietly.

She reached for his hand and kissed it quickly. 'Yes . . . I'm all right, don't worry.'

He squeezed her shoulder gently. 'Give me the gun, Leila.'

She picked it up and handed it back to him, glancing at him in the rear-view mirror. 'But how can you use it . . .?' She stopped as he rolled down his window and tossed the gun out of the car.

'I don't intend to, Leila. You are brave enough for both of us, but there will be no more shooting. You don't have to die to get me to Jounieh. If we get there, we must do it together.'

Leila sprayed the windscreen with water and switched on the wipers. The blood spread across the windscreen in ugly red blotches, then gradually began to fade.

CHAPTER

SIX

The anchor chain quivered, disturbing the sea bed of the marina; then it bit into the soft muddy bottom before pulling free, clouding the water, turning it from blue to thick murky brown. As the anchor surfaced the crowd cheered. Charlie caught the mood and jumped up and down excitedly, tugging at his nanny's dress and pointing to the anchor as it clattered into its moorings just below the bow. Ivy kept a tight hold on the boy's hand in case he attempted to dash to the edge of the dock.

Annabel leaned on the rail, watching her son in the fading light. Normally it would be a short trip, taking tourists along the coast to Fig Tree Bay and one or two other coves on the south side of the island. *Sea Victory* never ventured into the waters of the Turkish-held north. Sometimes they took Charlie with them, returning at the end of the day to their home port of Larnaca. Recently he'd started to go to play school and Ivy, his nanny, looked after him on the one or two days a week when they were busy.

Today was different. The lump in Annabel's throat would not go away. She tried to show none of the emotional turmoil she felt. It would not help Charlie if she were tearful or unhappy. Thank God he had no idea of what they were going to try to do, or the horrible choice she had had to make between her son and her husband.

Not that she'd had any real choice. She had been aware of Tom's growing dissatisfaction with the routine trips to Fig Tree Bay, and she'd lived with her husband long enough to know he wouldn't accept routine for long. He needed this opportunity, he needed change.

The purchase of *Sea Victory* itself had been a stab in that direction. Uprooted from friends and familiar surroundings in London, they began the slow drift down through the Mediterranean until she had found herself pregnant. After Charlie's birth they'd decided to look for something different, something that would provide an income for themselves and support the running of the boat. They had ended up here in Larnaca where they managed to get a licence to charter, and during the summer made a reasonable, but by no means huge, profit. *Sea Victory* took a lot of looking after and the costs were heavy, but they were just beginning to break even and, as usual, Tom was getting itchy feet again.

It was something Annabel was becoming used to. She didn't quite understand what it was that drove him, but until he had laid it to rest, this would be a recurring pattern. She only had to look at him now, striding back and forth from Rhys at the wheel to the rail, checking that Henshaw was slipping the lines forward and aft, making sure that *Sea Victory* got out of the overcrowded marina without mishap. Routine it may have been, but there was an underlying sense of excitement about him; something had come alive again that she hadn't really known was dead. Perhaps it was just the look in his eyes. That was what had attracted her to him in the first place and it tugged at her again now.

She turned to look at Charlie. Ivy had picked him up so that he could see over the heads of the onlookers. He waved to her as *Sea Victory*'s motor began to throb, pulling the stern away from the dockside. She could hear his high, tiny voice shouting to her, 'Bye, Mummy, bye . . .'

She covered her mouth with her hand, then raised it and waved to him, unable to risk a shout for fear her voice might betray her. She felt her husband's arm around her shoulders, his voice in her ear. 'He'll be all right, darling – don't worry.'

She slipped her hand around his waist and pulled him tight to her, finding comfort in his presence by her side. She heard him call out, his voice carrying across the widening gap between the boat and the dock. 'Be good, Charlie. We'll see you soon.'

Her son waved back. 'Bye, Daddy, I love you . . .'

The prow of *Sea Victory* swung slowly out into the harbour and Rhys switched the engines from reverse to slow ahead. The mud churned up from the shallow marina as the powerful thrust started to bite and the vessel began to ease forward.

Nazira Yammine had seen the look that had passed between husband and wife, and the protective arm he had put around her shoulders as they waved their goodbyes to the small, fair-haired boy on the dockside. It confirmed what Philippe Rousseau had said. The woman's anguish at being parted from the boy was plain, however much she tried to disguise it. There could be no doubt that their ultimate destination was Lebanon, and it gave Nazira a grim satisfaction. Finding a way into that beleaguered country had not been easy.

Running into the television crew at the hotel was fortunate. They were all stranded because of the shut-down of the airport, but now the charter gave them a chance. If Kemp and the others had been surprised to find a woman determined to get into the war zone, they had not shown it. Rousseau had tried to patronize her once, and had regretted it. She made her position clear.

The Palestinians in the camps had a right to their land, their country. None of them reacted to that – most French newspapers took that view editorially anyway. But her support of an active PLO had been received frostily by Rousseau. No one tried to take her on, though she would have welcomed the confrontation. They remained silent, and in that silence she sensed their disapproval. Not that she minded – it disturbed her not at all. It was what she had come to expect. That was why her task was so important.

It was crucial that what was happening in Lebanon was seen clearly in the West. And it could not just be left to television or so-called 'objective' reporting to present the truth about her people. She believed that the Israelis had made their first tactical blunder with the invasion of the Lebanon. Here, at last, was an opportunity to reverse their highly efficient public relations machine, and use the effects of the occupation to highlight her own country's agony. Instinctively she touched the camera that always hung around her neck. It was her weapon, the eye that would show the world the devastation of the Israeli advance into Beirut.

David Kass stood by the rail, near the stern, watching the muddy water foaming up beneath the vessel as the prop wash began to ease the boat forward. He was committed now, and with that sobering realization he suddenly felt better – the decision was made.

His eyes were drawn again to the woman in green battle fatigues, standing twenty feet away from him. He had noticed her almost at once when he had boarded, and he knew she had noticed him. Her eyes had fastened on him immediately, examining him without expression. She had said nothing, but he sensed her hostility.

It was a reaction he was unused to, and one he did not like. He didn't know her name, or where she was from. Only that she, like himself, was on this boat to reach Lebanon. He watched her from the corner of his eye as she stared at the receding dockside. She stood upright, her chin thrust slightly forward. What was it about her stance that puzzled him? It was so fierce, challenging, as if she had won a victory. Yes, that was it, a victory . . . but what victory?

Forester rejoined Rhys in the wheelhouse as they headed out for the breakwater. By now it was almost dark, but Rhys handled the wheel expertly, guiding *Sea Victory* through the bobbing lights that marked the presence of a clutch of small cargo vessels anchored outside the main harbour, awaiting clearance to proceed for unloading. The ship nosed slowly into the port basin, Rhys straining his eyes to see the customs building. It was tricky – not everybody took the precaution of lighting their vessels at night, and Forester kept a wary eye on the radar screen, just in case.

A faint glow from the street lights of the town outlined the buildings on the edge of the port area, and Rhys spotted what he was looking for. 'There!' he said, pointing. 'I think that's it.'

Forester looked in the direction he was indicating. 'You're right,' he affirmed.

Rhys glanced at him. 'The two Frenchmen are already talking to them?'

'That's right – Rousseau and Armand. They said they could sort it out.'

'Do you think they can swing it?'

'I don't know,' Forester said thoughtfully. 'We've never carried passengers into a war zone before . . .'

Rousseau stabbed his finger angrily beneath the nose of the customs official. 'But this is ridiculous . . .' He waved an arm at Armand, who was sitting disconsolately on a hard wooden chair. 'My colleague and I are part of a television news crew, and we're on assignment in Beirut. We have chartered this vessel quite legitimately. What right have you to refuse our request? It's outrageous . . .'

The Cypriot rubbed his forehead impatiently. It had been a long day and he felt tired, but his instructions had been explicit: *Sea Victory* was not to leave Larnaca. He took a deep breath, trying to hold on to his temper. 'I have every right – it is part of my job. My function is to decide these matters and I do not have to explain my reasons to you.' Before either Rousseau or Armand could protest further, he picked up his cap and started to walk towards the door. 'Now, if you will excuse me, I have to inform the owner of the vessel.'

Forester spotted him coming as Henshaw ran the gangplank on to the dock. Rousseau and Armand were bringing up the rear and Forester had been in Cyprus long enough to know he was about to face a problem. 'Rhys, get Annabel up here as fast as you can – I think we've got trouble.'

Rhys took one look at the agitated official as he stepped up on to the gangplank, then disappeared down the companionway below.

Forester lit a cigar and busied himself with the chart in the wheelhouse, waiting for the storm to break. He heard the Cypriot breathing heavily as he ascended the steps to the bridge. He turned, removing the cigar, and gave the sweating customs man his best smile. But before he could speak the official held up his hand.

'Mr Forester, there is no point in you tying up here. You will have to leave the port area immediately. Under no circumstances

60

will you receive permission to sail this vessel to Lebanon without a passenger-carrying licence, and that has to be processed by the Minister of Trade.'

Forester took a puff of the cigar and eyed him speculatively. He could hear Rousseau and Armand climbing the steps, and behind him Annabel and Rhys appeared as if by magic. 'And how long is that likely to take?'

The official smiled worriedly at Annabel. He had often dealt with her in the past and he tended to fantasize a little about the tall, blonde Englishwoman. Annabel smiled sweetly back. The Cypriot tore his eyes away from her and stared stonily at Forester. 'Several days . . . perhaps a week.'

Armand arrived. 'A week!' he expostulated.

'Yes, a week . . . Now I must go and so must you.' The official looked at Annabel and nodded politely, then turned and clambered back down the steps, leaving the bridge.

Forester glanced at his wife and puffed on the cigar. 'Well, I think it's up to you again.'

Annabel returned his gaze calculatingly, then with a swift change of expression she smiled confidently at the two Frenchmen. 'Don't worry, bureaucrats are the same the world over – only in Cyprus, more so.'

Rousseau looked quickly from Annabel to her husband. 'Is there anything we can do to help?'

Forester shook his head. 'No. Just leave this to her for now. Annabel has to deal with them all the time.' He picked up the manifest from the wheelhouse table and handed it to her. 'You'll need this.'

She glanced at the names on the list. 'Is everyone here?'

Forester nodded. 'All except the American, Kass.' He took Annabel by the arm and led her to the door of the wheelhouse, speaking to her quietly. 'I'll give you some time with them – see what you can find out, then I'll come in – the usual ploy, OK?'

Before she could reply Rousseau butted in. 'I think perhaps we all ought to be involved in this decision. It does affect us directly.'

Forester surveyed the small group for a moment, then made up his mind. 'All right, but let's give Annabel a chance first. It has worked before. Meanwhile you'd better tell the others that there is going to be a delay; maybe you'd better explain why.'

Rousseau looked at Armand, who nodded his agreement, then turned to Annabel. 'Good luck, madam . . .' He glanced at Forester. 'We'll join her later?'

'Of course.'

The Frenchmen left the wheelhouse and went below. Annabel waited until they were out of earshot. 'What are our chances?'

Forester pursed his lips, looking at Rhys, then back to her. 'Not good. This is coming from much higher up, otherwise the official would not have been so adamant, but' – he grinned – 'he does like you. See what you can manage.'

Annabel raised an eyebrow. 'Here we go again.' She kissed him quickly on the cheek, then slipped out of the wheelhouse, tucking the manifest under her arm.

Forester and Rhys watched her walk along the quay that glistened beneath the dock lights, up to the customs block. She turned and waved, then disappeared inside.

Rhys stared at the ugly building for a moment, then said without emphasis. 'She's a fine woman.'

Forester listened to the sea slapping rhythmically against the hull of the boat. He tossed his half-smoked cigar into the water. 'I know,' he said.

The room was harshly lit and poorly furnished, a few desks and chairs scattered over the wide uncarpeted floor. Not enough to accommodate Annabel, Kass, Nazira, the television crew and the two officials gathered there. Some were just sitting on the floor or leaning against the walls, waiting for the issue to be decided. Although late, it was still hot, and the solitary wooden fan that circled high above their heads did little more than stir the stale air around, hardly ruffling the tired official notices that hung limply from the board.

Nazira had unconsciously separated herself from the others, listening intently as the Englishwoman tried to reason with the officials. From time to time she became aware that the American was watching her, but she ignored him.

Annabel was getting no change out of the customs man. She leaned over his desk, trying to persuade him, but he was becoming increasingly irritated, glancing up at the clock on the wall, anxious to be away. It seemed to Nazira that they were on the brink of being ordered out. The other official continued to toy with the form he was supposed to be filling in, listening to the debate.

Outside, Forester was sitting on an upturned box. Annabel's voice filtered down through the muggy night from the high, open windows of the building. It was time to make his move. He stood up, stubbed out his cigar, then walked round to the main door. Annabel paused when she saw him come in. He strode purposefully towards her; she allowed him to take her arm, moving her to one side as he slid the chair from beneath the startled official, who scrambled hastily to his feet.

Forester sat his wife in it, then turned to face the customs man. 'Now then,' he said without apology, his smile gleaming brilliantly. 'What seems to be the trouble?'

The official was struck almost dumb by the sheer effrontery. He drew breath to launch himself, but before he could do so Forester continued, 'Is it not true that we have been chartering here in Cyprus for the last three years?' He held up his hand before the customs man could reply. 'And is it not also true that in the course of that time we have provided the port with a new amenity, that has not only been successful, but has made a lot of money in terms of trade and tourism for local businesses – not least, of course, yourselves?' He smiled and explained. 'Taxes and so forth.'

He drew the man towards him and put a solicitous arm around his shoulders. 'Now, all we want to do is take these perfectly respectable television people' – he nodded towards Nazira – 'and, of course, our lady photographer, across to Jounieh, and possibly bring back *more* trade and customers for the island.' Forester turned, leading him back to the desk. 'Now, why don't you be a good chap and sign the clearance, then we'll all get the hell out of here.'

The official stopped and glared at him. He flung Forester's arm from his shoulder and faced the Englishman, who stood at least six inches above him. He was furious and his finger quivered as he shook it beneath Forester's nose. 'You are quite mad,' he said tightly. 'You had better remove yourself from my office or I will call the police. You will also take your vessel from the harbour this minute.' Spittle formed on his lips. 'We do not need your custom, we do not want it. We would prefer to have some . . . some . . .'

'Local person?' Forester interjected.

'Yes, that's right!' he said, maddened by the interruption. 'You cause us too much trouble, and if it were not for your wife . . .' He paused, leaving the remark unsaid. 'You will not get permission to sail to Jounieh, now, tonight or tomorrow.' He stopped and looked angrily round at the others in the room. 'Why do you want to risk your lives?'

No one bothered to answer. He waved an arm contemptuously at them, then turned back to Forester. 'These people, they must go . . .' He picked up his cap from his desk, jammed it on his head and strode out of the door without a backward glance. A moment later they heard a car engine start. Then, gears grinding, the car sped off into the night, the sound gradually fading.

Annabel stood up and placed her hands on her hips. She stared accusingly at her husband. 'Well, that was terrific, really terrific. What do we do now?'

He didn't answer and Annabel sighed exasperatedly, turning upon the last remaining official. He recoiled as if she were about to strike him and held up his hands placatingly. 'Look, Mrs Annabel, why don't you go home? I have a small baby, my wife waits since eight o'clock for me. Look at the time.' He pointed imploringly at the clock on the wall: it was nearly midnight. He stood up addressing himself to everyone in the room. 'Why can't you leave? You all go now, we try to do something tomorrow.'

Nazira Yammine rose slowly from her chair. 'We stay,' she said matter-of-factly. 'We stay here in this room until we sail.' She sat down calmly and crossed her legs.

The Cypriot felt a hot flush of anger. Her assertive manner conflicted entirely with his culture and what he expected from a woman. It was an affront. He stood silently, feeling the eyes of the room upon him, his neck colouring with embarrassment. He sat down at his desk and picked up the phone, dialling a number. The room was quiet, waiting. A voice he recognized came on the line. 'I am sorry to have to call you at this time of night, sir, but the owner of *Sea Victory* and the television people are still here.'

He paused, listening.

'That's right, sir, they refuse to go.'

He listened again and gradually relaxed. 'Thank you, sir,' he said effusively, 'Thank you.' He put down the receiver deliberately and sat looking at it for a moment. Then he stood up and surveyed them with great satisfaction. 'Now you will go . . . you'll see.' He walked over to the door and stood with hands clasped behind his back, waiting.

David Kass eased himself up from a squatting position against the wall, and crossed the room to Forester and Annabel. He was puzzled, and worried. 'What's happening?'

Forester put his arm affectionately around his wife. 'Well, by a dint of hot and cold, not to mention a little rehearsal, we have finally persuaded the big white chief to get himself off his backside and down here.'

Kass gazed from one to the other incredulously. 'You mean all this was deliberate?'

Forester smiled. 'Some of it . . .'

Jack Kemp uncrossed his long legs and looked up at Rousseau. The reporter was staring at the back of the customs official, who was still in the doorway. The Canadian stood up and tapped Rousseau on the shoulder. Armand, who was sitting on the floor with his back to the wall immediately became attentive. Whenever Jack made a move, *he* was always the first to be affected. He listened.

Rousseau swung round and faced Kemp. The Canadian indicated the customs official. 'You thinking what I'm thinking?'

Rousseau smiled slowly. 'Well, he's obviously called in the big guns – the question is, can we cover it?'

Armand decided to stand up. 'Not if they know we're covering it,' he said.

Rousseau stared at him enigmatically. 'Exactly.'

The Canadian placed his hand on Armand's shoulder. 'However, if you and I were able to roll sound and camera without our bureaucratic friends being aware of it . . .'

Rousseau butted in, 'And, of course, without me being aware of it . . .' He grinned slyly at Jack and Armand.

'You bastard,' Jack said quietly, but with some feeling.

Rousseau shrugged his shoulders. 'How do you expect me to get you out of jail if I'm locked up as well?'

Armand shook his head, alarmed. 'I don't want to get involved in this, Jack.'

The Canadian digested that for a moment, then: 'But just think what we might get on tape if they don't know we're doing it . . .' He let the sentence hang there, waiting.

Armand's eyes began to shine with excitement – the challenge was irresistible.

Dimitri Xydias was very angry indeed. He did not allow it to affect his driving. The black Mercedes purred on steadily through the night, never exceeding a decorous forty miles an hour. It would not be appropriate for the Chief of Police to break the speed limit, particularly since he wanted no record of the journey.

And he was worried. He had not wanted to associate himself with this decision at all; now he was being forced into the open. It had been made clear to him that it was politically undesirable for *Sea Victory* to sail to the Lebanon. Cyprus was a crossroads, and it was vulnerable – it had been vulnerable for centuries. But now the economy was severely strained. Turkish forces had taken over the whole of northern Cyprus; many of the more profitable regions were under their control. Cyprus could not afford any more problems.

Sea Victory offered a dangerously attractive opportunity to the PLO forces in Lebanon looking for a route out. His government had no wish to offend Israel deliberately, and no intention of allowing itself to become saddled with the same kind of conflict that Lebanon was enduring. The spectacle of Beirut's destruction was all too evident.

In the right circumstances, a route out of Lebanon to Cyprus might be advantageous. There were certainly many wealthy businessmen in Beirut presently looking for somewhere else to place their resources, and Cyprus was right geographically and economically. But it must be handled carefully and, above all, under Cypriot control.

The Chief of Police eased the Mercedes through the dock gates and slowed down as he approached the customs block. *Sea Victory* was moored alongside, her lights reflecting brightly on the water, waiting to sail. They were going to be disappointed.

Xydias pulled up outside the building. A customs officer was standing in a doorway, watching his arrival anxiously. He switched off the engine and got out of the car. He had deliberately chosen to wear his full uniform and it immediately had an effect on the unfortunate official. He sprang to attention in the doorway as the Chief of Police strode through, pointedly ignoring him. The official followed disconsolately at a suitable distance.

Xydias stopped in the middle of the high-ceilinged room and turned abruptly to the customs man. 'You may go,' he said harshly.

The official swallowed hard and saluted. The Chief of Police didn't even bother to respond. The humiliation was complete, and the customs man left the building as quickly as he could, avoiding the eyes of the people in the room.

Xydias watched him go without expression. There was an expectant silence in the room, mixed with a certain amount of apprehension. He'd achieved the effect he wanted. He looked slowly round the bare room, mentally noting the presence of Forester and his wife and also the tall, striking woman in the green battle fatigues. There was something about her cool appraisal of him that he found interesting.

He decided to come quickly to the point: 'I'd like to make one thing clear from the start. I do not propose to discuss anything with you tonight.'

He waited to see if anyone would challenge that, but no one spoke. Only the swish of the fan in the still air above his head broke the silence. He looked at his watch. 'It's half an hour after midnight. You will leave these offices immediately.' He turned to Forester. 'The yacht will go back to its moorings in the marina. You do *not* have permission to sail . . . Go, and goodnight!'

The message could not have been clearer and there was a collective howl of protest from those assembled. Rousseau took advantage of the hubbub to glance at Kemp. 'Are you getting this?' he said from the side of his mouth.

Kemp had a holdall slung casually over his shoulder – his

hand inside it focusing the lens through a small hole cut in the canvas. He nodded imperceptibly, his attention concentrated on the Chief of Police.

The reporter looked at Armand, who was operating the sound recorder using a similar disguise – though in his case the bag was a gift from Cypriot Airways. A neat touch. Rousseau turned round and faced the room.

Forester was aware of what the television crew were doing. He didn't care. If the Chief of Police discovered that they were taping him, it might bring matters to a head. If *Sea Victory* was going to sail tonight, it could only be manoeuvred through the power of the media. He and Annabel had smoked out the man who could change the decision. Direct appeals were hardly likely to work; this might. He waited.

David Kass stared at the Chief of Police disbelievingly. He was shocked by the crude rejection, and the man's impassive face angered him still further. He found himself walking across the room, then standing directly in front of Xydias. The expressionless dark eyes studied him without curiosity. They irritated Kass – made him feel as though he were an insect waiting to be dismembered. 'Look,' he said, 'I don't know what this is all about.' He paused, aware of the sudden silence in the room. He felt his indignation slipping away. 'Maybe I shouldn't be poking my nose in . . .' He saw Nazira watching him, her eyes betraying her contempt. Incensed, he almost snarled at Xydias, 'Ah, to hell with it . . . I'm a doctor, and there are people in Beirut, in Lebanon, who are desperate for medical attention. I don't know what kind of politics are being played here.' He glanced at Forester and Annabel. 'This charter is not going to have any repercussions – we're not helping the warring factions.' He waved his arm around the room. 'These people are television, media. They don't do anything, they just report. I'm not going in there to help the military; they've got medical back-up. It's the hospitals, the civilians that need me, and their needs transcend any bureaucratic mumbo-jumbo. You've got to do something, don't you see!'

He stopped, and stared at the Chief of Police. His expression hadn't changed; it betrayed nothing.

Xydias had seen the American's name and US passport

number on the list. He knew that Kass was a Jew. It could be an elaborate cover for an agent, but he doubted it. In any case, it made no difference. He sighed deeply, almost regretfully. 'You Americans . . .' He shook his head. 'You always seem to think that if you bare your chest, wear your heart on your sleeve, that everything else can be swept aside.' His voice hardened. 'You do not live in the real world, Mr Kass. I am not concerned about whatever sense of guilt motivates your presence here. My people have not invaded Lebanon, have they?'

The barb went home – he saw it on the American's face. Xydias turned languidly and looked at the woman in the green fatigues. How would the Palestinian take it?

David Kass saw the gleam of triumph in Nazira's eyes. He knew he had lost. He stared bitterly at the Chief of Police. 'You bastard!'

Forester saw Xydias stiffen, then turn to face the American. He knew it was an insult that the Chief of Police could not ignore. He moved to cross the room, but felt Annabel's hand on his arm. He glanced quickly at her. She shook her head. 'No,' she mouthed silently.

Forester knew she was right, that they stood to lose everything if he angered Xydias, but somehow he felt responsible for the American. He shook his arm free, but before he could speak he heard a chair scrape on the floor as Nazira stood up. She faced the Chief of Police imperturbably. 'You do not seem to understand,' she said, and indicated the people gathered round the room. 'We have no intention of leaving this office tonight, not until you give us permission to sail.'

Xydias blinked, transferring his attention from Kass to Yammine. He was visibly surprised at her insolence; he had half expected some approval. Now the Palestinian was attacking him as well. 'You will leave.' His voice was hard. 'Leave or be arrested for refusing to do so . . . the choice is yours.' He moved to the desk and lowered himself into the chair, stretching out his hand for the telephone. He pulled it to him, then looked up at Nazira, waiting. 'Well?'

She actually smiled. Forester was impressed.

'That would be good,' she said. The sarcastic approval in her voice clearly irritated Xydias. 'Yes,' she continued implacably, 'that would make very interesting copy.' She paused and looked reflectively round the room. 'Do you know how many viewers and readers we represent here?' Nazira let the question hang for a moment. 'Two hundred million . . . Two hundred million people, plus whatever news bulletins our television crew concoct,' she said acidly. 'I imagine it would be something quite spectacular with such promising material, don't you?'

Kemp locked the trigger mechanism on the video to keep it running, then slid his hand down inside the canvas bag and pulled the focus tighter in on the Chief of Police.

Xydias didn't answer. He sat unmoving on the hard wooden chair. He was beginning to see that he had underestimated this woman. There had been political misjudgement as well. But he had his feelings under control now; he would not allow her to provoke him further. He heard Nazira's voice as though from a great distance.

'People will see and read that you, the Chief of Police, threatened to throw us into prison and stop a yacht carrying a foreign flag from taking us to a country that has been invaded and ravaged by war.' Suddenly her voice rose. Xydias looked at her. He saw the fanaticism in her eyes. 'Innocent people, *my* people, are dying while we stand here arguing about nothing.' She pointed an accusing finger at him. 'You stop us, Mr Chief of Police, and I will personally see to it that your name is heading a leader article about the "hospitality" of the Cypriot people and how you threatened to imprison a television crew, and a *Palestinian* photographer.' She stopped.

Forester felt like applauding, but confined himself to a studied lifting of his cigar. Even Rousseau was impressed. He glanced at Armand, raising his eyebrows admiringly. Armand crossed his fingers behind his back. The Chief of Police had not moved. Nazira took a pace towards him. 'I wish to make a phone call.'

Rousseau could feel the tension in the room – it was electric. What happened now was crucial; the woman needed all the help she could get. He stood up and walked deliberately across the room, stopping in front of Xydias, making sure he didn't block Kemp's view. The Canadian moved as casually as he could, changing focus, trying not to jump the camera about too much.

The Chief of Police ignored Rousseau's presence. The French-man stared down at him and spoke softly, so that only he could hear. 'I think you will be making a mistake if you assume you are only dealing with the woman. I assure you she speaks the truth – she speaks for all of us. You should not underestimate the power of the press and television.'

Xydias did not look up. Not by so much as the flicker of an eyelid did he indicate he had heard a word Rousseau had spoken. He sat in the hard chair, his back ramrod straight, staring down at the floor in front of him. Rousseau waited a moment longer for a response – there was none. He shrugged his shoulders eloquently. 'So,' he said, and turned away to face the others. He beckoned Armand and they began to leave.

Nazira reached for the phone. Before her hand could touch it the Chief of Police slammed his palm down on it with consider-able force. 'Wait!' he bellowed. His voice echoed from the bare walls, silencing everyone, and halting Armand and Rousseau in their tracks. Xydias rose slowly from his seat and faced them. His eyes were cold and calculating. Inside he was furious – contemptuous of the politicians who had backed him into this corner without thinking it through. His worse fears had been realized.

The order to block *Sea Victory* had been issued hurriedly, ignoring his warning about the possible repercussions. They had hoped, blindly, that it could all be accomplished quietly, without fuss. That was no longer possible.

He was faced with a stark decision. Either he put them in jail and risked the outrage of the world's press, or he let the vessel go. Whichever way he jumped, Cyprus could suffer.

Slowly he leaned down and picked up the receiver, dialling a number. The quiet whirring of the telephone was audible to everyone in the room. Someone answered, and the Chief of Police began to issue a string of orders in Greek. Forester was sweating. He knew the power this man possessed, and he had no desire to spend time in a Cypriot jail. He put his arm around Annabel and whispered something in her ear. She glanced at him and nodded imperceptibly.

Rousseau glanced at Kemp and Armand out of the corner of his eye – they were still taping. He tried hard to keep his

71

excitement under control. Whatever lack of technical quality there might be, what they had could be dynamite.

Xydias finished speaking and replaced the receiver. He looked up at Nazira and took off his cap, wiping his forehead with a handkerchief. 'You are a very brave woman. Perhaps foolishly so.' He paused and glanced around the room, including them all in his next remark. 'However, I have issued new orders. The officials will be back here within the hour to process papers for *Sea Victory*. Permission is granted.'

There was a stunned silence. The Chief of Police wiped his hat band, then replaced the cap on his head. 'I hope,' he said, 'none of you live to regret it.' He looked once more round the room, then walked with some dignity to the door and disappeared into the night. A moment later a car engine started and the tension broke.

Forester and Annabel congratulated Nazira, and they were joined by Rousseau. David Kass felt the Palestinian's eyes upon him. He turned his head and looked at her. She smiled arrogantly, knowing the victory was hers. Annabel was the only one to notice the look. She stared curiously at Nazira.

CHAPTER

SEVEN

Samra lay passively on the bed. It was hard and lumpy, but he hardly noticed it. He kept his head averted from the sight of the tube disgorging his blood into the bottle, but the cold, hard point of the syringe in his arm made him weak and nauseous. The pain was blunted by repetition, yet it still hurt, dull and aching – constantly drawing his strength away, impossible to ignore.

He tried to concentrate on the vague sounds of destruction high above him. There was an air of expectancy that had increased among the prisoners as the muffled noise of battle had grown nearer. The sounds were indistinct, just the ground vibration of an exploding shell, and occasionally a tremor of dust or masonry from the dark vault above as a high explosive bomb impacted.

The frequency of the blood transfusions had increased as the battle took its toll of the PLO. Samra was too weak to concentrate – his mind wandered constantly. He could hear the blood pounding in his ears. It seemed to get louder, mixing with the sounds of conflict, each hammering beat an explosion in his head. He tossed from side to side trying to make it go away. He felt a desperate longing for the silence of his underground prison, but the pounding of his blood gave him no peace.

In a brief moment of clarity he realized that he was relapsing into a coma – that soon he might be dead. But he did not want to die, not even to find relief from the horror of his incarceration. He had determined long ago that he would survive. He had found things to do. Helping others had somehow given him more strength than he knew he possessed. Other prisoners had looked to him, and he had seen death in their eyes: an acceptance of oblivion, a release from pain.

He rejected that relief. If the battle was real and not some figment of his despairing imagination, then it was possible that they might yet escape from this hell hole. He would sooner have the pain . . . He screamed, pulling his arm away from the cruel needle of the syringe. He felt a sharp, searing pain as it was jerked from his vein and a strange sense of elation. He was still alive. He covered his face with his arms, smearing himself with his own warm blood. The pounding in his ears suddenly stopped. He opened his eyes and stared at the blackness above. There was silence, a curious heavy silence that seemed to be pressing down upon his body on the bed, forcing the air from his lungs. Then the blast wave hit him. He screamed soundlessly, screwing his eyes shut as the bomb smashed in the roof of the vault. The structure collapsed into itself, burying prisoners and guards alike, leaving a huge, gaping hole in the street above. A cloud of dust rose gradually into the still air.

Samra lay upon the bed, his face a grimace of fear, waiting for death. More masonry crashed down; the stone floor shook. He cringed, expecting to be pulverized by the massive blocks. The vibration began to ease and there was an appalling silence: no shouts, no screams, nothing. He felt no pain. Miraculously, he seemed to be unhurt.

He coughed as a thick layer of dust began to settle, thinning slowly. Between his fingers, through his clenched eyelids, something bright permeated. He opened his eyes fractionally and it blazed into his eyes. He blinked, then shut them fast again. He could feel warmth on the back of his hands.

Oh, dear God, could it be the sun? The heat began to reach his body, penetrating his thin clothing, drying his cold sweat of fear, giving him strength. It was the sun – he knew it. He opened his eyes minutely, trying to adjust to the light he had not seen for six years, basking in the warmth of the life force.

He heard movement – earth sliding, rocks and masonry under stress. He looked around him. His bed seemed to be lying in an alcove formed by a partition of black rock lying half across him. He stared at it intently and realized it was macadamed, tarmacked

– part of a road. A huge slab had collapsed in one piece, forming a protective ceiling that had prevented the masonry from crushing him – had saved his life.

Carefully, he slid off the side of the bed on to the cold floor. Slowly he inched himself towards the gap through which the light was pouring. It was small, not much more than eighteen inches across, and if his body had not been so emaciated he would never have squeezed through.

The bomb had hit the street above squarely on the apex of the roof of the underground vault – at its weakest point – and the vault had collapsed in upon itself under the impact. A small hill of masonry and earth now filled one side of the prison and rose in a steep, jumbled pile to the edge of the crater above.

Samra gazed at the circle of blue sky. Sunlight filtered down through the dust that speckled brightly, shining in its shafts. On the still, warm air he could smell the faint, though distinct street odours of Beirut; it was to him as jasmine.

The light made his eyes water like tributaries down through the dust on his face. But he kept his eyes on the wide circle of blue sky. There was his freedom, his escape. Slowly, carefully, he began to climb the stairway of rubble.

CHAPTER
EIGHT

Forester gazed out over the sharp prow of *Sea Victory* as she creamed through the dark water, the bright lights on her superstructure diffusing a pale glow upon the sea around her. She was a handsome boat and he was proud of the work that he and Rhys had put in to restructure and restore her. He remembered the first time he had seen her lying on a mud flat near Portsmouth. An old Fairmile B, built in 1940 for the Royal Navy and used as a sub-chaser, the Admiralty lines still clearly distinguishable in her narrow hull, built of wood to give her lightness and speed.

He had fallen in love with the old hulk almost at once. In spite of the neglect and the years of inactivity, her graceful lines were still apparent and he had decided to find the owner. Once the search had begun and the owner had been found, the decision to buy had been arrived at without a second thought. He had worked hard and long on making her seaworthy. It had given him something concrete to do and turned his mind away from the distractions and disappointments of London – given him purpose and direction in his desire to try something different.

The day he had sailed *Sea Victory* out of Portsmouth under her own power had been one he would never forget. He had been filled with a mixture of apprehension and jubilation in about equal parts. The Mediterranean had been a natural objective and in Barcelona he had run into Annabel again. They had met once before in London, yet somehow it hadn't really registered. She seemed different on the boat.

Like him, she had fallen in love with *Sea Victory* and, when her modelling assignment had finished, they sailed down through the Med together.

In Port Suez they had met Rhys and his family for the first time. He, his wife Jan and their two teenagers David and Kirstie had made their way up from New Zealand in a small sloop, *Carnaervon II*. Later, they had unexpectedly met again on the slip in Haifa and since that time Rhys had worked on *Sea Victory*. Together they had rebuilt the vessel, making it more luxurious than it had ever been.

Forester glanced at the small, wiry man at the wheel. Rhys said little, but he was utterly reliable and understood the sea and ships with a professional seaman's expertise. Tom was glad of his presence on this trip.

He checked the radar screen. The sea ahead was clear. He was about to turn away when it flickered oddly for a moment, then cleared. He continued to stare at it, but could see nothing. He straightened up. 'Radar seems a bit eccentric tonight. Hope it doesn't give us any trouble.'

Rhys did not respond. He continued to gaze straight ahead, hands on the wheel.

'What time are we due?' Forester asked.

Rhys replied without turning around. 'Should see Mount Lebanon shortly after dawn.'

There was a sudden burst of laughter from the bar below. Forester smiled in the green glow of the radar screen. 'Sounds like they're having a good time.'

Rhys looked at him. 'Why don't you join them? I'll take the first watch.'

Forester glanced at the luminous dial of his watch. It was nearly two o'clock in the morning and they were well clear of the coastal waters now. 'OK, I'll relieve you in three hours. Do you want a drink?'

Rhys shook his head. 'No, I'm fine.'

Forester checked the radar once more. It was behaving normally. He left the wheelhouse and slid down the companionway, entering the saloon through the galley. As usual, Armand and Rousseau were in deep conversation on one of the bench seats. Annabel was behind the bar, serving. David Kass and Lee

Henshaw were on bar stools in front of her, and Nazira, holding a drink, was standing alone, staring out through one of the saloon windows into the night. The Canadian seemed to have gone to bed. Forester joined Henshaw and Kass at the bar.

The Australian turned and smiled effusively. 'Hello, Skipper. What would you like?'

Forester could see he was drunk. It did not please him. 'Let's get one thing clear, Henshaw. I *am* the skipper on this ship and if there's one thing I don't like, it's crew getting drunk first night out.'

Henshaw picked up the disdain in Forester's voice and raised his hand in a mocking salute. 'Sorry, sir . . .'

Forester eyed him coldly. The last thing he needed was a hungover member of crew, unable to function properly. They would all have to be on their toes and ready for anything.

Annabel sized up the situation quickly. Tom had a short fuse and she knew he would not tolerate this. She leaned across the bar to the Australian. 'Lee, I've fixed up a cabin for you. It's below in the stern next to ours. Maybe you ought to get some sleep. We have a long day tomorrow.'

Henshaw turned and looked at her blearily, then smiled and raised himself from the bar stool with as much dignity as he could muster. 'I'm sorry, ma'am. I take it I am dismissed.' There was a note of sarcasm in his voice and Annabel flushed slightly.

Forester deliberately took the glass from Henshaw's hand and put it down on the bar. 'Get below . . . I shall need you tomorrow and I want you stone cold sober.'

All eyes in the saloon were on the Australian. He decided to brazen it out. He lifted himself as though to attention. 'Yes, sir, Captain, sir.' He stopped. 'Beg your pardon . . . owner, sir.' He picked up the drink from the bar and swallowed it quickly in one gulp, slamming the glass back down again. He was tempted to throw up another salute, but the look in Forester's eyes made him change his mind. He turned and stumbled over the step before descending the companionway below.

Forester watched him leave, then twisted slowly round on the stool.

David Kass smiled. 'Here, let me buy you a drink. What'll it be?'

Forester glanced at Annabel. 'The usual . . .'

She was relieved, and poured a brandy sour from the flagon.

Kass raised his glass. 'Cheers.'

They both had a swallow and Kass broke the brief silence that followed. 'Seems you have a problem there.'

'As if I didn't have enough,' Forester said grimly.

'Will he be all right?'

'He'll be sober in the morning, I'll see to that.'

Kass twirled the brandy sour in his glass. 'These are pretty potent.'

Annabel interrupted. 'That's my fault, I didn't know he'd had so much.'

Forester shrugged. 'Some can handle it, some can't.' He smiled at Annabel. 'But don't let him have any more this trip.' He looked at the American. 'Still glad you decided to come?'

'I think so. It was a big decision.'

Forester stared contemplatively into his drink. 'I hope you made the right one.' He sipped the brandy, hardly aware of his surroundings.

'How will it be tomorrow?' Kass said.

It was as if the American had read his thoughts. 'Hard to say – we may get lucky and sail straight in.'

Nazira turned from the window and put her glass down on the bar. 'But that's not likely, is it?'

Both Kass and Forester sensed the challenge in her remark.

'I suppose not,' Forester admitted.

Annabel picked up Nazira's glass. 'The same again?'

Nazira ignored her. 'Won't the Israelis be blockading the entrance to Jounieh?'

Kass could see that Forester was annoyed by her rudeness to his wife.

'Yes,'

'And if they stop us?'

'Then we stop.'

It was Nazira's turn to be annoyed. 'But this is a British boat. What right do they have to stop us?'

79

Forester began to light a cigar and took his time answering. 'Guns, weapons, and a faster boat,' he said laconically.

Nazira eyed him levelly. 'So – might is right, just as it is in the Falklands.'

Kass intervened hurriedly. 'C'mon, that's not fair. Forester can't afford to risk the lives of his crew, his wife.'

Nazira interrupted him tigerishly. 'What do you know about risks, about lives? Have you any idea what it is like where you are going?' The questions were rhetorical and Kass did not answer. 'I'll bet you have a nice soft practice in New York, everything a good doctor would need. Well, you will not find that in Beirut. There will be no plasma or drugs. No pain-killers, perhaps not even bandages in some cases.' She paused, making no effort to disguise her contempt. 'Is this your holiday, part of your vacation? Instead of taking your wife and two children to Nairobi you come here. You talk about life! What kind of life do you think we have had in the camps all these years?'

Her voice rose, each accusation fuelling the next. 'You make me sick. You come here parading your conscience to the world. *You* are going to heal the sick, the innocent. What can you achieve? How do you equate your efforts against all the pain and suffering? But I will tell you, good Jewish doctor Kass. *I* will go in there and no Israeli will stop me. I will show the world with this' – she touched the camera that hung from her neck – 'what is happening to my people –'

She stopped in mid sentence, knowing that every eye was on her, knowing that she had said too much, revealed too much of herself – allowed emotions that she had carefully bottled away to show themselves in the fierceness of her tirade against the American. She turned on her heel and walked from the saloon out on to the stern, getting as far away from them as she could.

It was Rousseau who decided to break the embarrassed silence that followed. He rose from the bench seat. 'It seems to be a night for stating beliefs. I believe' – he paused fractionally – 'it is time for me to go to bed.' He put his empty glass down and nodded politely to Annabel. 'You serve an excellent brandy sour, madam. Goodnight.'

Annabel smiled, glad of the tactful intervention. 'Goodnight, monsieur.'

Armand quickly followed. 'I think perhaps he is right. Good-night, Forester' – he nodded to Annabel – 'madam . . . Good luck tomorrow.'

The bar suddenly emptied; only David Kass remained.

Forester took the cigar from his mouth and looked round the saloon. 'Was it something I said?'

Annabel smiled wanly, but she was not amused. 'I think they are all a little frightened.'

Forester glanced at her, surprised by the remark. 'Even the Palestinian lady?' He indicated the stern.

Annabel looked past him at the vague outline of the woman. Nazira was staring out at the sea, unmoving, curiously still. There was a fatalism about her, an inner compulsion that was inescapable. 'No,' Annabel said, 'I don't think she is frightened.' She paused, and in a voice that could barely be heard she added, 'I think she wants to die.'

Kass looked up from his drink, startled. Forester turned and followed Annabel's gaze. He knew instinctively that his wife was right. It explained everything: the fanaticism that motivated her, her cool destruction of the Chief of Police who had stood between her and the war zone, the fierceness of her verbal attacks on Kass. There was a death wish about her – it clung to her like a shroud.

He felt Annabel move close to him. She shivered slightly, holding him tight. 'Please . . . I'd like to go to bed.'

Forester put his arm around her shoulders, ignoring the figure in the stern. 'Come on.' He glanced at the American. 'Goodnight, Kass.'

Kass smiled briefly. 'Goodnight, see you in the morning.' He watched them descend the companionway together, then turned to look at the vague shape of Nazira. He didn't believe she wanted to die. She had a fanatical desire to defend her people, to attack those that she held responsible – and that included him because he was an American and a Jew – a sickening sense of injustice, perhaps – but a death wish? No, Kass sensed a deep vulnerability behind the hard face she presented to the world. He stood up and leaned over the bar to reach the flagon. He poured two fresh drinks and carried them silently through the saloon to the stern until he was standing behind her.

Nazira knew he was there, but gave no indication of it.

'I thought perhaps you might like a drink.'

When she turned to him her face was in shadow, making it difficult for him to gauge her reaction. 'Is that what you really thought?' she asked quietly.

The sea glittered behind her, disturbed by the passage of the vessel. He could not be sure of her mood.

'Probably not,' he said. 'I wanted to talk to you.'

'Why?'

'It seemed important.'

'Is it?' There it was again – defences up, a whiff of challenge in every question.

'Yes; it is to me,' he answered gently.

She did not reply – she was not going to make it easy for him.

'Some of what you said about me back there is true.'

'Only some?'

'Yes, only some.' He paused, wondering how best to make his point. 'You see, you make one fundamental mistake.'

'I do?' The warning sign was clear in her voice again.

'The fact is, I do care. However much contempt you feel about my efforts, it is possible that I can make a contribution.' There was a silence between them; the only sound was the engines throbbing beneath their feet.

'And that is my mistake?' she said levelly.

'Yes, in a way. There are so many injustices and cruelty. It is too much for one man – or one woman – to carry on his shoulders alone. We must do what we can – where we can, where it will do the most good.' He paused, then added, 'Your mistake is that you equate compassion with weakness.'

He waited for her response – to see if she would flare up, turn on him as she had before. Nazira said nothing. He held out the drink to her, moving one step closer. He could see her face now. Was there just a hint of uncertainty in her eyes? 'Take it,' he said. 'As a doctor I prescribe it.'

She studied his face, searching for deception, trickery. There was none. She accepted the drink and took a sip. It was good.

'Why are you so isolated from your colleagues?' he asked.

Nazira shrugged her shoulders. 'We have . . . different points of view.'

'Is that all?'

She glanced at him quickly, wondering what lay behind the question. 'No,' she said. 'They are professionals, they do a job; some of them do it very well. I have more than just a professional interest – I think it makes them uncomfortable.'

That was true, and it fitted in with what Kass had observed himself. But it was also true that France, the country she worked in, had shown itself to be more amenable than most to the claims of Palestine.

'And yet,' he said, 'are there not many who feel sympathy for the Palestinian people?'

She leaned against the rail and gazed out over the wake churning up from beneath the stern of *Sea Victory*. 'Sympathy? I don't know.'

Kass moved to the rail beside her. She looked at him, still not sure of his complete sincerity.

'I don't think it's possible for you to ever really understand. We have nothing any more – it is all gone and the world has turned its back on us. It wants it all just to go away. All we have left is ourselves.'

There was a long silence, but it was not uncomfortable. For the first time Kass had seen something of the real woman. There was an ineffable sadness about her as she gazed out, unseeing, over the dark water, a solitary desolation that made him want to reach out and hold her, protect her. Yet there was nothing he could say and he felt the moment slipping away.

'Thank you for the drink, Mr Kass.'

She did not look at him and he realized he had failed. He wanted to understand, to see her eyes soften, but if he pressed now he would lose her. He knew that. 'Goodnight,' he said, but she did not answer. He moved away softly, through the saloon and down to his cabin.

Nazira remained by the rail. She could feel the engines pumping away beneath her feet, drawing her closer to the conflict. 'Goodnight,' she whispered, the small sound of her voice whipped away by the wind and the sea.

Rhys hardly moved. His face was lit by the green glow from the radar. Occasionally he would make slight adjustments to the wheel, responding to the compass headings as *Sea Victory* ploughed on through the moonless night. The sea was calm and Rhys expected no change in the weather pattern. Not until August was it likely to get rough in these waters.

By dawn they would be nearing the coast of Lebanon and if the Israeli gunboats were blockading, they would pick them up soon after light. Rhys was glad of the opportunity to try their luck with the French television crew. Day charters up and down the coast of Cyprus were pleasant enough, and they provided an income. But they were repetitious and Rhys was a deep-water man. This trip, while not too far away in nautical terms, nevertheless carried a scent of danger.

The green glow from the radar flickered and he peered down at the screen. It was normal again, everything as it should be. But that flicker was worrying – it had never done that before. He looked at his watch: his spell at the wheel was over. He picked up the handset and dialled a single number.

Forester rolled over on to his side and lifted the receiver. 'Yes.'

'It's time,' Rhys said.

'Right, I'll be straight up.'

Annabel moaned softly in her sleep and he leaned over her kissing her ear.

'Everything all right?' she asked.

He could tell by her voice that she was still asleep – her eyes hadn't opened. It was an automatic reflex question. 'You go back to sleep. I'll see you later.'

Forester slipped out of the bed and put his clothes on quickly, splashing his face with cold water. He climbed the companion-way to the bar and was about to go through the galley when he saw Nazira lying on the couch in the saloon. He crossed quietly and stood looking down at her.

One arm was flung up half across her head, her dark hair spread out on the cushion. Her face had relaxed. Gone was the hardness, the constant defensive challenge. In repose he could see traces of the girl she once had been. Her lips were parted as if she were about to call out.

Forester knelt down beside her and pulled open the small cupboard beneath the bench seat. He reached inside for a blanket and covered her with it, trying not to wake her. She did not stir;

sleep had claimed her deeply. Forester studied her for a moment, remembering what Annabel had said earlier. She looked so vulnerable and calm that he wondered if his instinct had been right. He stood up, tucking in the blanket beneath her feet, then made his way through the galley and up to the wheelhouse.

Rhys heard him coming up the steps and checked the compass heading. 'Did you get some sleep?'

Forester rubbed his eyes. 'Yes, I'm fine.'

'Course is 240 degrees west. You will be in Lebanese waters shortly after dawn.'

Forester crossed to the radar and studied the screen. 'How is it?'

'I'm not sure,' Rhys replied, glancing at the scope. 'It flickered once or twice.'

'OK, I'll keep an eye on it.' He took the wheel from Rhys. 'Anything else?'

'No, it's as calm as a duck pond.'

'All right, you get your head down.'

Rhys nodded, then paused in the doorway. 'Let me know if you run into anything.'

Forester smiled. 'You'll be the first, Rhys. Now off you go. I'll see you at breakfast.'

Rhys ducked out of sight, disappearing below.

Forester made a slight adjustment to the course, then switched on the radio. He fiddled with the knob until he'd tuned into BBC World Service. They were halfway through a news bulletin. In the Falklands, British troops had reached the hills overlooking Port Stanley. Whatever happened, it was clear that soon the battle would be over, but probably not without a heavy loss of life. Forester switched it off, trying to concentrate on the job in hand, but the images of the British troops trudging endlessly across that cold, inhospitable terrain would not leave his mind. It didn't take much imagination to visualize the brutality of battle in those freezing conditions.

Unlike them he had a choice: he could at least turn back. Then, almost at once, he realized that he could not. It was not just a matter of what he wanted; he was committed, and whatever lay in wait for them in beleaguered Beirut he would have to see it through. The green light from the radar screen flickered, then came on again. Mentally Forester crossed his fingers; he needed that bloody radar.

The morning light came slowly, filtering blood-red over the horizon, diffused by the early morning sea mist that blanketed the sea into a pale watery glow. *Sea Victory* throbbed steadily on, her bow cleaving the flat, oily water. Occasionally the mast and upper parts of the superstructure would break clear of a thin tendril of mist and Forester would glimpse the lightening sky and the eerie layers of fog swirling in humpbacked ridges across the sea around them, while the rest of the ship beneath his feet was almost invisible. For a moment or two it would seem as if the wheelhouse were floating, ghostlike above the foggy tendrils, moving forward without apparent power. The ship beneath him was shrouded by the mist and cloaked in silence. Only the faint, muffled sound of the engines betrayed her presence. Then the vessel would be completely engulfed once more and the radar would be his only eyes. It was a disconcerting experience.

Forester was not a superstitious man, but like most people whose lives are directly affected by the elements, he had heard old seadog stories of portents and omens, and the strange conditions made him feel uneasy.

Gradually the heat from the sun began to burn off the vapour and their passage resumed a more normal pattern. As it did so Forester's spirits rose and he put his fears down to his lonely vigil at the wheel and the dead hours of early morning. He waited until the sun was warm on the deck, then picked up the handset. He heard Annabel fumbling with the receiver, then her sleepy voice: 'Hello.'

'Morning. How about a nice hot cup of tea?'

Annabel glanced at her watch: it was late. 'Oh God, I'm sorry, darling – I've overslept.'

Forester smiled at her confusion. 'It's all that night life, it doesn't agree with you.'

She laughed. 'Oh, I don't know,' she said. Then, with heavy seduction, 'I like it.'

Forester groaned. The open invitation to the warm bed and his wife was almost irresistible. 'Get into the galley, you wanton creature – you're needed for other purposes.'

Annabel sighed. 'What a pity,' she said tartly, then another sigh . . . 'Coming.'

Forester replaced the handset and checked his course, scanning the horizon. It was empty. No sign yet of the Israelis, or the coastline.

Gradually the vessel came alive as the breakfast odours permeated deliciously from below. The long table in the saloon became the focal point for most of the passengers as Annabel and Henshaw plied it with bacon, eggs, croissants and coffee. Henshaw seemed to have recovered from his heavy drinking of the night before, and Annabel was relieved to see he had also recovered his sense of humour. She made a mental note to keep the flagon of brandy sour as far from him as she could.

On the bridge Rhys took over from Forester, who made his way aft and broke out a brand-new ensign, hoisting it prominently on the stern. This aroused a few ironic cheers from the television crew round the breakfast table, which Forester studiously ignored. He joined them as Annabel put down a hot plate of bacon and eggs in front of him. He began to eat hungrily, glad that the night watch was over.

Annabel brought fresh coffee for all and David Kass proffered the sugar to Nazira, who shook her head, not answering. She seemed lost in her own thoughts and Kass didn't try to force the conversation. He sipped his coffee and glanced across the table at Forester, nodding towards the new ensign fluttering from the stern. 'Do you think it will do any good?'

Forester chewed his food. 'I don't know. It won't do any harm.'

Rousseau smiled and leaned back in his chair. 'Unless we were sailing for Argentina,' he said loudly.

The men laughed and Forester smiled too, enjoying the joke. The mood round the table was good – he hoped it would remain so. He didn't see Henshaw arrive, and only became aware of his presence as he leaned down over his shoulder to speak quietly in his ear. 'Rhys would like you to come up on the bridge – it's important.'

Forester looked up at him briefly, then rose from the table, grabbing a piece of toast and his coffee.

Kass watched him, concerned. 'Problems?'

The laughter drained away from the men round the table. Forester sensed an immediate anxiety. He grinned, shaking his head. 'No, just routine.'

Kass gazed after him and caught Nazira's look as she watched him go. There was a wariness in her eye, an anticipatory stillness.

The mood had changed abruptly. Philippe Rousseau signalled to Kemp and Armand, and they conferred quietly for a moment or two, then left to set up their equipment on the foredeck, leaving Kass and the Palestinian alone at the table.

Kass reached under his chair and picked up his doctor's bag, putting it down on his knees, checking the contents. Nazira watched him, then put her hand into the pocket of her fatigues and pulled out some half-dozen rolls of bandage. She handed them across the table. 'I found these in the medical cabinet.'

Kass took them, flabbergasted by the totally unexpected gesture. 'Thanks, but . . .'

She raised her eyebrows. 'But?'

Kass gestured with his hands. 'They may need them here.'

'You need them more. They can always rip up some sheets. Where you're going there may be none.'

He gazed at her, still not sure. Nazira stood up, taking them from him and stuffing them into his bag. 'Keep them.'

Kass looked up at her and shook his head, smiling slightly. 'You're crazy.'

He saw the expression change in her eyes, the swift glint of amusement to one of sadness, as though she knew something he did not. She turned away and walked towards the foredeck, leaving him alone at the table.

Forester peered at the dark, blank radar screen and banged it irritably with his fist, hoping the old-fashioned remedy would work on this reluctant apparatus; it did not. 'Jesus, that's all we need.' He stared at it, fuming. 'Shit!' Angrily he hit it again, harder. This time it came on.

Rhys looked across anxiously. 'Is it working?'

Forester continued to gaze at the offending machinery. 'Amazing!'

'Better than having a leaky boat,' Rhys said philosophically.

Forester picked up his binoculars and began to quarter the horizon. He spoke quietly to Rhys. 'Say nothing about this to anyone. As long as we can get in and get out we'll be all right. We both know these waters. When we get back to Larnaca I'll have it looked at; there'll be no one in Jounieh who can handle it, and it would only alarm everyone. OK?'

'Sure, Skipper.'

Visibility was good now, the atmosphere clear, but in the east, directly ahead, the sun was still low in the sky and glazed off the water, making it almost impossible to see. Forester tensed, then quickly lowered the glasses, rubbing the tears from his eyes. The glasses tended to concentrate the sun's rays, making vision difficult, but he had seen something. He tried again.

There it was – a white flash in the water, and behind it a dark grey shape. 'We may have that leaky boat sooner than you think.' He checked the radar. He was right, there were two blips, approaching, and closing fast.

Rhys raised a hand to try to shield his eyes. 'Gunboats?'

Forester confirmed. 'Yes, I can see one, coming up bloody fast; and there's another on the scope.'

The white foaming bow wave quickly grew as the Israeli gunboat bore down on them. The wild flurry of water indicated a very high speed, and as it got closer the thunderous roar of its engines began to vibrate across the water. Forester turned up the VHF receiver, waiting for their identification signal. It stayed ominously silent. Annabel slipped quietly into the wheelhouse and stood beside him, while on the foredeck Kemp and Armand were already taping the gunboat's approach. Rousseau stood beside them.

Nazira, her hair blowing out wildly behind her, was standing with legs braced, taking shots from the bow. It suddenly crossed Forester's mind that her green battle fatigues might be misinterpreted, but there was nothing he could do now. She was oblivious of everything around her. The gunboat's shape was nearly lost behind the spray from the enormous bow wave. Forester glanced at Rhys. He was staring grimly ahead, unruffled.

Forester let the glasses hang by their straps around his neck.

They were unnecessary now: the gunboat was streaking towards them at full throttle. Annabel gripped his arm anxiously as they all stood silently waiting, mesmerized by the onrushing bow wave. He expected the boat to throttle back, but the Israeli skipper seemed intent on passing them to starboard before circling. Rhys and Forester realized the danger simultaneously: behind the gunboat stretched a widening tidal wake that would hit them side on the moment the gunboat had passed.

'Hard to port!' Forester yelled.

Rhys swung the wheel desperately as the gunboat, with throttles wide, roared thunderously past them, throwing up the placid sea into a boiling cauldron as the four 3,000-horsepower engines hurled the displaced water either side of its passage.

The huge wake sped towards them faster than Rhys could get *Sea Victory* round. It would strike them broadside on. Forester sprang to the rail outside and screamed a warning to the camera crew on the foredeck. They saw the danger and flung themselves face down on the deck, Kemp gripping the legs of the tripod. Nazira did the same, grabbing hold of the anchor casing. Forester had not time to get back into the wheelhouse. He braced himself in the doorway as the wave struck.

The wooden hull creaked and vibrated under the impact as she heeled over at an impossible angle, her screws half out of the water, screeching a protest without anything to bite into. It seemed for one agonizing moment that the narrow-beamed vessel might completely turn over: the decks were but a few feet from the water as the giant wave passed beneath her and she began to tilt back. The ship groaned audibly as she began to right itself, throwing everything movable from one side to the other.

The gunboat swung in a wide arc, gradually easing off as several pairs of binoculars minutely examined every inch of *Sea Victory*. Rhys started to get some response from the wheel and pulled her round, keeping her prow head on to the slowly circling gunboat – he had no intention of being swamped a second time.

Forester helped Annabel to her feet. 'Are you all right?'

She smiled ruefully. 'Yes, but from the clamour below I'd say we've lost most of our crockery.'

The predatory gunboat continued to circle. Forester kept a wary eye, watching it through the curved window of the wheelhouse. 'Check everybody out, see if there are any injuries . . . do what you can.' Annabel left.

The VHF crackled, then sprang to life. The voice was hard, authoritative. '*Sea Victory*, this is Israeli naval ship. You will stop using cameras. I repeat, those people on the foredeck, they must stop immediately. Do you read me? Over.'

Forester leapt to the rail. Amazingly, the camera was still on its tripod, and Kemp and Armand were picking themselves off the deck, examining it to see if it were damaged. Nazira was standing forward, on the port side, lining up her still camera for a shot of what looked like an empty sea. Then Rhys pointed, yelling at Forester, 'Another one coming up on the port beam.'

Forester saw it. He grabbed the handset. 'This is *Sea Victory*. I read you loud and clear. No cameras.' He switched it off and cursed them under his breath. He crossed quickly to the door and shouted a warning. 'For Christ's sake keep down. They've ordered no cameras, and there's another bloody gunboat bearing down on us. Turn that thing off unless you want them to blow us out of the water.'

Philippe Rousseau tapped Kemp on the shoulder. Reluctantly, the Canadian stopped taping. He looked at the fast-approaching gunboat and took the camera from its mounting. They could take no chances with this situation.

David Kass was struggling up the still-heaving ladder from below, rubbing his arm where he had fallen against the bunk. He emerged with some relief on to the deck and heard Forester's yelled instructions. The first gunboat was beginning to creep up alongside, weapons bristling from its superstructure. Kass looked forward. Nazira had ignored Forester's warning and was still shooting film on the second approaching gunboat. Kass moved quickly, holding on to the handrail. He grabbed her arm. 'Come on, get below. Don't be stupid, you're risking the lives of all of us.'

Nazira glared at him and shook herself loose. Then she saw the first gunboat almost on top of her – she hadn't realized it was so close. She smiled suddenly at the American. 'Below, did you say? That's not a bad idea.' She left and disappeared into the saloon.

Kass stared after her. The grey, menacing silhouette of the Israeli ship was now alongside – he could have reached out and touched it. The steel helmets and dark glasses of the officers on the bridge surveyed him coldly. A trickle of sweat rolled uncomfortably down his side and he started to move fast towards the companionway. He climbed up it just behind Rousseau, and joined Forester and Rhys in the wheelhouse. Kemp and Armand had taken their equipment below.

The VHF came on again. This time it was the second Israeli captain. 'This is Israeli naval ship, do you read me? Over.'

Forester was about to acknowledge when Rhys grabbed his arm. 'Boss, take the wheel. Let me have the handset.'

Forester stared at him, puzzled. 'Why?'

Rhys held out his hand. 'Do as I ask, please.'

Forester gave it to him and took the wheel. 'Don't try anything stupid.'

Rhys shook his head. 'I won't, but we might just be lucky.'

The voice on the VHF boomed out again. 'Who is your captain?'

Rhys glanced at Forester and raised two crossed fingers. 'Hello, Israeli ship . . . My name is Rhys Williams . . .'

The VHF stopped crackling and went dead. Rhys stared at it, willing it back to life. Kass glanced across at Rousseau, who was watching Rhys carefully – waiting. Then it came on again. The hard note had gone. 'Rhys? What the hell are you doing here?'

Rhys sighed with relief. 'We are taking television people into Jounieh. Over.'

Forester smiled grimly at him. 'You old bastard, you know him.'

Rhys grimaced. 'We met on the slip at Haifa during the refit. I thought I recognized the voice.'

Kass stared at him incredulously. 'How the hell did you recognize it on that thing?' He gestured at the VHF set.

Rhys shrugged. 'You get used to it after a while.'

Forester was watching the two gunboats carefully. They had positioned themselves on either side of *Sea Victory*, and were moving forward, keeping abreast of the civilian craft. Even at this slow speed, the engines of the gunboats were so powerful that Forester could feel the vibration through the deck.

The VHF remained silent. Forester could imagine the conversation being transmitted between the two Israeli commanders deciding their fate. He remembered what he had told the Palestinian woman, how cool and matter of fact he had been. It was true – there was nothing they could do except wait and accept the decision whichever way it went. However, saying it to Nazira was one thing; standing here passively was another, and he didn't much like it.

The Israeli tactics had been extremely effective. Without using any weapons they had virtually incapacitated *Sea Victory* long enough to have them completely under control; a smaller vessel would have been overturned, or swamped. Yet they could still claim, truthfully, that no shots had been fired. An interesting manoeuvre, and one that could be valuable in the propaganda war.

Meanwhile Nazira was moving swiftly from cabin to cabin, using the different portholes to get as many angles as she could to photograph the gunboats and their sophisticated weaponry. The powerful ships fairly bristled with armour and antennae and while, from this low angle, their superstructures were mostly out of sight, nevertheless the number and trajectory of the torpedo tubes could clearly be seen; also the armour plating.

She continued to move around imperturbably, photographing everything she could, while the eyes of the Israeli marines stayed glued to the decks above.

The VHF came back to life. The voice was unemotional, calm. '*Sea Victory*, this is Israeli naval ship . . .' There was a pause and Forester picked up the handset to acknowledge, then the message continued, 'You may proceed to Jounieh. Shalom.' The line went dead.

No one in the wheelhouse spoke – the relief was too great, the fear still too strong. They waited silently to see what would happen.

The roar of engines on either side of them began to increase, and slowly the two Israeli gunboats drew ahead. Forester saw an arm raised from the bridge of the grey silhouette, port side. He nudged Rhys and they both returned the gesture.

It broke the tension in the wheelhouse. Kass turned to Rousseau and grabbed his hand, pumping it enthusiastically. Forester clapped Rhys on the back. 'You did it! My God, you bloody well did it . . . look at them go.'

The gunboats were peeling off port and starboard. Rhys allowed himself a brief smile of pleasure, then resumed his post at the wheel. Kemp and Armand appeared again on the foredeck and began to video the withdrawal of the Israeli gunboats until they were mere dots on the horizon. Then they turned and waved at Forester and Rousseau as though a war had been won.

Forester lit a cigar and enjoyed the small triumph. But he knew their problems were only just beginning. Yet . . . they were through the blockade. Now, at least, they could attempt a docking.

The studio cabin next to the galley was crowded. Everyone, apart from Rhys at the wheel, was jammed in to watch the playback. Jack Kemp had brought in their monitor, so that they could see the footage they'd shot with the Israeli gunboats. Rousseau was keeping the rest of the tape with the Chief of Police under wraps. He wanted no one to see that until he'd had a chance to evaluate it – he hoped to do that in Beirut.

Annabel drew the curtains of the small room, while Forester watched from the doorway, keeping a wary eye open for the Lebanese coastline. The picture quality was surprisingly good, despite the hasty set-up. The approaching gunboat could be seen clearly. Even on camera its speed was amazing. It was easy with hindsight to guess its intentions. But without prior knowledge of the tactic, the devastating effect of the huge wake was hard to anticipate.

The camera tilted at a crazy angle as it struck, a jumble of blue sky, heaving sea and flashing sun. Forester was disturbed to see that they had continued to shoot after going below. He was grateful the Israelis hadn't spotted it. They would not be on their way to Jounieh if they had.

There was a good deal of ribald comment as the shots of the departing gunboats came up. Then Forester heard something. He strode quickly across to the monitor and switched it off, returning to the doorway. He stood listening intently. This time they all heard it. A faint booming noise, heavy and insistent. Forester bounded up the steps to the wheelhouse.

Rhys pointed ahead. Rising above the early morning mist that still shrouded the shoreline was Mount Lebanon. The booming sound came echoing across the water again. Rhys nodded. 'Guns,' he said laconically.

Forester listened until he heard them again. 'Probably Israeli field artillery.'

Rhys made no comment. Forester levelled the binoculars, trying to discern the port. He adjusted them to as tight an image focus as he could, then he began to see the tops of some of the highest buildings emerging out of the ground mist that was dispersing fast in the morning sun. He took the glasses from his eyes and gazed meditatively at the oily sea ahead. He saw a silvery flash in the water, reflecting the light. He quickly brought the glasses on to them – then he saw another, and another . . .

'Jesus Christ!' He turned to Rhys. 'Half speed, there's a mess of partially submerged plastic bags dead ahead. If they foul up the water intakes we've had it.'

Rhys swiftly lowered the engine revs and steered *Sea Victory* in a wide arc away from the clutch of bobbing plastic bags lying in their path.

As they proceeded cautiously towards Jounieh the sea became choked with ugly blotches of flotsam, dumped from the shore or thrown overboard. It was a constant and irritating hazard. The port lay hidden in the shadow of Mount Lebanon as the sun rose steeply behind it.

Four miles out and everyone was on deck peering towards the shoreline and the sounds of battle. The blue sky became crisscrossed with high vapour trails as the Israeli jets stayed well clear of any heat-seeking missile. Through the glasses Forester was able to distinguish two large vessels anchored in the bay outside the port. Around them, yet giving the anchored vessels a wide berth, dashed a number of speedboats towing water skiers. It was a bizarre spectacle and one that Forester had not expected to see.

He glanced worriedly at Rhys and picked up the handset. It was time to make contact and establish identity. 'Hello, this is

Sea Victory calling Jounieh Port Control. Permission to enter harbour is requested. Over . . .'

Forester waited. Static crackled from the radio, but no reply. He tried again. 'This is *Sea Victory* calling Jounieh Port Control, permission to enter harbour . . . Over.'

Forester could see Rhys's knuckles clenched white around the wheel as the silence lengthened. He was about to try again when they answered.

'*Sea Victory*, this is Port Control. You have permission to enter. Over.'

Forester relaxed. For a brief moment he had wondered if they had found the right place. He switched on the handset. 'Thank you. We expect to be off the harbour entrance in about half an hour. Over . . .'

'*Sea Victory*. A service boat will come out to you when you are in sight . . .' The voice on the radio sounded relieved. 'Please await its arrival before coming in. Over . . .'

Forester acknowledged. He put the handset down and took a long pull on his cigar. He grinned at Rhys. 'Well, we're in.'

Rhys did not reply. Like Forester, there lurked at the back of his mind the obvious fear. Would they get out again?

Kemp and Armand were set up on the foredeck again and Rousseau was directing their attention to the harbour area that lay ahead. As they drew closer, a faint but distinct smell of sewage drifted downwind from one of the ships anchored there.

It was soon apparent why. They were both cattle boats, one empty, the other crowded, not with animals, but with people. They jammed the decks and companionways to the railings, where they waved pathetically at *Sea Victory* as she sailed closer. The smell of effluent and urine grew stronger.

Now it was clear why the water skiers were giving it such a wide berth. They now started to buzz around the British ship shouting and waving unconcernedly while the guns continued to boom out from behind Jounieh.

Sea Victory had to pass close to the cattle boat in order to reach the entrance to the channel that led to the port. The stench and the cries for help from the women and children crowding the rails were overpowering. Annabel came rushing into the wheelhouse, taking hold of Forester's arm. 'We must do something, they need help.' She gazed, horrified, at the children who were holding out their hands to their mouths, indicating their need for water.

Forester stared grimly ahead, ignoring them. 'Steer well clear of her, Rhys.'

Annabel was shocked. 'If we could just give them some water.'

Forester could not bring himself to look at her. 'We don't know how long we shall be in harbour, or what the conditions are like. There may be none available. We have to hold on to what we have.'

Annabel looked at him incredulously. His face was set, implacable. It was a side of Tom she had not seen before and it frightened her. She turned and left the wheelhouse without another word. Forester wanted to stop her, to explain. But he didn't move. There was nothing he could say. He tried to concentrate on the job in hand. Once upwind of the cattle boat, the foul smell grew fainter.

Jack and Armand recorded the cruel images in the blue sea with professional disinterest, trying not to allow the plight of the refugees to affect them. Nazira used roll after roll of film, moving her camera around endlessly. David Kass watched her silently, saying nothing – seeing the outrage and the hate glittering in her eyes.

The carefree water skiers continued to crisscross their path, yelling their greetings enthusiastically, while Forester paced the bridge, deep in thought. The conditions on the cattle boat were appalling. He went outside. He was angry with himself, yet he knew he had no choice. His own passengers came first; he had to be sure there was enough water for them to get back.

He turned his binoculars on to a large, three-storey building that overshadowed the port. It was heavily sandbagged. Two military helicopters stood on a concrete apron. It looked like a military barracks. Incongruously, back to back with it, was another building: the Jounieh Yacht Club, its flag fluttering proudly above its smart exterior. The marina was lined with expensive motor cruisers and yachts. Suntanned men and women basked on the decks or lay in rows on the beach, sipping iced drinks while, behind him on the cattle boat, the refugees suffered in the heat. Forester lowered the glasses. He didn't want to see any more. He felt a hot surge of anger welling up inside him and glared helplessly across the water. How could they ignore the foul conditions on the cattle boat – sip their drinks and sunbathe as though the refugees did not exist – when men, women and children were lying out there in that stinking hulk desperate just for water? And yet, had he not sailed past them in his beautiful white yacht, ignoring their cries himself? Oh yes, there were any number of practical reasons for doing nothing, but how much did that weigh in the mind of a child thirsty for water? He thought of Charlie, and of Annabel's face when he had refused them aid.

The juxtaposition of images was weird, nightmarish. The artillery barrage continued to thump away beyond the port. Further down the coast, nearer Beirut, he could see columns of smoke, flickering red with flame, rising high in the hot, still air, while around him the water skiers still buzzed and, in the yacht club, the sunworshippers basked. It was disorientating.

Only the stench on the wind that occasionally drifted down from the cattle boat gave the lie to this deliberate charade of normality in Jounieh. He felt someone lean on the rail beside him. David Kass shaded his eyes from the sun and stared at the yacht club. Forester sensed his anger.

'Are we in the right place?' he asked, his voice edgy.

Forester didn't look at him. 'We'd better be.' He was about to turn away when a weatherbeaten old service boat rounded the bluff that guarded the entrance to the port and chugged towards them. Forester could see two Phalangist soldiers standing in the stern. In front of them was a short, stocky man wearing a sober grey suit that seemed oddly out of place in the garish, bright colours of Jounieh. He stood, solid, feet apart, unmoving. Forester glanced inside the wheelhouse. Rhys had seen them. 'I'll go down and find out what they want.'

Rhys nodded his acknowledgement and lowered the revs still further, keeping the engines ticking over just enough to give him steerage. Forester slid down the steps and made his way aft; the service boat was just pulling into the stern ladder.

The man stepped gingerly from it and climbed carefully up the steps. He smiled when he saw Forester and held out his hand. Forester clasped it briefly.

'I'm Kevork Makarion,' he said, 'from Inter-Travel. Gemino telexed us from Larnaca to say you were coming. We are very glad to see you.'

Forester looked at the two soldiers who had followed him up the ladder. 'You run the shipping agency here?'

'No, but I represent them. Mr Hatan asked me to meet you. I shall be looking after your passengers and arranging the manifest. You are the first to get through the blockade. Were you stopped by the Israelis?'

Forester ignored the question. 'That cattle boat in the harbour, whose responsibility is that?'

The smile slipped from Makarion's perspiring face, and his eyes flicked uneasily to the Phalangist soldiers standing behind him. He took Forester's arm and Tom allowed him to walk him out of earshot. 'They are Egyptians. They were given permission to embark by the Army,' he said quietly, 'then the Israelis radioed that they would not be allowed to go to Alexandria.' He shrugged dismissively. 'I suppose they think the PLO could be hiding on board.'

Forester kept his feelings under tight control. 'Then why aren't they ashore?'

Makarion touched his arm placatingly. 'Please,' he said, 'not too loud. The soldiers, the Phalangists, they will not permit them to come back.'

Forester stared at him expressionlessly. Makarion shifted uncomfortably beneath his gaze.

'And that's it?'

Makarion did not reply at first, but Forester waited implacably for the answer. He held out his hands. 'There is nothing we can do.'

Forester grabbed the top of his arm and squeezed it brutally. 'Oh, yes there is. If you want to do business with me, first you see that those refugees get fresh water, food and some decent sanitary arrangement.' Makarion squirmed painfully in his grasp, but Forester did not relax his grip. 'When you have done that, then we will discuss manifest and passengers. OK?'

Makarion nodded his head vigorously. 'Of course, we will do all we can.'

'You'd better; otherwise there's no deal.'

Forester relinquished his hold and Makarion rubbed the spot, trying not to attract the attention of the Phalangist soldiers. He looked at Forester pleadingly. 'I understand your concern, Captain, but you do not fully comprehend the situation.' He rubbed his arm again, grimacing with pain. 'Perhaps when we are ashore you will see what I mean.'

Forester nodded. 'Perhaps. First you have to get us around the point and into the docks. Follow me.'

He led the way up to the wheelhouse. 'This is a Mr Makarion from Inter-Travel,' he said shortly to Rhys. 'We're going in . . .'

Forester was worried. He did not like the presence of the two soldiers on his boat, and the remark Makarion had made about conditions ashore was ambivalent. It could indicate trouble there, too. But there was only one way of knowing, and only one way to find out. He moved quietly out of the wheelhouse and stood by the rail at the top of the companionway, where Rousseau had joined David Kass and Annabel. Nazira was standing by the prow, occasionally using her camera.

Sea Victory nosed slowly forward, while two bikini-clad girls in a paddle boat called up to Jack and Armand, trying to attract their attention. High overhead the jetstreams crossed the sky above Beirut, dropping their distant messages of death. The vessel rounded the point into a channel that led to the dock area. As they cleared a long, concrete building, a sound began to intrude above the steady throb of the engines. At first it was impossible to identify: a strange, surging, wailing cry. Forester looked at Makarion. 'What's that?'

Makarion stared straight ahead, pretending not to hear. Forester was about to force an answer from him when he heard Kass exclaim behind him. He turned round. The port was just coming into view and the cause of the strange noise was staggeringly clear.

The dockside was a sea of faces, and the road leading to it was choked with a jostling mass of people, all trying desperately to remain on their feet as they surged helplessly in the pull of the crowd. Phalangist soldiers near the water's edge were using their belts as whips, brutally trying to keep order in the chaos and confusion. The volume of noise was unimaginable – a wall of shouts, screams and crying children. Annabel turned to her

100

husband, her face blanched with shock. It was the first time he had seen real fear in her eyes. She pressed her hand in his, holding it tightly, staring grim-faced at the howling mob.

People were somehow holding on to their possessions and shouting encouragement as *Sea Victory* eased slowly towards the dock. Forester could see a small party of Europeans sitting beneath the shade of two trees, surrounded by their luggage, which they had made into a protective wall around them. No one on *Sea Victory* spoke: the enormity of the misery shocked them into silence. Only the television crew continued to function.

Leila Khalil held tightly on to her brother's good arm as the crowd swept back and forth around her. It seemed to have a will of its own, as though intent upon separating them, tearing them apart. She was tired, exhausted, her clothes damp with sweat and fear. She talked constantly to André, knowing that in his darkness and pain the sound of the wailing crowds around them, pushing them first one way, then another, must be a waking nightmare of terror. She could see above the heads of the people the white superstructure of the vessel coming gradually into dock. Off to her right were the buildings that housed the shipping agents, but hard as she tried she could not force a passage through the mass of people whose sole attention was fastened on the arrival of *Sea Victory*. Her arm ached from the constant strain of hanging on to André. She tried to move around behind him and get to his other side. In that brief moment the crowd surged, snatching him from her. Leila heard him cry out and she screamed at him. 'I'm here, André.'

He tried to turn and force his way back to her, but the crowd jostled him as he did so and she realized he was moving further away. She screamed once again, but her voice was drowned in the howling excitement of the crowd. Panic rose in her throat as he was inexorably pulled further away, in constant danger of being pushed and trampled to the ground. She clawed and pulled at the people around her, trying to get back to him. Tears of fear and helplessness ran down her face.

She felt a hand on her arm and turned. A man, his face white and gaunt, dark eyes deep in their sockets, started to push a gap in the crowd around them. He pointed towards André and she nodded frantically. The man pushed sideways past one person and pulled her after him. Then another and another . . . Slowly, terrifyingly slowly, they began, between them, to forge a tortuous path through the surging crowd. She kept her eyes glued to her brother, praying he would not be forced to the ground. The gap narrowed and the old man beside her yelled in her ear. 'Call him now. I think he might hear you.'

She screamed his name again and again. She saw him stiffen and turn towards her voice. Again she called. He started to come to her. The man slipped her between two more people and suddenly she was only an arm's length from André. She grabbed him and pulled him towards her, holding him tightly in her arms.

André patted her back, murmuring her name over and over. The old man took his other arm and slowly they started to push towards the shipping offices. In the jostling, heaving mass Leila looked at the man and tried to convey her thanks. Samra could not hear what she was saying, but he could see the gratitude in her eyes. He smiled and pointed at the ship. She nodded vigorously, trying desperately not to give in to the mounting tide of hysteria she felt within her. If they could gain passage on the boat she knew they would survive this horror. They broke through the edge of the crowd and staggered the last few paces to the shipping offices. Inside, incredibly, it was cool. Leila sat down abruptly on a chair and buried her face in her hands.

Samra stood silently with André, waiting for her to recover.

CHAPTER
NINE

Forester followed Makarion down the gangplank into a space that had been cleared on the jetty by the Phalangist troops. The soldiers immediately surrounded them and began to club a way through the swaying mass of refugees. Forester was sickened by the brutality.

Those in the forefront caught the full force of the militia's tactics. They fell back before them, trying to protect themselves as the canvas buckled belts and wooden batons were wielded unmercifully. No distinctions were made. Men, women, children . . . all were cruelly assaulted.

A space opened up before them. Makarion and Forester were bundled quickly into it. Their progress was slow. The cries of the refugees washed around Forester, pleading, begging for a passage, a way out. Forester was fighting to stay on his feet, keep close to Makarion, whose head bobbed in front of him.

The single, most clear impression was the smell of fear. It was pervasive, overpowering, and seemed to remove any feeling of pain from the poor wretches around him who caught the full force of the Phalange soldiers' progress. Unable to escape the onslaught, they simply reached out, trying to touch Forester, screaming at him, 'Captain, Captain!'

He tried not to see them; there was nothing he could do. He concentrated on staying upright, using his elbows and his height to make progress. At last the pressure eased, and suddenly he burst free. The Phalange re-formed around him and Makarion then led them towards the shipping offices. Forester didn't look back; he didn't want to see the pleading eyes. He felt shaken, angry, and something else that he found hard to identify. It was shame.

The agency's offices were cool, and mercifully quiet. He saw a young woman slumped on a chair. Two men stood passively either side of her. She looked up as Forester came in, gazing directly at him. He saw a flash of hope in her eyes – he was beginning to recognize that look. She stood up and moved towards him. The soldier next to him waved her away, raising the belt in his hand to strike her.

Something snapped inside him. His hand shot out, grabbing the belt, jerking it from the grip of the Phalangist. The girl flinched, holding up her arm protectively, but Forester threw the belt clattering to the floor, and led her back to the chair, ignoring the militiaman. It had all happened so quickly that neither the old man nor André had moved. Then Forester saw that the younger man was sightless.

Leila collapsed into the chair and looked up at Forester gratefully. 'Thank you,' she said.

Her voice was quiet, almost toneless. Forester could see she was close to tears. He smiled encouragingly. 'Can I help?'

She took her brother's hand and held it tightly. 'We have come a long way. My brother, as you can see, has been . . .' She paused fractionally. 'Has been injured. We' – she glanced up at Samra – 'all three of us are hoping to find a way out. We saw your boat.'

Forester felt a hand grip his arm. He turned. It was Makarion. He pulled Forester slightly away from the girl and the two men. 'My employer is waiting to discuss your manifest with you. There are a number of substantial commitments already made for your voyage out.' He smiled ingratiatingly. 'I think you should talk to him first, before you make any promises to this girl.'

The hard knot of anger inside Forester swelled. The urge to hit Makarion was almost irresistible. He jerked his arm free and stared coldly at the Lebanese. 'You concentrate on getting supplies out to that cattle boat, otherwise there is no passenger list for anybody. Is that clear?'

His eyes glittered with suppressed fury and Makarion stepped back a pace, averting his gaze. 'I'm sorry, Captain,' he said, putting more space between them.

Forester turned his attention back to the girl. 'I'll do the best I can. Stay here, all right?'

Leila nodded dumbly, biting back the tears. Forester smiled, then turned and followed Makarion.

Samra watched him go, hardly daring to believe that his ordeal might be over. His face remained impassive, drawn. Only his eyes revealed the hope that had suddenly been kindled there.

Makarion led Forester down a cool, tiled passageway. Their footsteps echoed back from the walls, the sound magnified until it seemed as if a small troop of soldiers were marching along it. He stopped in front of a glass panelled door and tapped deferentially. He waited, smiling anxiously at Forester. A thin, high voice called to them in Arabic. Makarion opened the door, waving Forester in ahead of him.

The thin voice belonged to an equally thin, wizened old man, sitting behind a desk that engulfed him. Makarion inserted himself between the Englishman and the desk to make the introductions. His eyes shifted uncomfortably from one to the other. 'This is the captain, sir – Mr Forester.' He glanced at Tom and gestured to the frail figure behind the desk. 'Albert Hatan . . .'

Hatan was wearing a tropical suit that had once been white and a shirt with a separate collar that was too big for his scrawny neck. The Adam's apple bobbed. 'Forgive me if I don't get up,' he said to Forester. The voice had changed. Using English it was surprisingly melodic. 'I'm afraid I'm not as sprightly as I used to be.' The sunken eyes shone mischievously from beneath his grey, bushy eyebrows. He indicated a cane chair. 'Do sit down.'

Forester did so – he still towered several inches higher than Hatan.

'You must be thirsty. What can I offer you?'

Forester realized the old man was right. His throat was dry – he could use a drink. 'Something long and cool.'

Hatan spoke brusquely to Makarion in Arabic. Once again

Forester noted the difference in the tone – it was sharp, imperious. Hatan was clearly a man used to command.

Makarion left the room.

Hatan smiled toothlessly. 'He won't be long.' He surveyed the Englishman quietly.

Forester became aware of the low-pitched hum from a VHF radio behind Hatan. He indicated the set. 'Did you monitor our transmissions on the way in?'

Hatan shook his head. 'No – I don't play with it. We have it tuned into channel sixteen, the international open line. But I am curious . . .' He paused, studying Forester. 'How did you get through the Israeli blockade? No one else has succeeded.'

Forester smiled. 'We were lucky. My engineer knew the Israeli captain. Besides, we were coming in – not trying to get out.' He watched Hatan carefully. 'What are our chances?'

Hatan sucked thoughtfully on a fingernail, then waited as Makarion's footsteps echoed down the passage outside. He tapped on the door once more and Hatan called out, this time in English, for him to enter. He was carrying a tray. There were two drinks – a tall glass, misting on the outside, and a small tumbler which he gave to Hatan before passing the other to Forester. He withdrew silently.

Forester took a sip from the glass – it was lager, icy cold. He glanced up. 'It's good.'

Hatan raised his drink. 'To a fruitful relationship.'

Forester nodded – then sank half the glass, quenching his thirst. Hatan sipped delicately, then swirled the golden liquid around the tumbler. 'They say whisky is good for the blood, but I must confess I enjoy it simply for the taste.' He put the glass down on his desk. 'However, to answer your question as best I can. No ship, thus far, has been allowed to leave Jounieh. And, to my knowledge, none has been allowed to leave Lebanon at all.'

Forester took another swallow from the lager. 'Have any tried?'

Hatan shrugged. 'Probably many, but only one that I know of has tried to go without permission.'

'What happened?'

'I listened on this.' He indicated the radio behind him. 'It was

106

a Turkish captain. He was ordered to stop by the gunboats – he refused, claiming he had no part in the war. They warned him several times.' He paused, then sighed. 'His radio cut out – we never heard from him again, and he did not come back.' Hatan let that sink in, then, 'The only chance you have is by getting permission from the Israelis.'

Forester looked questioningly at the old man. There had been something in his voice. 'How?'

Hatan's eyes glittered. 'There *could* be a way . . .'

Makarion closed the door and stood for a moment outside. He heard Forester's comment on the drink, and Hatan's toast to a fruitful relationship. He could not risk standing there any longer. Age had not dimmed Hatan's sharpness. The old man would have been aware of his presence if he'd stayed outside the door.

He walked deliberately up the passage, his footsteps signalling his retreat. He came to the well of a wide staircase and ascended the three flights to the top floor of the shipping block. The last flight narrowed. At the top was the door to his office. Once inside, the hesitant and obsequious manner dropped from him like a cloak. The room was not large, but it had a fine view of the dock area. He watched the crowd still seething around the approaches to the quay where *Sea Victory* was docked. The wailing had died down, but for the occasional cry of pain or fear as people surged aimlessly back and forth, controlled by the Phalangist soldiers.

A group of Europeans were standing by the gangplank at the stern of the vessel, preparing to leave. It was clear from the cameras and equipment they were carrying that they were media people. His eyes were drawn to the dark-haired woman in battle fatigues. Curiously, the clothing seemed to accentuate her femininity, rather than disguise it. She was ceaselessly photographing the crowd and the actions of the militia. She, he knew, was not European.

Eventually the four men and Nazira were escorted off the boat and through the crowd to a waiting taxi. The old Chevrolet drove off in the direction of Beirut.

Makarion stood thoughtfully by the window for some time,

gazing absently at the dock. Then he glanced quickly at his watch: it was time. He moved to the door and turned the catch, locking it. His movements were automatic, unhurried, as though he had done it a thousand times before. He picked up a wooden chair from the corner and placed it against the wall, then climbed upon it. His hands reached up to the air ventilation grille, his fingers sliding through the vents. He pulled sharply upwards, jerking it out. He climbed quietly down and stood for a moment listening . . . nothing. The grille was placed carefully on the floor so that it would not slip and make a noise, then he clambered back up again and reached into the wide, dark hole of the shaft. His hand touched the hard surface of the leather-covered case and found the handle. He pulled it from the shaft: it was undistinguished and rather battered. Leaving it on the floor, he picked up the grille and replaced it in position over the shaft, then carried the case to the front of the desk where it could not be seen from the window.

He sat down crosslegged on the worn strip of carpet and opened the suitcase. Inside, it was divided into several compartments. A dismembered machine pistol occupied three of the spaces; the oiled gunmetal shone dully in the light. He ignored the weapon and carefully removed a pair of headphones and a transmitter. From the inside lip of the case he extended a telescopic aerial, then checked the power level of the batteries. Again he looked at his watch. Satisfied, he began to tap out an identifying signal in morse. He received an acknowledgement, then began to transmit in earnest. The muted bleep of dots and dashes lasted only a minute or so. His task completed, Makarion quickly replaced the transmitter into the suitcase and returned it to its hiding place in the shaft. When the grille was back in place he moved the chair back to the corner and glanced swiftly around the room: everything was back to normal. He padded silently across to the door and turned the lock, then sat down behind his desk. He swivelled his chair around and gazed out of the window at the white vessel nestling against the quay. The sun was at its zenith now and the heat haze shimmered off the oily water of the dock, undulating slowly in the swell. *Sea Victory* looked like a mirage – a ship of dreams. But it was real enough – real enough to be a threat; or a promise?

108

Makarion wasn't sure yet. It was not for him to decide. The decision belonged to the Commander.

It was hot in the back of the taxi, and crowded. Nazira had to sit well forward on the seat, with Kass and Rousseau on either side of her, and they just squeezed in. That taxis still plied their trade at all, in the chaos and confusion around them, surprised Nazira. In time she would come to accept this surface of normality, to realize that just by continuing to go through the motions of doing what they had always done made the horror easier to bear for the Lebanese. In a curious way it removed some of the fear, took the sting away from the imminence of death . . . if not the pain.

Nazira wanted to use her camera, but it was difficult to move and find a position. Kemp had the front seat, which irritated her. Armand was squeezed between him and the driver. As they approached Beirut on the coast road the devastation became more apparent. The driver had to slow the car down to avoid craters, caused by mortar and rocket attack, which pockmarked the road. She lifted the camera from around her neck and tried to get a few shots, but it was impossible to keep her balance.

Kass watched her struggle for a moment, then touched her arm. 'Stand up . . . you sit here, next to the window.'

She glanced at the American – then raised herself to allow him to slide into the middle, while she took his place without comment.

Kass perched himself as best he could. 'Thanks,' he muttered mockingly. 'Thanks a lot.'

Nazira ignored the sarcasm; she was so involved in her work he doubted if she had heard. He glanced at Rousseau and raised an eyebrow. The Frenchman smiled and spoke quietly. 'Perhaps the patient needs different treatment, Doctor?'

Kass smiled at the allusion, but didn't comment. He looked out past the Frenchman at an apartment block they were passing. One side had been completely ripped away, like a doll's house with the front removed. Each room was open to the elements and some of the furnishings were still, amazingly, in place. Tables were laid, waiting for diners who would never arrive.

For the first time the enormity of the destruction struck home.

Soon, he knew, all of this would seem commonplace. He would look, but not see. How quickly would his mind adjust, horror lose its impact? He shook his head: one thing at a time. It was *he* who had decided to come, to leave New York and his comfortable practice; no one had forced him. He didn't want to think about why he was here, but his mind was racing – too many thoughts, the old images crowding in again, making him sweat profusely in the stifling heat of the taxi.

There was no escape. He'd always known that sooner or later he would have to face up to what he believed in, and here in Beirut he'd finally reached his point of no return. Only two people in New York knew of his trip to Cyprus – Evie and Paul. Both of them had told him he was stupid to go, though Evie had phrased it differently. She had tried to understand his reasons but, in the end, had rejected them. There were too many risks, she said, and he could not deny it. They outweighed any argument he could put forward. It had been impossible to explain – he wasn't even sure in his own mind. There were so many reasons, in themselves insubstantial, which, taken together, became an irresistible urge to *do* something, to be involved where the issue was dramatic and stark, before he was too committed by family or wife to do anything that might endanger his responsibility to them. For the moment he was still a free agent.

He didn't know if he loved Evie. Her reaction had somehow disappointed him, though it was perfectly reasonable for her to be concerned about what might happen to him. Every time he examined a reaction, or his own motivation, he only became more confused.

Why was he here? What had persuaded him to leave his budding practice in New York and sail into this? He could still turn round and go back on *Sea Victory*. Instinctively he rejected that; it would be a failure. He examined that thought. What did he mean? Yes, it was failure in a way. He would be failing to be the man he thought he was. That was it – failing himself.

But wasn't that simply ego – self-esteem? Were all those long student debates about freedom and justice, his disagreement with his own country's role in Vietnam in the early seventies just so much hogwash? Had he simply been kidding himself?

He hadn't had to go any more than he'd had to come here. He'd missed the draft because of his commitment to medicine. That bugged him too. He suddenly felt the old flush of anger and humiliation. It was unchanged. It surprised him that it could still be there, so strong, so powerful in its effect.

He'd almost forgotten the shame, buried it in his desire to qualify as a doctor and set up a decent practice. Yet here it was again, rising to torment him because he sensed the danger . . . the possibility that he, young Doctor Kass, might be involved in something that was a risk to himself.

Maybe he had finally pinned it down, maybe this was it: he had to discover the truth about himself. Did he really want to help the suffering in this city, or was it merely a means to an end? It was probably a bit of both. But if he turned back now he would never know, and he would have to live with that. In the end, did it matter *why* a life was saved?

Surely not. Only to him, perhaps. But what really mattered was that a person had lived, when that life would otherwise have been extinguished. He remembered Tom Forester's reaction in Larnaca − how he had seemed to understand his confusion; how he had shared the same confusion. His own explanation for the voyage had hardly been rational, yet Forester had accepted it instinctively. There it was again. An instinct, a gut reaction that defied logic.

He knew then that *Sea Victory* would sail back without him, and somehow he felt better.

CHAPTER

TEN

Forester studied the old man, waiting for him to continue. 'Well,' he said, 'I'm listening.'

Hatan leaned forward in his swivel chair. 'You will have no chance if you simply take on board as many as your vessel will carry.'

Forester's face hardened. 'I *want* to take as many as I can – I can hardly leave with space on board, when there are refugees out there desperate to get away.'

Hatan clasped his bony hands together fastidiously. The delicate blue veins shone through his ancient, freckled skin. 'That is not what I am suggesting,' he said reprovingly. 'The Israelis are blockading because they do not want the PLO to escape from the country.'

Forester grew impatient. 'I know that.'

Hatan held up his hands. 'Then bear with me for a moment. They will never allow you to take out Lebanese.'

Forester tried to keep his voice level. 'You expect me to *leave* them here?'

'For the moment,' Hatan said softly. 'Just for the moment. Take only those who have dual-nationality passports. I can assure you that we can fill your vessel several times over. Most of them will still be Lebanese, but this way they can claim another nationality – otherwise . . .' Hatan shrugged, leaving the possibility hanging in the air.

Forester knew the old man was right. He reckoned he could squeeze about 120 on board *Sea Victory*. He would have to take the Europeans, and if the remainder were dual nationality there was a good chance the Israelis would let them through. He nodded. 'That makes sense – and once I've got through it creates a precedent. It will be that much easier next time.'

Hatan smiled delightedly. 'Exactly – at least you will have a chance.'

Forester took another swallow at his drink. He wasn't sure about the old man – not yet. It was possible he had certain people he wanted to get out – money was no object in these circumstances. There would be those willing to pay high for a passage out of the war zone. 'I will give you a list of names for the manifest as soon as I have them.'

The old man continued to smile, his expression unchanging. 'As you wish.' If there was an ulterior motive, he disguised it well.

Forester indicated the radio. 'Will you try to contact the gunboats – tell them we are coming?'

Hatan nodded. 'Yes, I'll get Makarion on to it right away; see if we can get permission. You will be taking the Europeans on the dock?'

'Yes, I'll deal with them first.' He stood up. 'Let me know as soon as you have made some contact.'

'Of course.' Hatan reached across the desk for the switch on the intercom. 'Shall I get Makarion?'

Forester shook his head. 'No, no need – just make sure he gets on to those Israelis.'

Hatan looked up at him steadily. 'You can rely on me, Captain.'

Forester studied him for a moment, then turned and left, shutting the door behind him.

Hatan stared at it, deep in thought. He reached out to the intercom. Makarion's voice answered, and Hatan rapped out a command in Arabic.

As Forester emerged from the passage, the girl stood up expectantly. He slowed fractionally – he'd almost forgotten about her and the two men. The girl took her brother's arm and pulled him close to her, as if sensing Forester's lack of decision.

Well, he would have to decide – make a start somewhere. He smiled encouragingly, stopping in front of them. 'I shall be

113

returning to Larnaca, getting under way as soon as I can get clearance. Is that a suitable destination for you?'

A smile of relief lit Leila's face, erasing the tension from around her eyes. 'Anywhere,' she said, 'anywhere will do. Just as long as we get away.'

Forester realized that he'd made a tactical mistake. 'I'm sorry – first I have to see your passports. Do you have them with you?'

She turned and picked up the bag that was lying on the seat. The flask Mr Frangieh had given her was still inside – she wondered if he was all right. She fished around inside, searching apprehensively. She found them and heaved a sigh of relief, handing them over to Forester.

He examined them briefly – they were Lebanese. He kept his voice casual. 'Do you have any others?'

Leila glanced at her brother, then back at Forester. 'No, they are ours – they are in order?' She looked anxiously at him.

'Yes, they're fine, it's just that . . .' He stopped. She was biting her lip and he sensed her rising panic.

André spoke for the first time. 'You wish to know if we have dual nationality?' His face was set – his eyes staring sightlessly ahead.

'That's right – without them the Israelis will not let you through.'

A smile flickered briefly across André's face. 'Then you had better have these.' He reached into the pocket of his jacket and handed Forester two French passports. 'I work for a bank – I often have to go to France. They provided me with these when things started to get bad out here.' He put his arm around his sister. 'They also gave me one for her.'

Leila hugged him. 'You never told me.'

'No – it would only have increased your fears.'

Leila laughed for the first time, and Forester smiled, sharing her relief – yet realizing in almost the same instant just how tough and hard some of the decisions were going to be. He glanced at the old man.

Samra Asaker had remained silent and motionless, listening to the others. When he had escaped from his prison it had seemed like a miracle – something he had not even dreamed about. The circle of blue sky that had lit his darkness was an unthought-of beacon of freedom; just staying alive had been enough. Now he was free. He could see the sun, and feel its warmth.

He realized that the others were looking at him – waiting. He shrugged, holding out his hands, palm upwards. 'I have no passport, Captain, but it's of no consequence. I will go to the mountains – this will end some day. I fear you will have to sail without me.'

Forester eyed the white-haired man before him. His clothes were in tatters, his skin like parchment, and there were dark circles beneath his sunken eyes. Yet there was something about the man – a spirit and dignity; no pleading for help, nor yet anything of the martyr, just a calm, philosophical acceptance – almost as if he had expected it. Well, *he* was not prepared to accept it – not yet. There must be a way to get this man out. 'You'd better come with me, all of you. We'll see what can be done when we get on board. Stay close and leave the talking to me. OK?'

Samra nodded. 'Thank you, Captain.'

Forester led the way from the building. The heat outside hit them like a solid wall. Immediately he was bathed in perspiration. One of the two Phalange militiamen who had escorted Makarion came towards him, looking at the others curiously. Forester cut short the question on his lips. 'They are with me – we are going back on board.'

The Phalangist stared at him uncertainly for a moment.

Forester pointed at André. 'This man is badly injured – he needs medical treatment.'

The militiaman glanced at the bloodstained bandage wrapped around André's hand, and made up his mind. He turned to the other Phalangist, who was standing by the edge of the crowd, and called him over. Then, one in front and one behind, they began to push a way through the swaying mass of people.

Leila and Samra stayed on either side of André, trying to protect him, while Forester and the Phalange militiaman cleared a path for them.

Once again the wailing started, the cries beat about Forester's head. But he ignored them, making sure he kept his small group

115

together. It was less difficult this time. The crowd were getting used to Forester having to make his way back and forth and they fell back before him, allowing a passage to open up, perhaps hoping that by co-operating they had a better chance of boarding his vessel.

They reached the edge of the dock. Forester could see Annabel and Rhys waiting anxiously in the stern. He waved cheerfully. The gangplank sloped quite sharply up on to the deck, and he stood at the bottom, helping Leila and her brother to negotiate the first steps. Then he led the way, holding carefully on to André's arm.

Annabel and Rhys took over as he stepped clear of the gunwale. Forester took his wife's arm and put his face close to her ear. 'Take them below – do what you can with his injured hand. They are brother and sister so they can share a cabin. I'm going to talk with Rhys – we have a lot to sort out. Come back up to the bridge as soon as you can.'

Annabel didn't say anything, though there must have been a thousand questions she wanted to ask. Calmly she helped André and Leila through the saloon to the stairs below.

Samra looked at Forester questioningly.

Forester smiled. 'Go with her.' He paused. 'I'm sorry, I don't know your name?'

The white-haired man stared at him for a moment. He seemed to be trying to express something. 'Forgive me,' he said finally. 'I'd almost forgotten myself. My name is Samra Asaker.'

Forester nodded. There was something in the man's eyes that did not need expressing, an immense mantle of suffering that had lifted for a moment. He turned and slowly followed the others through the saloon.

Forester gazed after him. Whether he liked it or not he was being drawn in deeper – he knew that. But what was the alternative? Skip out as fast as he could and leave them to their fate? *That* was no alternative at all. He turned quickly to Rhys. 'Come on, we've got work to do.'

CHAPTER
ELEVEN

The decoded telex was brief and to the point, but the message cheered him considerably.

The day could not have started worse. He had chased several enquiries round the department, but in the end had made no progress. He felt stymied and frustrated, and he recognized the pattern. It was going to be one of those days. The harder he pressed, the less he was likely to get results. Now this. Perhaps it had broken the chain; maybe the log jam would ease. He picked up the phone.

The voice was as smooth as ever – urbane and polite, giving nothing away.

'Good morning, sir,' he said. 'I'm on scrambler.'

'Ah, hello, Hank.'

It never ceased to surprise the Director that he always recognized his voice instantly. He wondered if it were the same with everyone. He smiled to himself . . . you could bet on it.

'What can I do for you?'

The Director relayed the telex from Beirut.

'That is good news.'

'Yes, sir, it is. They've got into Jounieh – we couldn't help them on that. But soon they will have to get out.'

'What can we do?'

'Well, sir, obviously the Israelis will be on the look out for PLO. My feeling is they will only consider letting Sea Victory out of Lebanon if they are certain that no Palestinians are on board. We have been monitoring the radio traffic closely, and the shipping agent in Jounieh has been trying, unsuccessfully up to now, to get clearance from the Israeli gunboats.'

'They've not replied at all?'

'No, sir, not yet. I think they're just waiting to see what Sea Victory will do.'

'Can we help?'

'Yes, sir, I think we can.' He began to explain . . .

CHAPTER
TWELVE

As they entered the outskirts of Beirut, the muffled explosions of gunfire began to grow louder. Nazira glanced at the Lebanese cab driver, who seemed unconcerned. He drove casually, one hand on the wheel, negotiating his way through the wrecked suburban streets of the capital.

Amazingly, a few shops were still open and people queued in an orderly fashion for what little there was. Outside wrecked buildings some of the shopkeepers had set up stalls and were selling vegetables and whatever else remained of their stock.

Nazira checked her film – she had bought as much as she could carry, but she had been assured that there would be plenty available. Why not, she thought? This was the media war to end all media wars. The men in this taxi, with the exception of David Kass, were all here to get the pictures and send them home, where they would be presented in whatever political context that country represented. She understood the attitude of Kemp, Armand and Rousseau. It was a straightforward, professional approach, but it was not hers. She knew why she was here, and it hardened her resolve.

Kass watched the Canadian in the front seat, his video ever at the ready, occasionally taping some of the devastated buildings. Kass liked the two Frenchmen, but he was less sure about Jack Kemp. The impassive Canadian worried him slightly. His silence, his lack of comment, disturbed him – though he tried to dismiss it as another symptom of his own insecurity.

As the sound of the shelling got louder, the tension in the cab increased. The driver must have sensed it, too. He half-turned in his seat and spoke to no one in particular. 'It's all right, the fighting is not in this area. The Israelis are bombarding the airport over there.' He waved an arm towards the west, where a column of smoke and dust could be seen rising up to the stark blue sky. There was a harsh rattle of machine-gun fire and, in the distance, mortars added to the sounds of conflict.

Kass glanced at Nazira from the corner of his eye. He wondered if she felt as tense as he did. There was no sign. She sat calmly next to him, her shoulder and arm touching his, on the crowded back seat. No sense of fear from her. Was it possible that she could feel *his* fear simply by sitting close to him, their bodies touching? Medically, it was an interesting question. Animals conveyed fear physically by gesture and facial expression. But what if they tried to disguise their anxiety as he did? Would the species still be able to detect it? The lie-detector worked on the basis of increased physical stimulation: the heart, sweating and so forth. It seemed impossible to him that the others in the cab could be completely unaware of his own fear, though, curiously, pondering the medical aspects of the question had calmed him down.

The driver looked round again. 'We are coming to the green line. You have to cross here on foot, it is impossible for me to drive you.' He must have anticipated their alarm. 'There is nothing for you to worry about, it's not a long walk, and when you get to the other side you will find another driver waiting.' The cab slowed down, then stopped. The driver pointed to some military personnel standing beneath a dusty clump of trees. 'Speak to them.'

Rousseau paid the driver as Kass and the others gathered their luggage. Kass watched the taxi turn round in a cloud of dust, then head back towards the coast road. 'We should have held on to him until we've sorted this out.' He indicated the militiamen, who were watching them curiously. Nazira picked up her travelling bag and camera cases and marched across the road – the men trailed after her.

None of the soldiers wore insignia, so it was impossible to tell who was the senior officer, although the uniforms were more complete than those of the Christian Phalange they had seen on the dock in Jounieh. In fact they were units of the Lebanese Army.

Nazira addressed herself to one of the soldiers, taking out her identification. 'We are journalists and television reporters.' She showed him her press card. 'We want to go to the other side.'

The soldier stared at her, realizing she was Semitic, but unsure of her nationality. He examined the card.

Kass watched nervously. He had no press card. How much weight did his doctor's qualifications carry?

The soldier studied the offering without much interest. He waved his arm down the long, straight road. 'That way . . .' He shrugged. 'They will kill you, but if you must go . . . You walk about a mile, then you come to the PLO. Then, if you are lucky, you come to West Beirut.' He smiled sardonically. 'Stay in the centre if you want to stay alive.' He turned his back on them and looked at the other soldiers, putting his finger to his head to indicate that they were mad. A couple of them laughed.

Armand swallowed nervously. 'There is danger?' His voice was pitched high with fear.

The soldier looked at him contemptuously. 'Yes, but we haven't lost a newspaperman yet.'

Nazira picked up her bag. 'Come on, let's go.' She moved off without looking back, unconcerned as to whether they followed or not.

Kass admired her spirit, in spite of himself. Rousseau and Kemp began to follow. Armand picked up his own things reluctantly, wondering whether he should turn back. He stood in the dusty road, staring morosely after them. Then he realized the soldiers were watching him, waiting to see what he would do. He could hardly fail to go where a woman was leading the way. Disgruntled, he picked up his heavy suitcase and tape recorder and trudged after them, forgetting his fear in his irritation.

The road stretched away in front of them, dipping in the middle, before rising slightly the other side. They all kept conspicuously in the centre, making their intention clear to any watching militia. Kass felt naked and exposed. It only needed one jumpy, trigger-happy guerrilla and they were all dead.

121

He could see why it was called the green line. Nothing had driven down this deserted stretch of no man's land for months. Weeds and vegetation were forcing their way up through the cracks in the road surface. And, as it receded from them in the shimmering heat, the colour spread, giving it an unnatural green lustre. The heat was unbelievable. It seemed to rise from the cracks in the concrete surface, making Kass blink the sweat from his eyes.

Nazira kept up a steady pace. Not too fast or too slow... Nothing in the least suspicious. The ground began to rise from the dip. She could see the earthworks of a tank-trap thrown up across the road ahead of them. In front of it a small chicane had been constructed, twisting the road so that everything had to slow down before it reached the barrier. The PLO had done a good job.

Rousseau tried to absorb everything – it was important for him to do so. He had spotted the troops dug in behind the trees on either side of the road where they had spoken to the Lebanese Army soldier. The deep rift between the rival militia was very evident. East and West Beirut were, for all practical purposes, two different cities.

They threaded their way slowly through the chicane towards the tank-trap. If the PLO were guarding this point, he could not see them. Then, quite suddenly, as they walked past the earth-works, a militiaman leapt down from it in front of them, shouting at them, 'Come on, get behind this – they're all crazy down there – they will kill you!'

Kass wanted to laugh. It was bizarre. Word for word, the utterance had been almost the same. Yet there was nothing funny about the sub-machine-gun this man held, pointing steadily at them.

The PLO man studied the camera cases around Nazira's neck. 'You are a journalist?'

'Photographer,' she corrected.

He was wearing a battered hat, sweat-stained and wide-brimmed, and dark glasses. The glasses were impenetrable, mirroring the small party standing before him. They gave him a vaguely sinister appearance. But they served a useful purpose, protecting his eyes from the glare and disconcerting those he talked to.

Nazira heard a splash; some men laughing raucously. She glanced to her right but could see nothing.

The militiaman had noticed her look. He leered, his eyes sliding up her body. 'Better turn your head the other way when you walk by, lady.' He gestured towards the road with the machine-gun, inviting them to continue. 'You'll find some Lebanese drivers up there, looking forward to lifting your money. But if you want to write about us, don't forget you will require press accreditation from the PLO.'

Nazira lifted the wide-angle camera from around her neck. 'Do you mind if I take a picture?'

The glasses stared at her. 'No, I don't mind.'

He held the weapon in the crook of his arm, posing slightly. Nazira took a couple of shots, then picked up her bag. 'I think that's enough.' She smiled at the militiaman. 'Maybe I shall use you on my centrefold.' She turned to the others. 'Let's go . . .'

As they moved up the road the reason for the laughter suddenly became clear. A huge bomb crater had filled with water from a burst main, and several naked men were taking dives from a makeshift springboard, constructed from an old door, one end of which was jammed beneath some debris.

Nazira looked back at the PLO man and laughed. 'You mean this?' She raised her camera and, continuing to walk, shot some more film. The naked swimmers, far from being abashed, flexed their muscles, posing suggestively. One of the PLO men called out something obscene in Arabic.

Nazira stopped and lowered the camera. She began to walk towards the man who was posturing crudely to the others, laughing. As he saw her coming closer he stopped, his partial erection drooping foolishly. She halted in front of him and spoke in Arabic. 'You disgrace your country. You come here to resist the Israelis; instead you make crude suggestions to me with that.' She looked down contemptuously at his penis. 'You don't deserve me, you don't deserve any woman. All that is good for is a boy. Maybe I should find you a boy.'

The silence after she had spoken stretched agonizingly. While

123

Kass and the others did not know what she had said, it was not difficult to guess. The automatic rifles were lying only a few feet away from the PLO men. The tension could be cut with a knife. It broke as one of them laughed derisively, pointing at the limp penis hanging between the man's legs. The others joined in, leaping into the makeshift pool, dragging the unfortunate man with them.

Kass felt like applauding, but he didn't. That would have stretched providence too far. Nazira rejoined them.

Three hundred yards further down the road they heard an engine start up, and an old, battered American Buick pulled out of a side road and stopped beside them. The driver grinned. 'You wanna taxi?'

Armand heaved a sigh of relief. 'Thank God,' he said, climbing in and hiding himself in the furthest corner.

The Lebanese driver smiled broadly at Nazira. 'My name is Yussef.' He was portly and middle-aged, and he seemed to be enjoying a joke. His eyes twinkled, and he was delighted when Nazira sat beside him: he'd seen the episode with the naked swimmers. The others clambered in the back. 'Hotel Commodore?' he asked her.

She nodded her assent, keeping a straight face.

The gears crunched and they started to move, then Yussef slammed on his brakes, jerking them forward, stopping the big car. The barrel of a sub-machine-gun was sticking through the driver's window. Yussef sat rigid with fear and Nazira looked past him. It was the PLO man who had stopped them by the anti-tank barrier. Her face set hard. 'Yes?'

He removed the weapon and leaned forward through the window, ignoring the driver. 'If you want me to, I can arrange for your press accreditation.'

She studied him for a moment.

He smiled. 'Otherwise you will *all* find it very difficult, I promise.'

Rousseau spoke from the back. 'That's very kind of you. Shall we contact you?'

The PLO man continued to stare at Nazira. 'I will find you, I know where you will be.' His glasses never left her face. He waited. The silence lengthened.

124

Christ! Kass thought, why the hell doesn't she say something? It was unbearable.

'Yes,' she said finally, 'I would like to see you at my hotel later today.' She even made her acceptance sound like an order.

His head turned, and he looked at the others, fixing their identification in his head. Armand was paralysed with fear. His smell was heavy in the back of the car. Then the PLO man stepped back and waved the driver on.

Yussef needed no second bidding. The gears crunched appallingly, and once more they began to move. The PLO man stood in the middle of the road, watching their departure. The woman was interesting, and she was undoubtedly Palestinian . . .

Yussef drove carefully. The incident had shaken him and he felt compelled to explain: 'You have to be very careful with these people, you understand. It is not possible to be sure what they will do . . .' He waved a hand at a bombed-out building. 'You see all this? The Israelis bomb us all the time because they are here.' He relapsed into silence for a moment, then said bitterly, 'I wish the PLO would go – maybe then we would be left in peace.'

No one in the taxi spoke. Yussef had obviously not realized that Nazira was Palestinian. Kass hoped she would not turn her wrath on the friendly Lebanese driver. Thankfully, she did not respond. He felt sorry for Yussef, and he understood his sentiment. He too wished the Israelis had not become embroiled in Lebanon's internal struggle – instinctively he felt it could do no good.

The traffic began to increase and the cab turned down a narrow, dirty street, then slowed. Yussef indicated a tall building. 'We are here, that is the hotel.'

The Commodore showed few signs as yet of any damage. Some windows were broken, but already workmen were repairing the damage. The car stopped and Kass eased himself out, relieved to have arrived safely. He tried to pay Yussef the fare, but Rousseau would have none of it, dismissing his protests. 'It's all on expenses, Doctor. I don't pay.'

Yussef smiled up at the Frenchman. 'If you are here for some time, you will need to have a regular taxi – everyone does. I know this city, monsieur . . . I've lived here all my life. I can make myself available, either on a daily or weekly basis.'

Rousseau turned to Kemp. 'What do you think?'

The Canadian shrugged. 'We're gonna need transport quickly when things start to happen. It sounds like a good idea to me.' He leaned down and spoke to Yussef. 'Could you be available from tomorrow?'

Yussef nodded vigorously. 'Oh yes, for a fee I take no one else – just yourselves.'

Rousseau decided. 'OK, be here in the morning not later than eight a.m., all right?' He stopped. 'By the way, how much?'

Yussef smiled. 'Normally for a week I charge the Americans three hundred dollars; for you, two hundred and fifty.'

'Two fifty it is . . . Remember, be here tomorrow at eight.'

Yussef was pleased to have negotiated the deal. He waved away the money Rousseau was proffering. 'Forget it. Consider it part of the fee. Au revoir . . .' He checked they all had their baggage, then drove off.

The street outside the hotel was busy with cars and vans constantly loading and unloading. Many, like themselves, carried video equipment and sound recorders. Kass felt slightly out of it, holding only a small suitcase and a doctor's bag. Inside it was cooler, though no less frantic. British and American voices predominated. Bits of information were being relayed: the war, the siege, the airport . . . How long before the Israelis reached this part of the city?

It took some time for him to register and find himself a room, and in the general hubbub of the reception area they all went their separate ways. He caught a brief glimpse of Nazira studying a Reuters wire machine which spilled out information in the corner, then the elevator doors closed.

His single room was on the top floor. Although he didn't know it then, this was the most vulnerable position in the hotel. But it was customary: the longer he stayed at the hotel, the further down he would be placed. It was the same for everybody.

Nazira stayed in her room. She waited; she knew he would come. First, she picked up the telephone and ordered a bottle of whisky and some mineral water. Then, unhurriedly, she began to unpack. It did not take long – she travelled light, with the exception of her cameras. She always carried three. They were

Nikon, motor driven. A wide-angle lens for the closer shots, a middle-range 200 millimetre, and a long lens at 400. Nazira sat on the bed and checked them all thoroughly. If any of them failed to operate in a war zone, then the one picture that might have made this long and dangerous journey worth while could be lost. From now on she would carry all of her cameras, all of the time. On the boat it had not been necessary, they had been close at hand. Film went into an old ammunition belt which was strapped around her waist. The small boxes were perfect, carrying all the stock she would need. Then she had a bath, washed her hair and cleaned her teeth. She felt better after that, towelling her body hard and slipping into a dressing gown.

She took a large-scale map of Beirut from her bag, and spread it out on the bed, studying it to familiarize herself with the layout of the city. She worked out where the green line crossing point was, and marked it. Also the position of the Commodore, and the route they had travelled. It was beginning to fit together.

The knock on the door was heavy, commanding. Nazira folded the map and left it on the table. The knock was repeated, impatiently. She looked around the room, then crossed and opened the door.

The glasses stared soullessly at her. 'About your press accreditation,' he said.

She left the door open and walked back into the room. 'You'd better come in.'

He did so, then stood, confidently, studying her.

Nazira helped herself to a glass of water. 'Maybe you should shut the door.' She smiled wickedly. 'Otherwise people might talk.'

He slammed it violently. She was unimpressed. She lifted the bottle of whisky. 'Would you like a drink?'

He nodded shortly.

Nazira poured a medium-sized amount into a glass and held it up. 'Is that big enough for you?'

He said nothing, holding out his hand imperiously.

She crossed the room, but did not give it to him. 'Look, if we are going to discuss' – she paused, emphasizing the next word sarcastically – 'accreditation, don't you think you ought to take off your hat?'

He did not reply.

Nazira reached up and swept it away, pressing her body close to his. 'There now,' she said, looking at him directly. 'Isn't that better? You have nice hair.'

He slid his arm around her waist, pulling her tightly to him. She could feel his erection rising hard against her stomach. He bent to kiss her.

She was still holding the drink away from him, arching her back. 'Please,' she said, 'the sunglasses. I keep seeing myself in them.'

He took them off and threw them on the armchair. He kissed her hard and brutally, his stubble scratching her face. His hand went inside her dressing gown, sliding quickly up her leg. Nazira pulled away. 'Just a minute – I'm going to spill this drink.' She thrust it into his hand and went to the bedside table, picking up her glass. 'Cheers.' She took a sip and watched him swallow his in one gulp. She handed him the bottle. 'Help yourself.'

He poured another and swallowed that too. He began to take off his gunbelt and shirt.

Nazira picked up the map of Beirut and spread it on the bed. He stared at it, surprised. 'What is this?'

'What does it look like?' She saw the suspicion begin to cloud his eyes and held up a hand. 'All right, let's clear this up right away.' She took her shirt from the back of a chair, removed a small, plastic folder from the breast pocket and threw it on to the bed in front of him. 'That's my identification.'

He picked it up and glanced at it curiously.

'As you can see,' Nazira continued, 'I am a party member, and my purpose is to get as much coverage with these' – she tapped her cameras – 'as I can. The more civilians the Israelis kill, the stronger world opinion will be against them.' She smiled wryly, anticipating her cliché . . . 'And a picture is worth a thousand words . . .'

He handed back the plastic folder. 'What do you want?'

'First, your name.'

'Elias Mourad.'

'Right. I need that press accreditation, not just for me but for the others, too.'

He bristled. 'Why? They are French, not Palestinian.'

She strode over to him, her eyes blazing. 'Because, you idiot, we need the publicity. It is the Israeli Army that is invading Lebanon. It is their first major blunder. This country has never been militarily active against Israel. It has a fine colonial tradition,' she said contemptuously, 'the Paris of the Middle East. The more the French and the world see the way it is being destroyed, the more powerful will be the voices against the Israelis.'

He did not try to deny it; he couldn't. He felt deflated, physically and emotionally. Nazira had undermined him as she had the naked swimmer. Intellectually and emotionally he was flattened. His erection had subsided. Sex with a superior woman was not a part of his tradition. Nazira knew that.

She pulled him down on to the bed to study the map. She had complete control. 'Now, tomorrow I want you to take us to wherever the fighting is. I don't care about the danger, that isn't important. We must go. I have to have pictures.'

Mourad nodded and pointed to a spot on the map.

CHAPTER
THIRTEEN

Sea Victory was crowded, jammed from gunnel to gunnel, every inch of space utilized. At the last count they had crammed 120 men, women and children on board.

Some of the decisions regarding who would go and who must stay had been the most harrowing Forester had ever had to make: wives and husbands split because some had dual nationality and others did not; parents chose to separate rather than lose the opportunity of getting their children out of Lebanon.

Annabel had been close to tears many times, but she knew it would not help the refugees to see her distressed – much better to insist that they would be back as soon as all the passengers were ashore in Cyprus. This had helped; as long as there was hope, people could bear the pain and the fear of separation – though it had not been easy.

Now Forester wanted to get away as quickly as possible, before daylight ended. He did not relish having to deal with the gunboats in darkness. He checked for the sixth time with Hatan on the VHF. 'Any response yet?'

Hatan's voice came through clearly this close, and Forester knew immediately by the tone that there had been no contact. 'I'm calling them every five minutes, Captain, but they do not acknowledge.'

'Have you made it clear that all we are requesting is permission to leave harbour? I'm perfectly willing for them to check the passenger list.'

'Yes, Captain, I've repeated that several times – but still nothing.'

Forester glanced at his watch. It was six-thirty. It would be dark in three or four hours. He made up his mind. 'OK, transmit that I will wait until seven o'clock. If we hear nothing by then, I intend to leave anyway.'

Hatan was concerned – Forester could hear the warning in his voice. 'I hope you realize exactly what risk you are taking.'

'I understand . . . tell them.'

'All right, Captain, as you wish.'

Forester replaced the handset back in its position. He stared out through the wide, curved-glass pane of the wheelhouse, overlooking the open foredeck.

Annabel was distributing a trayful of cold drinks in paper cups to a group huddled near the rail. They looked up at her, saying nothing, but accepting the drinks gratefully. They were glad to be on board, already feeling a sense of security in the vessel itself.

Those refugees to whom Forester had been unable to offer passage had dispersed themselves around the dock area, staying close in case another vessel came into Jounieh. Only the immediate relatives of those on board remained on the quay, talking quietly, anxiously, to their loved ones who lined the rails.

Henshaw was busy providing blankets and seats for the women and children. It would grow cold during the night at sea, and those on the open deck would need whatever comfort he could give them. The Europeans – about fifteen of them, mostly women and children – were in the saloon. There were only two men, both British. They had been in Lebanon on business and were unable to leave on the last plane two days before. There was also one American lady – Joan Drucker. She was large, middle aged and very loud. Her small son, Bernie, was equally obnoxious and had been demanding a hamburger ever since he had set foot on deck. Both Annabel and Henshaw had tried to steer clear of him as best they could. Unfortunately, the galley was next to the saloon, and every time Annabel returned for more drinks, she expected Mrs Drucker or her son to waylay her. Thankfully, some of the other women were helping her to fill the cups and prepare the food.

Rhys emerged from the engine room and made his way slowly

to the bridge, carefully stepping over the outstretched legs of those sitting on the decks. Some were already asleep. As he began to climb the companionway to the wheelhouse, he felt somebody tugging at his trouser leg. He looked down. It was a small, dark-haired boy, his eyes gleaming with suppressed excitement. 'We leave soon?' he asked.

Rhys looked around – as far as he could tell none of the other refugees had heard the question. He stepped back down on to the deck. 'Maybe,' he said quietly.

The boy sensed the confidentiality of his tone. 'What you think?' he hissed, enjoying the possibility of a secret.

Rhys tapped the side of his nose. 'If I find out anything I'll let you know, OK?' he said conspiratorially.

The boy grinned, white teeth flashing in his dark face. 'OK,' he repeated, 'I promise to say nothing.'

Rhys tried to keep a straight face; he didn't want to spoil it for the youngster. 'Have you had anything to eat yet?'

'No, but the white-haired lady has given me some orange juice. She says the food will come soon.' He clutched himself around the stomach. 'I hope so.'

Rhys nodded. 'Where are your parents?'

The boy pointed towards the bow. 'Up there – I am with my mother. We do not know what has happened to my father.'

It was said matter-of-factly, but Rhys could see the fear in the boy's eyes. 'Don't worry, he'll turn up. Dads always do, just like a bad penny.' He indicated the door to the wheelhouse at the top of the companionway. 'When we get under way, would you like to come up there?'

'Could I?'

'I'll see what I can do.'

Rhys started to climb again, then stopped. 'What is your name?'

'Alexis, sir.'

'Good . . . you be where I can find you, now.'

'Yes, sir.'

Rhys smiled. 'Aye aye, sir,' he corrected.

Alexis repeated it with a salute, then rushed away to tell his mother.

Rhys climbed the last few paces to the wheelhouse and pushed the door open.

Forester, who had been gazing pensively out towards the channel entrance that led to the harbour, turned and faced him. 'I want to get under way at seven. Is everything all right?'

Rhys nodded. 'Yes, we're in good shape – though if we hit any rough weather she'll wallow like a pig in a trough with this kind of load.'

'I know. Let's keep our fingers crossed.'

The radio suddenly burst into life. It was Hatan.

Forester picked up the handset and acknowledged. 'Yes, what is it? Have you heard anything?'

'Not from the Israelis, but the international waveband just broadcast a signal from the American Embassy in Beirut, saying that the ambassador would be sailing shortly to Cyprus . . . on your vessel!'

Forester stared incredulously at Rhys. 'On *Sea Victory*?'

'That's right,' Hatan said. 'I'm as bewildered as you are. I've been given no information.'

Forester heard a muffled voice in the background. 'What is it, what's happened?'

Hatan came back. 'Makarion has a message. I'll put him on.'

Forester waited. He heard the microphone waffle slightly as it changed hands. Makarion sounded excited. 'Captain!'

'Yes, what is it?'

'I've just taken a call from the Embassy. They are already on their way. They ask if you will wait. They anticipate that they will be here not later than 1930 hours.'

Forester looked at Rhys. 'Tell them we will wait, Makarion.'

Rhys nodded his agreement. Then Hatan came back. He was elated. 'Hello, Forester?'

'Yes, I'm here.'

'This could be the breakthrough – what we need.'

Forester let his breath out slowly. 'I know,' he said.

CHAPTER
FOURTEEN

They crouched in the wide entrance of the ruined shoe shop. The high-heeled, sophisticated footwear lay strewn around the shop front, where it had been blown by the blast. It was of no value to the people because it had no practical use.

Elias Mourad watched from the corner of the entrance, and then pointed down the street to a T-junction at the bottom. 'We have set up defensive positions in that area.' He paused as machine-gun fire ripped through the brief lull in the constant barrage of noise. 'This is as close as I can take you.'

Nazira began to protest, but he cut her short. 'This is as far as you go. There is street fighting here with some of the extremists.' He shrugged. 'It happens all the time, but it's nothing we can't deal with.' He looked up and down the deserted street, then at the three men. 'Now I must go!'

Rousseau nodded. 'Of course, we understand. Thank you for your help.' He smiled. 'Good luck.'

The PLO man ignored him and looked steadily at Nazira. He could see the suppressed excitement in her eyes. 'Be careful – a bullet kills, no matter where it comes from.' He pulled the chinstrap of his hat tighter and checked his automatic weapon – then dived quickly from the doorway. He stayed close to the walls, making as much use as he could of whatever cover there was, gradually working his way down the street.

Kemp had already positioned himself in the entrance and was taping Mourad's progress. Armand poked the long gun microphone out and checked his levels. Rousseau had his mouth close to Armand's ear so that he didn't have to shout. 'Did you get any of that conversation?'

Armand gave him a grin. 'Yes, I got the sound, but Jack didn't get any visual.'

'I know . . . it was not possible.'

Nazira was finding it difficult to use her camera. The Canadian occupied the best position, blocking her view. She caught a glimpse of Mourad as he dodged from one doorway to the next. He had still not reached the junction.

She reached her decision instantly. She leapt from the cover of the entrance before Rousseau could stop her, and ran down the street, clutching her cameras tightly so that they did not hinder progress. Rousseau swore.

Kemp suddenly became aware of her as she moved into his foreground, and quickly adjusted focus so that he could see her clearly. He could hear Rousseau behind him. 'Stupid bitch, she'll get herself killed.' Then, a moment later, 'Are you getting this, Jack?'

The Canadian didn't answer; he was trying to cover both the PLO man and Nazira.

Rousseau watched tensely as the militiaman, oblivious of her pursuit, reached the junction, then disappeared from view. Nazira was making much less effective use of the cover, and when Mourad turned the corner, she began to run faster – ignoring it altogether.

Kemp swore quietly to himself, trying to keep her in shot. 'Use the cover, dammit, use the bloody cover.' He saw puffs of dust begin to kick up around her feet, and realized that she was now under fire. The sound of a sub-machine-gun echoed loudly up the street.

It was close. Kemp held his breath, continuing to film.

Nazira didn't seek the doorways, or deviate an inch from her objective – running faster, her feet flying over the ground, keeping her eyes on the corner. She could not distinguish the sound of the automatic firing at her from the general level of gunfire, but she could hear the bullets ricocheting from the walls. She felt something dash into her face – it stung, but didn't hurt.

The corner seemed to retreat in front of her and her legs grew tired and heavy, as if she were running through glue. Each moment hung like a globule of water, suspended, seeking to slide down a pane of glass. It was like a nightmare, timeless, endless. Had she been hit? Was she dying? Is this what it was like?

Then she was round the corner, and the gunfire suddenly stopped. All she could hear was the harsh sound of her breathing as she gulped in the hot, dry air through her open mouth. She felt something wet on her cheek. Her hand came away bloodstained. She stared at it, fascinated, wondering how bad it was. She felt her face again. She was lucky, it was only a scratch. A fragment of masonry blown from the wall by a bullet had nicked her. It was her only injury.

Nazira ignored it and reached for her camera. Of Mourad there was no sign. The PLO man had disappeared.

Kemp released the trigger on the video camera and stood up. All three of them stared down the street. It was empty and, once again, deceptively quiet. They listened, but no sound broke the lull in their immediate surroundings.

Rousseau looked questioningly at Kemp. 'Did she make it?'

'Yes.'

The Frenchman turned to Armand for confirmation. He gestured briefly. 'I don't know, I couldn't see clearly past Jack.'

The Canadian continued to stare impassively towards the junction. 'She made it all right – but she might have been hit.' He glanced at Rousseau. 'We'd better go and look.'

The reporter stared at him. 'You heard what the PLO man said – you saw what happened!'

Kemp didn't take his eyes off him.

Rousseau tried to hold his composure, but he knew Kemp was right – they had to go. He threw his arms wide in exasperation. 'All right, all right. Be it on your own head. But don't try to shoot while we get down there. We must move fast.'

Kemp smiled, but did not reply. He adjusted the weight of the camera, then glanced at Armand. 'You OK?'

The sound man looked from one to the other, perplexed. 'You are going down there?' He was incredulous.

Rousseau nodded reluctantly. 'Yes.'

Kemp helped Armand to his feet. 'Come on, I'll go first – you stay right behind me.'

The sound man swallowed nervously. 'Oui . . . after you, yes?'

Jack smiled. 'Keep the tape running – we can use it as background noise.' He waited while Armand set his levels, then, holding his camera loosely down by his side, he moved quickly along the street to the next doorway. The others followed him in with a rush.

Kemp poked his head out. The street remained quiet, deserted . . . deceptively so? 'OK, so far so good.' He pointed to another doorway about fifty yards away. 'That one there . . . let's go.'

He ran effortlessly, his long legs carrying him swiftly over the rubble littering the street. Armand and Rousseau stayed as close as they could. Again they reached the doorway without attracting any fire. Two more doorways and they turned the corner. They stopped, breathing heavily, their backs to the wall. There was no sign of either the PLO man or Nazira.

Rousseau glanced irritably at Kemp. 'Now what?'

There were more signs of conflict here: a number of burnt-out vehicles and the remains of an armoured car, its camouflage peeled off, blackened by fire. The road was wide, long and straight. On both sides were a number of tall buildings – apartment blocks, many of them gutted or partially demolished. As the road receded into the distance, to the west, Kemp could see a pall of black smoke rising from behind a tower block. He knew that neither the militiaman nor Nazira could have got that far. They had to be in one of the apartments.

There was something odd about the line of buildings opposite. He stared at them, puzzled. At first he could not decide what it was. The walls were pockmarked with bullet holes, as were most of the structures, but there was something else . . . Then he realized: the windows were empty; there was nothing behind them except blue sky. The entire rear of the buildings had been blown away. The frontage was merely that – like a street in a Hollywood studio. There was nothing solid about it.

He motioned to Armand. 'Come on.' Without waiting for a reply, he crossed the road towards an alleyway on the other side. Rousseau yelled something after him but he took no notice, moving fast into the alley. He stopped – he was right: the backs had gone. The front wall stood bare and ridiculous when seen from this angle. He let the camera roll.

Rousseau came rushing up beside him, complaining. He stopped, staring at the gutted building. Armand joined him. 'Jesus Christ, it's amazing.'

Kemp lowered the video camera and gestured Armand to be quiet. He'd heard something. He listened intently . . . there it was again. Faintly, in the distance, he could hear the siren of an ambulance – it had to be an ambulance: civil law enforcement had collapsed and police cars were non-existent. The siren got louder, closer. The ambulance was coming down the street they had just negotiated. They moved out of the alley into the road.

Kemp saw some movement further down. A woman dressed in traditional black garb was standing close to a car ramp entrance by one of the apartment blocks. He tapped Rousseau on the shoulder and pointed to her. 'I think she is waiting for the ambulance.'

The siren was much louder now, and they could hear the engine revving as the driver dodged the obstacles in the street behind them. Finally it burst round the corner into view. Large red crosses were prominently displayed on either side.

The Lebanese woman stepped out into the road and waved. Kemp was already taping the incident and started to move in closer as the ambulance skidded to a stop beside her. The dust partially obscured her for a moment, then cleared as the white-garbed medics leapt from the back of the ambulance, carrying a stretcher. They followed the woman down the ramp into a car park below the apartment block.

Kemp switched off the video and yelled at Rousseau to get the arc lamp out of the case. The Frenchman struggled with it as he ran down the ramp after Kemp and Armand.

It was dark and cool in the car park, and it took a while for Kemp's eyes to adjust after the brilliance of the sun outside. He could see the white uniforms of the medics as they followed the woman to the far side of the car park. Then, as his eyes got used to the gloom, he saw Nazira standing beside a solitary vehicle in the corner. Her camera flashed as the medics approached.

138

Kemp called out to Rousseau behind him to get the arc on and light flooded the area in front of them.

As Kemp got closer he could see several people clustered round the car, including two small children. The back door of the vehicle was open, and stretched out on the seat was the body of a man. The Canadian ignored Nazira and shot as much footage as he could. The man was bleeding heavily from a chest wound, and one of the medics examined him briefly before binding it tightly with a large pad.

A boy was crying, his voice distorting strangely in the underground car park. Kemp hoped Armand was getting that. The other child was a girl, about five or six years old. She tried to cling to the wounded man as the medics lifted him on to the stretcher. Her mother pulled her gently away, holding her close, trying to soothe her.

Armand and Rousseau were just behind Kemp, keeping out of shot as the cameraman followed the stretcher back up to the ambulance. Once outside, the medics bundled the wounded man as quickly as they could into the ambulance, pushing the stretcher on to one of the racks. As soon as they were all inside, the driver gunned the engine, and the dusty white ambulance fled from the war zone, back into the city, leaving the black-garbed woman standing forlornly on the kerb, clutching her two children. Her face was set, stony, masking her despair from her children.

Nazira focused her camera on the woman's face, taking picture after picture. The Lebanese woman was oblivious of her and of the cruel, intrusive camera. She stared after the departing ambulance.

Kemp continued to record, while Rousseau was concerned to get in his reporting of the event as quickly as possible on the spot. As soon as the Canadian had finished, he began to discuss the details animatedly with the other two. He knew they had a good story.

None of them, it seemed, had time to comfort the woman or her two wailing children. Nor did they ask if they could help. The camera, having recorded its human drama, was about to move on, seeking fresh images of war for the evening bulletins and the front page.

The Lebanese woman stood bewildered and uncomprehending in the blinding heat. Her children clutched her skirt. She did not know what to do, or where to go, except to the hospital – to discover if she was still a wife, or just another widow . . .

CHAPTER
FIFTEEN

Makarion watched *Sea Victory*'s slow progress from the quayside. She nosed her way carefully towards the narrow channel that led to the harbour and disappeared behind the featureless building of the naval barracks.

The small crowd of relatives who had waited right to the end began to drift sadly away, leaving the quay to the remaining Phalange militia. People crowded round the shipping office below him or thronged the road into the town itself, still hoping to board a vessel – straining their eyes, looking back to the distant harbour which was empty of craft except for the Turkish cattle boat.

Makarion continued to stare at the spot where *Sea Victory* had disappeared from view. What chance did they have? The odds must have shifted now that the American ambassador was on board. That development had been entirely unexpected, but what was its significance? Clearly, it must be an attempt to break the blockade. The ambassador certainly did not need *Sea Victory* to get out of Beirut. The American Sixth Fleet was nearby – he could be airlifted out at any time. Thus far the Americans had stayed out of the conflict, so this must represent a change in policy. But *what* precisely, and how important was it?

Makarion turned his back to the window and glanced up at the ventilation grille, checking his watch. It was not his usual time, but the information could be vital. The Commander was utterly ruthless, and would not appreciate any delays due to procedure. He made up his mind. He would call him now.

CHAPTER

SIXTEEN

Hardly a breath of wind disturbed the flat, unruffled surface of the harbour as *Sea Victory* gradually picked up speed and headed for the open sea. The water skiers and sunworshippers of the Jounieh Yacht Club had gone. They were back in their club house or aboard the motor cruisers and yachts that lay still and calm in the marina. The Turkish cattle boat swung loosely at anchor. The refugees crowding her deck picked up what shade they could from the sun but were too hot and too tired to even try to capture the attention of the British vessel. They had already attempted to reach Alexandria, and had been sent back. What happened to *Sea Victory* didn't interest them.

It *was* hot. In the galley, where Annabel was coping with the continuous demands for food and drink, it was stifling. All the portholes and doors were open, and she was glad of the first breath of air that stirred through the ship as their speed increased. She had given the ambassador and his secretary her cabin – the only one unoccupied. There was one other American who had arrived with the ambassador: a Colonel Bridges, whose presence was clearly a security measure. He had ensconced himself at the bar, where Henshaw was helping out and serving the drinks. It had crossed Annabel's mind that it might not be the best place for the Australian, but there was nothing she could do about that – her hands were full.

She glanced curiously at the woman who was constantly washing the glasses and dirty crockery which arrived in a never-ending stream. She was in her forties, a small woman with intensely blue eyes emphasized by her deeply tanned face. Her name was Erica Graham. She had been the last person to board after the entourage bringing the ambassador had pulled up at the dockside. She was English and lived near Newmarket, and – Annabel had glimpsed at her passport – she was an author. The name rang a bell, but Annabel could not place it. However, there were no airs or graces about her. She had immediately offered her help – though her face revealed the exhaustion and stress she had been under.

Annabel accepted another glass from her and dried it on the damp cloth. The woman didn't look at her and focused all her attention on washing each glass until it was meticulously clean. Annabel sensed that this automatic, familiar routine was helping to ease her tension. She wanted to ask questions, help if she could, but thought better of it. The woman wasn't ready yet. She seemed happy with the washing up. Much better to let her talk when she wanted to.

Annabel put the cloth down and started to fill up the glasses with more orange juice, placing them on a tray. She offered one to the woman. 'Would you like a drink?'

The writer stared at her uncertainly.

'It's cold,' Annabel encouraged.

The woman took it from her and sipped it slowly without speaking.

Annabel picked up the tray. 'I'll be back soon.'

She nodded, reassured, then turned to stare at the sink, placing her hands in the warm, soapy water. Annabel stood in the doorway of the galley, watching her. She was concerned.

Then the boy who had accosted Rhys tugged at her shorts. 'Will the food be long, miss?'

She turned to him and smiled. 'Not long. I'll call you when it's ready.'

Alexis grinned up at her and ran back excitedly to communicate the news. Annabel made her way carefully along the side of the vessel, squeezing past the refugees crowding the rail, and handed out drinks to those who had not yet received any. She kept a couple back for the girl and her mother in the stern.

The wheelchair had been wedged against the bulkhead so that it would not move. The Lebanese girl in it stared wide eyed at the wake of the ship, feeling the thud of the engines beneath the deck. Her mother welcomed Annabel, accepted the drink gratefully and held it to her daughter's lips. The girl gulped it down automatically, her eyes fixed on the sea creaming back from the propellors beneath the stern. Her mother looked up at Annabel, her eyes betraying anxiety.

Annabel gave her the other drink. 'That is for you,' she said firmly.

The other woman nodded. 'Thank you.' Her voice was low, almost inaudible.

Annabel sat her down on the bench seat and knelt beside her. 'Is she all right? Is there anything I can get? I have some sedatives.'

The mother shook her head. 'No. She is just a little frightened, I think. She has never been to sea before.'

Annabel looked at the girl in the wheelchair. She was in her late teens. Her body was rigid in the chair, her fingers gripped the wheels tightly and, in spite of the heat, she trembled involuntarily. It was not just fear of the sea that terrified her. The girl looked as though she might be in shock.

Annabel crossed the deck into the saloon. Leila was sitting quietly next to her brother. She smiled at the blonde Englishwoman. 'We are on our way at last.'

Annabel nodded. 'Yes. Could you and André stand up for a moment, please?'

Leila took her brother's arm obediently and helped him to steady himself against the faint roll of the vessel.

'I just want a blanket for the girl in the wheelchair,' Annabel explained. Quickly she opened the cupboard and removed one, then indicated to Leila that she should sit down again. 'There are more there if you need them.'

André gazed in Annabel's direction. She found it hard to cope with his sightless eyes – they seemed so natural and unaffected.

'It is kind of you to look after us,' he said. 'Will Samra be all right?'

Annabel leaned down close to him and spoke quietly. 'He is in the wheelhouse with my husband and Rhys. He'll be safe there.'

André shifted his position slightly to make himself more comfortable and inadvertently used his injured hand. The pain

144

was intense. He sucked in his breath, gritting his teeth so as not to cry out. He held the hand up, clutching it to his chest, rocking slightly back and forth to ease the pain. He waved both women away as they sought to help him. 'It's my own stupid fault – leave me, I'll be all right.' He smiled grimly up at Annabel. 'It seems my memory as well as my eyesight is going.' It was perhaps as well that he could not see the distress his self-mocking remark caused his sister.

Annabel squeezed her arm sympathetically. 'I'll be back soon.' She took the blanket and wrapped it around the knees of the girl in the wheelchair, then made her way back to the galley.

The sun was dropping swiftly down below the western horizon – its rays diffused by heavy dark clouds. It would be night soon, but it seemed no cooler. At least the sea was calm . . . but it was a flat, oily calm that boded ill.

In the wheelhouse Forester tapped the barometer. Rhys, who was at the helm, looked at him enquiringly.

'It's falling,' Forester said shortly, offering no further comment. None was required: Rhys knew as well as he that a storm was in the offing and, with a vessel crowded with refugees, that was the last thing they wanted. It seemed the ordeal was not over for them yet.

Rhys was talking to Samra, instructing him in the use of the wheel – how to keep the bow cleaving straight through the water. They had dressed him in a T-shirt and a pair of Rhys's dungarees. The shirt was monogrammed with *Sea Victory's* name, and they were all wearing similar shirts to identify themselves more clearly as crew. If they were going to be boarded by the Israelis, Samra would have to take the wheel. That way there was a chance that he might pass for a crew member.

Forester stared moodily out over the crowded sundeck, watching the horizon, checking the radar. Occasionally he raised his binoculars, looking for the first sign of the gunboats, the first white speck of an enormous bow wave. They were out here all right, and they would come – it was just a question of how soon. He felt a sense of helplessness. All he could do was wait.

He envied Annabel's non-stop activity. She had done marvels, almost emptying the supermarket in Jounieh, and purchasing all the blankets and foam mattresses she could lay her hands on. He had hated his own task of separating those who had dual nationality from those who had not. People had begged and pleaded, sometimes with tears in their eyes. He'd had to harden his heart and take only those with some chance of escape.

One decision had been bitterly harsh. A charming, good-looking Lebanese man who worked in the USA had brought his American wife and their two young children on a vacation to meet his parents who lived in West Beirut. Suddenly the nightmare had begun, and they had been caught up in the conflict. They'd sensibly made their way to Jounieh as quickly as possible, then, with escape within their grasp, Forester had discovered the man only had a Lebanese passport; the wife and two children were all right. And so the cruel decision had been made: the father would have to stay behind.

Forester could not forget the face of the man's son. The boy clasped his elder sister's hand and looked up at his father as he kissed his mother goodbye, and the tears ran down his face.

Forester had not enjoyed playing God. Caught in the emotion of that moment, he had made a promise; he'd clambered on to the roof of the work boat and told all the refugees that if he got to Cyprus safely, he would be back within thirty-six hours. He did not regret that promise, but he knew he had no right to risk the lives of his wife, Rhys and Henshaw without their consultation. They had said nothing, given no hint that they would not return with him – but he intended, if they reached Cyprus safely, to give them the opportunity of refusing.

The sun had gone and the short twilight was rapidly changing to night. Forester scanned the diminishing horizon once more: there was nothing to be seen but an ocean empty of ships. One look at the radar showed how deceptive that view was. There were a number of blips scattered on the screen, any one of which could be the gunboats. They would come soon now, before the storm.

He went over to the chart table and checked their position: they were nearing the edge of the twelve-mile zone . . . Maybe that was what they were waiting for. He crossed quickly to the radar. He was right: two blips, one each side of *Sea Victory*, were closing rapidly. He turned to Rhys. 'Give the wheel to Samra; we've got company.'

Swiftly they changed places. Rhys stood beside Samra, keeping an eye on the course. Suddenly the vessel was struck by two blinding lights, port and starboard. Forester rushed to the door. The powerful engines roared as the gunboats closed in fast.

The VHF snapped on and a voice ordered them to stop engines. Forester picked up the handset and identified himself as Rhys cut the power. Slowly *Sea Victory* wallowed to a stop.

The two gunboats reduced their speed, keeping their spotlights trained on the decks of the converted Fairmile B. Every detail of the craft was laid bare, every shadow penetrated, washed away by the bright beams of light. Behind the glare the two gunboats circled slowly, invisible to Forester and the passengers on *Sea Victory*. It was eerie – their engines had almost stopped and gave only the faintest whisper of sound as they continued to inspect the British vessel.

Forester waited.

The harsh voice blared from the radio again. 'Clear the deck in front of the bridge . . . I repeat, clear the sundeck.'

Forester protested. 'They are only refugees. We have no space anywhere else.'

'Find it. Clear that sundeck or I shall be forced to take action.'

Forester glared at the circle of light. 'I will do my best.' He slammed the receiver back into its rest and looked at Rhys. 'OK, let's see what we can do.' Then to Samra, 'You stay here at the wheel – check the radar from time to time. If the radio comes on, don't answer it, call me.'

Samra nodded. 'I will, Captain.'

As Forester and Rhys turned to go Major Bridges came rushing into the wheelhouse. He grabbed Forester's arm. 'What's the situation?'

Forester stared coldly at him. 'We have to get those people off the sundeck. I expect the Israelis will be boarding soon. Tell the ambassador to stay below until he hears from me. I'll keep him informed.'

The major glanced anxiously at the glaring searchlights. 'Are you sure they're Israelis?'

'I'm sure,' Forester said. 'I'd know those engines anywhere. Now you'd better get below as well.'

Bridges slid back down the companionway and disappeared below.

The emotionless voice clicked on to the VHF again. 'I'm waiting, Captain.'

No doubt the American major's presence had been observed from the gunboat. That should have reassured them; Bridges was hardly likely to be present with PLO on board. However, the Israelis were taking no chances. They obviously feared a possible attack from the sundeck. It commanded the water between the vessels, and anything crossing would be vulnerable if PLO were using *Sea Victory*.

The only people on the sundeck were terrified women and children, crouching down behind the corner of the bridge and the railings.

Forester tried to reassure them. 'It's all right. Let's go down to the saloon – you'll be safe there.'

No one moved; they continued to cower from the expected attack.

Rhys caught sight of the boy who had spoken to him earlier. He was kneeling down beside his mother. Rhys crossed the deck and knelt beside him. 'You and your mother come with me, we'll go first.'

Alexis looked to his mother.

Rhys smiled. 'We'll go down to the galley. You remember that food I promised?'

The boy nodded eagerly.

'Well, it's ready now.'

Alexis's mother looked anxiously at Rhys. 'There's no danger?'

Rhys shook his head. 'No . . . but there will be if we stay here.'

The woman took her son's hand and stood up. Rhys led them across the deck to the companionway that led below. It was the move the others needed: one by one they stood up and followed the boy and his mother.

Forester shepherded them towards the stairway and they slowly climbed down, crowding into the saloon below. He checked the sundeck. It was deserted. Then he turned deliberately into the glare of the searchlights and cupped his hands to his lips. 'It's clear . . .' he yelled.

From the open door of the wheelhouse he heard the radio snap on again. 'Thank you, Captain – now, would you be kind enough to go back into the wheelhouse.'

Forester gazed contemptuously at the unseen gunboat and slowly went inside, pushing Samra away from the helm and wrapping his arms around it. He was seething, but he knew it did no good to show it. He had to remain cool and calm; the next few minutes would be crucial and he owed it to his passengers not to let his anger and frustration get the better of him.

Into the circle of light around *Sea Victory* a Zodiac inflatable suddenly appeared. It was crowded with Israeli marines and it churned its way alongside, disappearing below the bow.

Forester waited no longer. He moved swiftly from the wheelhouse, slid down the companionway, and raced up to the bow, where about thirty frightened refugees stood looking nervously at the handrails. Forester tried to calm them down: 'There's no need to worry, it's just a routine inspection.'

He didn't know how much effect his words had, for at that moment six tough, athletic Israelis came tumbling over the rails. They were all armed to the teeth with automatic rifles and hand guns. They lined up, crouching in a semicircle, facing the small crowd of refugees. Then a tall, lean man in battle fatigues and wearing a black patch over one eye vaulted on to the deck.

What happened next was utterly bizarre, yet curiously effective. It rooted everyone to the spot. He whipped aside his eye patch, smacked the back of his head with one hand, and deftly caught the glass eye that popped from his head with the other. He glanced at the assembled refugees with his one good eye and proceeded to toss the glass one up in the air. It flashed and shone in the harsh white light, glaring evilly and hypnotically at each one of them as it rose and fell continuously.

Then, without a word, the Israeli rammed it back into the empty socket the wrong way round, then pulled the eye patch back over the white, staring orb. He looked quickly round the bow area and rapped out some orders in Hebrew. The marines fanned out to search the refugees and make sure they were not armed.

The man with the eye patch carried no rank insignia; he didn't need it — his authority was self-evident. Forester addressed him: 'Is there any way I can help?'

The Israeli surveyed him quizzically. 'You are?'

'Tom Forester. I own and run this vessel.'

'You have a manifest of all your passengers?'

'Shall I get it for you?'

'Later. Just try to keep your passengers calm and co-operative.' He turned his back on Forester, and waved his arm at the gunboat on the port side of *Sea Victory*. It was the signal they had been waiting for.

Almost immediately two more inflatables materialized out of the darkness and approached the stern of the British vessel. Forester started to move off in that direction. The Israeli officer waved his hand gun casually. 'You will stay here with these refugees — tell them they have nothing to fear. How many crew have you?'

Forester spoke calmly, controlling the hard knot of anger in his gut. 'Three, in addition to myself, and one woman — my wife.'

The Israeli smiled broadly. 'Ah yes — that is the blonde lady — Annabel, I believe.'

Forester did not reply. He wondered just how much the Israelis knew about them. Would they know that Samra Asaker was not one of his crew?

Annabel was in the galley when she heard the girl's high-pitched scream. She dropped the breadknife and ran through the saloon towards the stern. She could see the camouflaged uniforms of the marines clambering silently over the handrails, spilling on to the stern deck. The girl in the wheelchair continued to shriek, her voice shrill with fear.

Annabel burst through the open doorway as three marines swung their sub-machine-guns in her direction. She could see into the menacing black barrels. She stopped. The girl's fists were clenched tight, held up on either side of her head, and she screamed uncontrollably, her mouth wide. Her mother stood, too shocked to move, gazing at the blackened faces of the Israeli marines. Annabel heard some of the Lebanese women behind her in the saloon begin to wail, their voices rising. She knew that at any moment they might panic, and throw themselves over the side. It would only take one . . .

Annabel ignored the marines and strode across the deck to stand in front of the wheelchair. The girl was beside herself with fear – her eyes wide, unseeing. Annabel struck her sharply, twice across the face. The scream died in the girl's throat and her face froze as she suddenly focused on the woman before her. Annabel knelt down and took her hand, slowly unlocking her fist. She spoke softly, reassuringly, as though to a child. 'There now, it's all right. No need to feel afraid – we are all here with you, to look after you.' She saw the girl's eyes flick for an instant to one of the marines who was watching her silently. Annabel turned to him angrily. 'Will you please move away from her, before she starts again.'

Almost sheepishly the Israeli moved himself and the others away from the stern towards the saloon. Some climbed swiftly up the steps to the upper sundeck. Slowly but firmly, they began to move all the refugees towards the bow.

Annabel turned back to the girl. 'See they've gone now – there's nothing to worry about.'

The girl stared at her wide-eyed. Her face slowly crumpled and she started to cry, sobbing painfully. Annabel gave her a handkerchief, which she clutched gratefully, murmuring her thanks haltingly through the tears. Annabel tucked the blanket around her legs and looked up at her mother. 'I think she'll be OK now.' She stood up and added quietly, 'I'll bring her a drink and a sedative.'

The Lebanese woman nodded, close to tears herself. She knelt beside her daughter and held her close, rocking her back and forth in her arms.

The foredeck gradually became more and more crowded as everyone was pushed towards it by the Israeli marines – everyone except the American ambassador, his secretary and Major Bridges.

Rhys, Henshaw and Samra joined Forester, but there was no sign of Annabel. Erica Graham pushed her way through the crowd. She told him that Annabel had gone to the stern when the girl screamed and had not come back.

Forester was worried. He could see Leila Khalil holding protectively on to her brother's arm and was about to make his way across to them, when Rhys gripped his arm. He pointed to the side rail, midships . . . The Israeli with the eye patch was helping the American ambassador and his entourage over the side into one of the inflatables. Worse, Annabel was with them.

Forester shouted out and began to push his way to the bulkhead door that separated the bow section from the side passage. A marine barred his way. Forester pointed to the small party boarding the inflatable. 'Where are they going? Why are they being taken away?'

The Israeli marine made no reply, merely shifting his sub-machine-gun so that it pointed directly at Forester.

There was nothing he could do. He watched helplessly as the inflatable pulled away, disappearing into the darkness behind the glare of the searchlights. He gripped the solid wood top of the rail and stared after them, trying not to show his anxiety. He could hear the American woman, Joan Drucker, protesting loudly in the crowd behind him that she was a US citizen, and they had no right to do this to her.

Forester felt a hand on his shoulder. He turned. It was the Israeli officer. 'I will have that manifest now, Captain.'

Forester indicated the bridge. 'It's up there.'

The officer motioned him to proceed. The marine stood aside and Forester climbed the steps to the upper deck, closely followed by the Israeli. Inside the wheelhouse he took the clipboard down and handed it over. 'All the names are listed. There are no Lebanese passports – I'm carrying one hundred and seventeen passengers in all. As far as I can see, you have them all in one place.'

The Israeli smiled. 'All except two, Captain: the girl in the wheelchair and her mother.'

Forester took a cigar from his shirt pocket, slid it from its container and bit off the end, spitting it out. 'You also have my wife, the ambassador and his entourage.'

The Israeli shrugged. 'Just a routine check and a little hospi-tality – they will be back soon.'

Forester lit the cigar and drew in a long breath. 'I hope so.' He kept his tone non-committal. He did not want to challenge the

Israeli's authority – not yet. But he knew the Israelis could not afford to offend the Americans – and this was a British vessel: not much against a pair of powerful gunboats and a small company of marines, but it was all he had.

The officer waved his pistol nonchalantly towards the door. 'Now, if you will accompany me, Captain, we will check out your manifest and see if what you say is true.'

The cabin was small and sparsely furnished, the steel walls undecorated; a man's room – undoubtedly the Israeli captain's. On the small table beside the single bed that doubled as a couch were a pair of photographs. Annabel examined them: a woman in her late thirties or early forties, and a boy, hands clasped behind his back, of about fifteen; he was looking very serious, like most boys of his age. There was a writing desk – bare, except for a pad and a pencil, and a single chair in front of it. A small refrigerator in the corner completed the spartan image of the room. To be fair, she thought, there was little room for anything else.

She heard someone coming down the passage outside. She turned to face the door as the lock clicked and it opened.

He was tall and had to stoop to avoid crashing his head on the bulkhead. His hair was crinkly, greying slightly – as was his beard. He wore a khaki shirt and trousers; sweat marks stained the armpits. He flung his cap on to the bed and smiled – he had good teeth, she noted. 'Sorry to have kept you waiting, but there was a lot to do.'

'I'll bet,' Annabel said tartly. 'Do you always stop and board neutral civilian vessels in the middle of the night?'

He looked at her steadily, his eyes neither friendly nor unfriendly.

Annabel felt a little uncomfortable beneath their gaze. She spoke hurriedly to break the silence. 'My name is Forester – my husband is the captain of *Sea Victory*.'

He inclined his head deferentially. 'Forgive me. I am Aaron Gould, senior officer on this vessel.'

He held out his hand, and Annabel took it briefly. 'Can I offer you a drink?' He moved to the desk, taking out a pair of glasses from one of the drawers, then he leaned down and selected a bottle of white wine from the fridge.

Annabel had been about to refuse, but the bottle was so cold the outside had already misted over. She changed her mind. 'Yes, I will have a little wine.'

He smiled. 'Good.' He poured out two glasses and handed her one. He raised his glass. 'Your health.'

'And a safe voyage,' Annabel added.

Gould paused momentarily, then drank.

Annabel took one swallow. It was cold and delicious, but she had decided to take the offensive. She was not here to enjoy good wine; better to strike first. 'Why have I been brought here?' she said curtly.

Gould casually finished his wine and indicated the chair. 'Perhaps you'd like to sit down?'

She shook her head impatiently. He sighed. 'Then I shall. My feet are killing me.' He sank tiredly into a chair, and Annabel was hard pressed not to smile.

She changed her mind again and sat down on the edge of the bed. 'I hope you are not going to take those off,' she said, pointing at his heavy shoes.

The captain shook his head. 'No . . . I think in a cabin this small it might be overpowering.'

This time she did allow herself a fleeting smile. 'Yes, quite so, Captain. But, more to the point than your, er . . . tired feet, what am I doing on board this ship?'

He took another swallow of his wine, then placed the glass on the desk and turned to face her. 'I believe your first name is Annabel?'

'Yes . . .' She was puzzled. 'How did . . .?'

He interrupted. 'How did I know?' He paused for a moment. 'When *Sea Victory* was on the slip in Haifa for repairs a couple of months ago I happened to get talking to your engineer, Rhys.'

Annabel remembered what her husband had told her – how Rhys had identified himself to the Israeli captain on their way in. 'You intercepted us before?'

'That's right.'

'I still don't understand.'

'Then let me explain.' He proffered the bottle. 'Would you like some more?'

She shook her head. He put some in his own.

154

'My earlier meeting with Rhys in Haifa was not entirely accidental – I wanted to talk to somebody from the vessel to get a better idea of the people involved.'

'You were spying,' Annabel said grimly.

'No, not exactly. It was my own initiative; I could see the way things were going.'

'You knew there would be an invasion of Lebanon?'

He shrugged. 'I was not alone in thinking that.'

'So, you checked us out.'

'Yes, that is not unfair. It seemed to me the more I knew about the vessels who worked regularly in this part of the Med the better.'

'Get to the point, Captain.'

'Why are you getting involved in the Lebanon, trying to break this blockade?'

Annabel answered unhesitatingly. 'Because we were asked to take in some media people – mostly French. They could not get in any other way. As you know, the airport is besieged and under fire.'

The Israeli captain gazed at her thoughtfully. He knew that was true, as far as it went – but there were other elements. 'And now,' he said, 'all these people you are bringing out. What of them?'

'They are refugees – none have Lebanese passports. We made sure of that so there could be no possible objection.'

Gould sipped his drink. 'And the future?'

Annabel shook her head. 'I don't know, Captain. There are hundreds of people trapped in Jounieh. Some of them are husbands, wives, parents of people we have on board. What do we do – just leave them to rot?'

She was tired and much more angry than she realized. She leaned forward. 'There is a Turkish cattle boat in the harbour, jammed with people. It has been there for days, trapped by this blockade. The ship is unsanitary – they have hardly any food or water. The Phalange will not let them back into dock. They are Egyptians, they want to go to Alexandria. Why do you stop them?'

Gould stood up and stared through the porthole at *Sea Victory*, wallowing gently – held between the twin beams of the searchlights. He turned to face Annabel. 'Let me make this absolutely clear. It is my job to stop and search anything coming in or going out of Lebanon. If there is any doubt at all about who is on board, I send them back.' He paused. 'You do not seem to comprehend the danger you are in. There are dozens of different factions fighting for control in Beirut. If, however inadvertently, you were to carry someone they did not approve of, they would have no compunction about destroying *Sea Victory*. We do not intend to allow any PLO to escape from Lebanon, and if that means sending this ship back to Jounieh, I will do so.'

He crossed the cabin and picked up his cap from the bed beside her. 'Now, if you will come with me.' He opened the door and politely gestured her through.

Annabel gazed defiantly at him for a moment, then slammed her glass on to his desk and preceded him from the cabin.

The Israeli marines had searched *Sea Victory* from stem to stern, making certain that no refugees were hiding anywhere else. Only the girl in the wheelchair and her mother were not in the forward bow section. They had already been checked and cleared.

Then the Israelis began to go through the passengers one by one. It was careful and meticulous: each passenger was checked against his or her passport, then body-searched for arms. Forester heard a number of weapons being dropped surreptitiously over the side. If the Israelis heard it also, then they paid no heed. It suited their purposes either way.

Rhys, Henshaw and Samra were with Forester, and he knew he had to make a move. The Israelis would not expect him to remain here with the refugees. The vessel needed to be under command – there was always the danger that it might drift too close to one of the gunboats.

He signalled to the others. 'Come on, let's get back to the bridge.'

He glanced at Samra, and suddenly realized how pale he was compared to himself and the others. The glare of the searchlights made it worse. 'Wait,' he hissed. 'This way.' He began to sidle carefully across the crowded foredeck. The others followed, puzzled by his action. The refugees provided good cover, and the marines were too immersed in their checking to notice the movement.

Forester reached the anchor cable mounting and leaned down, getting some of the grease on to his fingers. He smeared a little on his face, then wiped his hands clean on his trousers. He pointed to Samra and the others. 'You do the same – not too much. Just enough to make yourself look dirty.'

Silently they all rubbed the smelly grease on to their hands and faces, realizing just how close they had come to making a crucial mistake. They had all got used to the pallor of Samra's skin, but it could easily have raised suspicion. Forester checked them over quickly. It was not perfect, but it did disguise, to some extent, the parchment-like skin of the Lebanese. It would have to do.

He began to ease himself towards the marines by the bulkhead door, the others close behind.

A hand gripped his arm tightly, and a high nasal voice shouted in his ear. It was the American woman, Joan Drucker. 'Listen, I dunno what the hell is going on here, but my boy needs to go to the lavatory pretty damn quick, or he's gonna do it in his pants.'

Forester looked down at the kid, who was clutching himself and looking pained. Whether the boy was faking it or not was immaterial; it was clear his mother was not going to let him out of her sight. He smiled. 'All right, Mrs Drucker, you come with me.'

He pushed her in front with the boy and approached the door. The Israeli with the eye patch was watching the check from just inside the passageway. He heard the complaining voice of the woman before he saw Forester. He stepped forward into the light. 'Yes, Captain?'

Forester indicated the proximity of one of the gunboats. 'I have to get back to the bridge – we are drifting a bit too close – and this boy needs to use the lavatory.'

The single eye studied him intently for a moment, then checked the distance between the craft. They did seem to be closer. He snapped out an order to one of the marines and turned back to Forester. 'The marine will stay with you all the time, Captain. We should be finished here in about an hour. I will let you know if you can proceed. Meanwhile I'll deal with the woman and get them through as quickly as I can.'

'Bet your damned life you will,' Drucker snapped. Then to Forester. 'Thanks, Captain.'

Forester nodded and pushed past the Israeli, the others following behind, Samra last.

The eye examined them all unblinkingly as they filed by. He called out sharply. 'Captain!'

They stopped. Forester turned slowly and faced the Israeli. He tried to keep the tension from his voice. 'Yes?'

The officer's nose wrinkled in distaste. 'Get your lot cleaned up, will you? They smell disgusting.'

Forester shrugged. 'It's been a hard day.'

The Israeli waved him away exasperatedly. 'Bloody sailors.' He turned to Mrs Drucker. 'Now, your passport, please.'

'Passports!' she said loudly. 'You ought to be damn well ashamed, he's nearly crapping his pants.'

The ambassador was a small, podgy man, and he was having considerable difficulty climbing up the stern ladder on to the heaving deck of *Sea Victory*. Annabel got herself wedged below him and gave him a shove with her shoulder. It was undignified but effective, and Forester was able to grab his arm and haul him safely aboard. Annabel followed, then came Major Bridges. Two marines clambered down the ladder, taking their places in the Zodiac inflatable, which was rising and falling on the heavy swell beneath the stern of the British vessel. It was not easy for the marines to keep the light rubber craft close to the ladder, but they held on.

The Israeli officer swung his leg out on to the top rung, then paused, looking back at Forester. 'Goodbye, Captain, I hope we do not have to do this again.'

The searchlights from the gunboats were swinging wildly now as the wind increased, casting strange shadows over the vessel.

The Israeli saluted, his one eye glittering in the reflected light from the water.

'Shalom,' he said. He clambered swiftly down the bucking ladder, waited for the inflatable to rise, then stepped expertly into it, seating himself as the marine pushed the craft away and sped back to the gunboat.

The ambassador looked inquisitively at Forester. 'Are we free to go now?'

'Yes.' Forester put his arm around Annabel's shoulders and held her close. 'Are you all right?'

She smiled. 'I'm fine'; then shivered slightly. 'Just a little cold.'

'Right, let's get inside, it's warmer there.' He turned to the others. 'Major Bridges, Ambassador, I suggest you go into the saloon. We're getting under way at once.'

The ambassador nodded his acceptance. 'Of course; let me know if I can be of any help.'

'Without your help,' Forester said grimly, 'I think we would be heading straight back to Jounieh right now.'

The two Americans disappeared into the saloon. The wind gusted suddenly, heeling the narrow-beamed vessel over. Annabel gripped her husband's arm, steadying herself. 'I've got work to do here, darling. You get up to the bridge.'

He held her close for a moment as the rain began to spatter on to the upper deck above them. 'Can you manage?'

'Yes.' She kissed him quickly, then ran into the saloon, slamming the door shut behind her.

Forester moved down the outside passage and climbed the companionway to the bridge. He heard the engines of the two gunboats burst into life as they got under way, then, suddenly, the searchlights snapped off. Darkness enveloped the ship; the wind gusted again, causing the antennae above the wheelhouse to sing. He pushed the door open and stepped inside towards the familiar green glow from the radar. He shut the rising gale out and switched on a light. Samra was sitting by the chart table. He looked frightened by the imminence of the storm. Rhys was already at the wheel, his hand poised above the starter. 'OK?'

'OK,' Forester replied. 'Get some speed on here as fast as you can. Head her straight into the wind. I'll check our position.'

Annabel was in the galley when she heard the reassuring vibration of the engines beneath her feet. She leaned on the table and closed her eyes, gripping the edge in an effort to hide

159

her relief. The door from the packed saloon opened and she felt a hand on her arm. She turned and stood up.

It was the writer, Erica Graham. 'I'm so glad to see you, Mrs Forester, so glad.' The concern in her eyes was genuine – she was close to tears. The two women hugged each other silently, finding comfort in their embrace. The vessel began to move forward through the choppy water. *Sea Victory* was alive again.

Annabel broke free. 'We've got lots to do. You get the blankets – they're stored under the bench seats. Give them to as many people as you can. It's going to be a rough night.'

Mrs Drucker had seen the ambassador come into the saloon and watched him make his way to the bar, followed by Major Bridges. Someone offered him a seat, which he courteously refused, but he did accept a drink from Henshaw, who was tired but sober.

Mrs Drucker was seething. Her son was lying on a blanket reading a comic. She grabbed his arm. 'You stay here,' she commanded. 'I want you here when I come back. Is that understood?'

The boy didn't even look up. 'Sure, Mom – no sweat.'

That irritated her still further. 'And don't *say* that – I hate it.'

Bernie's interest in the comic didn't waver. 'Sure, Mom,' he said again, almost repeating the offending remark. He glanced up at her and grinned. 'Sorry.' It averted the clout which was imminent. Only the glint in her eye told him how close he had sailed to the wind. He understood his mother pretty well.

Mrs Drucker headed for the ambassador. This was the moment she had been waiting for. She tapped him firmly on the shoulder.

He turned and looked enquiringly at her. 'Yes?' he said politely.

His good manners annoyed her still further. She suspected that most people who were in the public eye were fags anyway. 'What the hell,' she said peremptorily, 'is going on?'

The ambassador opened his mouth to reply, but that was as far as he got.

'Do you realize just what I've been through?'

He didn't attempt an answer this time – it seemed better to say nothing.

She poked at him with her finger. 'You are the American ambassador?'

He nodded hastily. 'Yes, I am.'

Major Bridges felt compelled to place himself in the firing line. 'Now just a minute, Miss . . .'

She gazed fiercely at him. 'Mrs Drucker,' she said with icy emphasis.

The major fell back a step beneath the verbal blow. 'Well, Mrs Drucker, I'm sure the ambassador will do all he can to help.'

She poked the unfortunate major heavily in the chest with her steely finger. 'Get your – ass – out – of here. I ain't talking to you, I'm talking to him.'

The ambassador was close to half her size and weight, but he wasn't without courage. 'How can I help?'

'Help!' she said contemptuously. 'Help! Would you mind telling me what the USA is doing making refugees out of its own people?'

The ambassador was bewildered. He looked from the major to Henshaw – then at the woman. 'I'm . . . I'm sure you are mistaken, Mrs . . . ?'

'Drucker . . . Am I, indeed?' She leaned forward to add emphasis to the *coup de grâce*. 'Then how come a goddamn bomb landed in my garden in Beirut with Michigan stamped all over it?'

At that point he was saved from further embarrassment by the arrival of a huge bowl of grilled chicken pieces, which Annabel placed upon the bar. The smell was delicious, and the argument died a natural death, hunger overcoming ruffled feathers. First in the queue was Mrs Drucker, followed immediately by her ravenous son.

Forester tapped the barometer; it was still falling. The wind was gusting more frequently now, churning up the land-locked sea. It was going to slow them down, but at least it was from the north-east, and they could keep their bows into its teeth and still maintain their course for Cyprus.

Forester turned to Rhys. 'I'm going to check that everyone is under cover before this gets any worse. Stay on our present heading.'

161

Another gust of wind whistled round the bridge and through the cracks, making Samra jump. Forester smiled encouragingly. 'Don't worry, its bark is worse than its bite. We've survived a lot worse than this.' He wasn't sure how much the words reassured Samra: his face revealed no expression, and he continued to hold grimly on to the handrail, wedging himself in the corner.

Rhys rolled the helm expertly through his hands, anticipating as much as he could the drift and movement of the rising sea. Forester was glad of his presence – his seamanship could not be questioned. He patted him on the shoulder. 'I shan't be long.'

Rhys continued to peer through the pouring rain. 'Mind those decks, now – they'll be slippery till the sea cleans them off.'

'Right,' Forester acknowledged. He took a flashlamp from the shelf above the table, then grabbed the handle of the door and slid it open.

At once the rain whipped into his face, stinging, driven almost horizontally by the wind. He jerked the door shut and gripped the wet handrail, pulling himself along it on to the sundeck. He flashed the torch on. The deck was awash, the rain pouring down the companionways either side. It was deserted. He decided not to use the forward ladder – it was too exposed. Instead, he slid down the companionway, the rain cascading round him like a waterfall.

He worked his way forward until he was clear of the super-structure. The gale hit him full force, nearly breaking his hold on the handrail. He wrapped his arm around one of the pillars supporting the upper deck, and used the torch again. The bow lifted, then dropped, plunging itself into the next wave. A blanket of white spray lashed him with salty water and made his eyes smart. Thankfully, nobody had been foolish enough to stay in the open.

He moved back into the lee of the cabins and worked his way past the windows of the saloon. Inside, through the streaming glass, he could see it was jammed with people, most of them sitting on the bench seats or lying on the floor. He reached the stern . . . It was clear. That just left the exposed upper deck.

Carefully he climbed the rear companionway until his head was level with the deck. The wind force had increased considerably. He tried to raise himself to get a clear view. The ship lurched heavily to starboard as a huge wave caught her beneath the port beam. Forester was flung against the awning, losing his hold on the rail. His feet slid from under him and he crashed back down the companionway on to the stern deck, the fall completely winding him.

The torch bounced from his hand and rolled over the side beneath the rail. Before he could grab a hold, the vessel rolled sickeningly again, sliding him across the streaming deck towards the stern. He wallowed like a stranded whale, desperately trying to hold on to something. His flailing hands missed the table support by inches as the bow of the vessel rose steeply in the heavy sea, pitching him relentlessly towards the white-flecked water.

If the stern ladder had not been raised, blocking the gap in the rails, he would have been thrown straight into the maelstrom of threshing water beneath the vessel. He crashed, feet first, into it, the metal scraping the inside of his leg. He was unaware of any pain as his fingers scrabbled to get a hold on the guard rail before the bow slid down again. His hand closed around a steel stanchion and he pulled himself sideways on to the rail as the deck sloped away from him again. He held on grimly, trying to get his breath as the rain and sea spray tore at his clothing, as if the storm itself had decided to wrench him from his precarious hold.

Through the misted windows of the saloon door he could see the vague figure of his wife as she moved slowly amongst the refugees, totally unaware of his danger. He wanted to shout – scream for help, but he knew it was useless. The wind would simply tear the cries from his throat, and whip them into the blackness of the night.

The bow began to rise again. His hands were cold – losing their grip. He wrapped his arm around the stanchion, bracing his feet on the deck to try and get some support. He waited until the deck levelled off and, still gripping the rail tightly began to ease himself round the stern towards the side passageway. Three times he had to stop and hold on grimly as *Sea Victory* crested mountainous seas – then, blessedly, he found himself in the cover of the superstructure and he was able to haul himself groggily to his feet.

For a moment he contemplated going into the shelter of the saloon, but there was blood streaming down the inside of his leg and he feared his appearance could easily cause a panic among some of the refugees. The Lebanese were not the best sailors in the world, and they were probably feeling utterly sick and miserable as *Sea Victory* rose and fell like a drunken lift in the heavy seas.

Annabel had enough to do dealing with them. He would patch himself up. He carefully eased his way back along the side of the vessel, then slowly clambered the steps to the wheelhouse. Inside, distorted by the rivers of water streaming down the windows, he could see the two figures of Rhys and Samra lit by the glow of the radar. He slid open the door and staggered inside, shutting it behind him.

The howl of the wind cut off, and the warmth of the interior was a huge relief from the biting rain. It felt like home.

Sea Victory was not too well endowed with lavatory facilities: one on the main deck, and another below, next to Forester's own cabin. They were both of the hand-pump variety, and certainly not adequate enough to deal with the needs of nearly 120 passengers. Inevitably, the one on the main deck, which was nearest to the refugees, became blocked and foul.

Annabel, Henshaw and Erica Graham had their hands full trying to cope with seasick and inexperienced travellers. As the night dragged on the crowded saloon and cabin areas became a nightmare of crying children and frightened adults. The best they could do was simply to be on hand, cheerful and confident, supplying towels, buckets, containers – anything they could lay their hands on – and allaying fears that the storm-tossed vessel would not survive.

It was Henshaw who came up with the most startling piece of news. The ambassador was mucking in too. Quite literally, in fact: he was endeavouring to unblock the lavatory. Annabel rushed upstairs to the main deck and found him with his sleeves rolled up and armed with a bucket. She grabbed the bucket from him and filled it from the tap. 'You should not be doing this,' she protested, wrinkling her nose. The smell in the lavatory was vile.

He took it back from her and flushed it down the pan. 'Nonsense! Someone has to do it, and you are needed elsewhere – you're doing a marvellous job, young lady.'

Annabel steadied herself as the boat pitched, then took the bucket from him once more, refilling it. 'You keep on calling me young lady and I won't mind.'

She flung the water into the pan. He jerked the pump up and down several times and, quite suddenly, it cleared. 'There,' he said, 'it worked . . .'

He was as pleased at accomplishing this onerous task as anything else he could recall. In a sense, he reflected, his job was as much a cleaning-up operation, after others had dumped on him, as this.

He took the bucket from beneath the tap again and poured it down. 'Clear as a bell,' he said with some satisfaction. He looked curiously at Annabel. 'We haven't had a chance to talk. I was wondering what happened when we got split up on the gunboat.'

'Not a lot. They kept me down in the captain's cabin for some time, then he came in and asked a few questions.'

The American ambassador rolled down his sleeves. 'Well, he must have been satisfied with your answers, because here we are.'

Annabel was tempted to say something rude about precisely where they were but she wasn't sure how strong he was on dirty jokes and, after all, he was an ambassador. 'He also warned me about the dangers of trying it again. I don't think we could have got through this time if you hadn't been on board.'

The ambassador looked at her quizzically and smiled. 'Oh, I don't know. Seems to me, on a neutral British vessel you stand a better chance than most. Besides, I have found it most useful, and I dare say other Embassy staff as well as our own will need something like this while the airport is out of action.'

He indicated the open door. 'Perhaps we ought to abandon this now, in case it is required.'

Annabel smiled. 'Yes, it's the first time I've ever had a meeting in the smallest room – least of all with an ambassador.'

He closed the door firmly behind him, then faced her. 'True, but I wish all my meetings ended as satisfactorily as that one.'

Annabel noted with pleasure that there was a definite twinkle in his eye.

The gale blew steadily throughout the night, and was still gusting strongly as the grey sky began to lighten off the starboard beam. It took a long time before any perceptible light filtered across the white-flecked sea. It always surprised Forester how little, in these conditions, it resembled the image of the Mediterranean. The dark sky and sea, the scudding low clouds were more fitting to the north Atlantic than these waters. But traditionally, as the morning advanced, the grey skies lifted and the hot sun began to shine through in bright shafts between the vanishing clouds.

The wind slowly died away as they approached the eastern toe of Cyprus, and by the time they were closing on the harbour that gave access to Larnaca the storm had disappeared completely. Like a mirage, the night and the gale had gone. The only trace of its presence was on the tired, stressed faces of the crew and passengers, though the joy and exhilaration of their imminent arrival lifted the refugees.

They lined the rails, gazing at the coastline of Cyprus as though it were the promised land. Total strangers hugged each other with relief. They pointed to the harbour and the dusty oil refinery that gleamed in the sunshine, distance disguising its down-at-heel exterior.

Having seen something of the turmoil they had endured, Forester could understand their emotional response. The last twist of fear had been the storm, but they had survived that, too. They were more than entitled to their moment of joy.

Annabel had cleaned and dressed the wound on André's hand. He would never have complete use of it again, but at least there was no infection. 'There,' she said, ripping the end of the bandage in two, and tying it neatly. 'That should look after it until you get to a hospital.'

Before she could rise, André took her hand and lifted it to his lips, gently kissing the palm. 'I hope,' he said quietly, 'I hope I can come back one day to see you. My sister and I know how

166

hard you have worked to help us. I would like to know your face.'

Leila saw that the blonde Englishwoman was closer to tears at that point than any other during the long, interminable night.

Annabel rose, pulling him up from the bench seat, putting her arms around him. 'You will,' she whispered, 'I know you will.'

On the bridge, Samra had relaxed at last. He stood outside the open door, basking in the sun, the cool breeze ruffling his white hair. Already there was a trace of colour in his cheeks.

Forester called to him from inside the wheelhouse. 'Feel any better?'

Samra smile happily. 'Oh yes, Captain – this is much better, and not just because the storm has gone.'

Forester studied his profile against the azure sky. It was clear now that Samra was by no means an old man – certainly not the age he had seemed in the shipping agent's office in Jounieh . . . was it only yesterday? It felt more like a week – a month.

For Samra, time had gone into reverse, wiping away the suffering, the years of incarceration beneath the streets of Beirut. He could feel it – the blood stirring, like sap rising, beginning to live again. He looked inside the wheelhouse. The Englishman had said something. 'Sorry?'

'I asked what will you do?'

Samra thought about it for a moment. 'I don't know, I don't care.' He shrugged. 'I used to have a friend here – maybe I will find him.'

Forester handed over the wheel to Rhys, and joined Samra at the rail, gazing at the low flat coastline. 'Do you need any money – a small loan perhaps?'

Samra touched his arm, staring at him gravely. 'Please, Captain, no more. You have done enough; you brought me here.'

Forester would have liked to insist, but he understood the Middle East well enough not to try. 'Perhaps I shall see you again?'

'Yes, Captain – you will, and it will be my pleasure.'

It was very odd. Annabel and Forester leaned over the rail on the upper deck, near the wheelhouse, and it was silent. Well, almost silent. Just the usual sounds a boat makes when it is tied up: the creak of the timbers; the occasional slap of water between the quay and the vessel; and the faint sounds of the traffic in the distance. But, other than that, silence.

And it did seem odd. Apart from themselves the vessel was deserted. All their passengers gone: Mrs Drucker and her son, still as loud and complaining as ever; the unfortunate ambassador who had taken the brunt of her fury – and who had proved such a godsend; with him, his taciturn security officer, Major Bridges. Erica Graham had gone, hugging Annabel emotionally before climbing down the gangplank; the Lebanese lady and her daughter in the wheelchair – they had, surprisingly, been driven away in a very expensive Mercedes; and, of course, Samra Asaker. He would stay longest in Forester's memory. There was something infinitely sad, yet enduring, about Samra. They had all gone, relieved, exuberant and, for the moment, happy. Now the vessel seemed strangely quiet.

Henshaw and Rhys had both got away as soon as they could. Only Forester and his wife remained. And, as the adrenalin slowed down, tension eased, so a sense of heaviness swept through Forester. He felt as though he could sleep for a week.

Then he heard something and he was wide awake again. Annabel pointed. It was Charlie, running down the quay towards them ahead of his nanny, who was toiling along behind, trying to keep up. They waved and shouted to their son, then descended the rear companionway into the stern as he came running up the gangplank. They picked him up and hugged him between them. He plucked at Forester's collar impatiently. 'Can we go to the beach, Daddy?'

Forester knew that more than anything else they both needed to sleep. He glanced at his wife.

Charlie saw the look. 'You did promise, Daddy – just before you sailed.'

Annabel kissed him. 'Yes, of course we can.' She looked at Forester. 'We'll all go together.'

Charlie's voice raised itself another decibel of excitement. 'Oh, 'triffic, Mummy . . . 'triffic!' He kissed her, then quickly

168

turned back to his father. 'Was it a great adventure, Daddy?'

Forester lifted his son from Annabel's arms and sat him halfway up the steps leading to the upper deck. The same steps that had nearly cost him his life. 'Yes,' he said seriously, 'it was a great adventure, Charlie.'

CHAPTER

SEVENTEEN

It was chaotic. The power for the lifts had gone and Kass was trying to help the medics carry a stretcher up to an emergency casualty room. The main one on the ground floor had been wiped out when the area had been blanket-shelled, prior to the siege.

It was difficult to climb the stairs. People sprawled everywhere, crowding every space. The wounded man on the stretcher was unconscious, suffering from a high-velocity bullet wound that had entered his body just below the ribcage. He was soaked with blood and Kass knew it was going to be touch and go. They had already treated more than 150 casualties that day – mostly flesh wounds requiring stitching. He had lost count of the number of operations. Eighteen had been dead on arrival.

Several blocks away an ammunition dump had been hit and a continuous round of explosions ripped through the hot evening air. No one reacted; experience had taught them when to take cover and when there was no immediate danger.

Kass was utterly exhausted. His clothes were bathed in sweat. He could not remember if they had stopped to eat or not and he knew he was in no fit state to perform anything but the most rudimentary first aid. But the rest of the medical staff in this West Beirut hospital were in a far worse state than himself. They had barely acknowledged his presence and no one had questioned his medical qualifications – they were merely grateful to have a helper who seemed to know what he was doing.

They reached the first-floor casualty room and a nurse in a stained uniform helped him and the medics lift the wounded man from the stretcher on to a table. The medics rolled up the bloodstained stretcher and, without speaking, disappeared back downstairs. Kass didn't envy them their task of trying to drive an ambulance through the war-torn streets. His own ride here in the early hours of the morning had convinced him of that.

A Lebanese man had been hit by a shell splinter outside the Commodore. He had been able to treat the man before the ambulance arrived and had stayed with him in the vehicle on its way to the hospital. Not even the high-pitched wailing of the siren as it tore through roads littered with debris and burnt-out cars had been loud enough to drown the rattle of gunfire all around them. He had wondered if his Odyssey was going to end ignominiously before it had even begun, but the ambulance seemed to have a charmed life. Bullets had ricocheted close several times, but nothing had hit the vehicle. Perhaps the militia hadn't even tried . . .

Kass removed the sodden cotton-wool swab from the wound. The bullet had lodged behind the back of the ribcage and the man was going to require major surgery. The nurse rigged up a blood-transfusion bottle while Kass inserted the needle, making sure the transfusion was effective. The operating room was still being used, but Kass knew that if the patient was not treated immediately he would die. He made the decision instinctively, and ordered the nurse to prepare the badly wounded man for surgery. He washed his hands in a basin, trying to get them as clean as he could. The towel was damp and used, but it would have to do. He turned back to the table.

The nurse stood silently beside the wounded man. There was a stillness about her that made him call out sharply. She looked round at him and shook her head mutely. Kass examined the man briefly: he was dead – he'd never really had a chance. An overwhelming sense of tiredness and depression swept over him. He turned away and walked slowly down a passage, looking neither left nor right.

Nurse Setta watched him go. She said nothing. She knew what he was going through. There had been a lot of foreign doctors in this hospital before. Some had stayed, others given up in despair. There was no way of knowing if the American would come back or not. She covered the dead man with a sheet

171

and picked up the telephone to call the mortuary. They would come as soon as they could. They were very busy.

Kass turned off the passage into one of the wards. Both sides of the long room were lined with beds; all were occupied except the one nearest to him by the open door. He slumped on to it and fell instantly into a sleep of deep mental and physical exhaustion.

As the shadows lengthened, street dust blown through the shattered windows glittered in the evening sun, settling over everything in a fine white film. Outside, the explosions from the ammunition dump slowly faded. There was the occasional outburst, then it stopped altogether. Gunfire began to ease, as though welcoming the night, exhausted by its day of killing, needing rest before resuming its carnage with first light.

Only the ambulances continued to siren their way to and from the overburdened hospital. Kass heard none of it. Sleep had kindly claimed him.

CHAPTER
EIGHTEEN

Nazira sat and waited. The lobby of the hotel was busy. The war seemed to have abated, the battles had moved away – at least for the moment. And, as always, people grabbed the opportunity to get as much done as possible before the next alarm. The lulls between fighting were what passed for normality in Beirut, and the civilian population seized on them avidly.

Nazira had seen the pattern repeated a hundred times in the streets outside: broken glass was swept away; queues would suddenly materialize wherever food could be bought or bartered; information was exchanged; children played amongst the rubble. It was a startling example of the resilience of ordinary people amidst the devastation. And of the incredible strength of the life force – survival was paramount.

It was reflected, too, in the somewhat exotic atmosphere of this hotel. The faces around her were animated: there was tension, certainly, and fear; but there was excitement, too, a sense of living for the moment.

Nazira remembered the camps in Palestine – no sense of excitement there; only the deadliness, the soul-destroying uniformity of each day without hope or escape; her mother's face, her despair. She had closed her mind to her mother's disapproval. There was only one thing that mattered – she had to get out, fight back, do something for her people – even for her mother, who tried to burden her with guilt. Her mother did not understand.

There was only one way. She used what she had. Her good looks were in demand, men liked her and she knew how to please them. Nazira felt no sense of guilt in using the only viable asset she had. If it distressed her mother, then so be it; it distressed her not at all. She used the Israeli officers the way they used her. And, eventually, she had succeeded in reaching France. It had helped that her father had been French, an official of the United Nations who had come to help – then helped himself and disappeared when he realized her mother was pregnant. The irony did not escape her. And so she had manipulated these same desires to achieve her own ends . . . she had made it to France. Her mother was still in the camp; she could do nothing about that – not yet.

But soon they would all pay for what they had done. Her camera would be the eye that exposed them to the world, until the disintegration of her people could no longer be ignored or swept away. Here in Beirut the Israelis were making their biggest mistake. This was where the balance would begin to swing against them. She intended to be a part of that, to make it happen.

At last she saw Rousseau come down the staircase, inevitably accompanied by Armand. Nazira had placed herself carefully so that she could be seen from whatever direction they might come.

Rousseau paused as he saw her, and she smiled. He and Armand crossed the lobby and stopped in front of her. 'Good morning.' He indicated the camera round her neck. 'Are you getting the pictures you want?'

Was there just the slightest ambivalence in his question? She wasn't sure. In any case, she decided to ignore it. 'Oh yes,' she said enthusiastically. 'The agency seem to be pleased. I spoke to them on the telephone this morning and I think they like them.'

Rousseau knew it was better than that. Her modesty was false and did not suit her. One of the photographs had already been on the front page of *France-Soir*. He could feel Armand getting impatient beside him. 'We are just about to have some breakfast. Would you like to join us?'

Nazira rose and smiled charmingly. 'I'd be delighted.'

Armand's face fell. He didn't like Nazira – he didn't trust her – and he liked even less having his breakfast interrupted by a

174

hard-nosed lady photographer. 'Shall we go?' he said ungraciously.

He led the way across the lobby and into the large room that served as a breakfast lounge. He chose a table as far away from the windows as he could get. He'd already been warned about blast. They ordered a light continental breakfast and Rousseau studied Nazira curiously.

She was still wearing the green battle fatigues; he had never seen her in anything else. But that did not seem to trouble her. She made no concessions to femininity, and yet there was nothing unfeminine about her either. She was good, there was no doubt about that. *France-Soir* did not print many pictures by freelance photographers.

'Have you seen anything of the American doctor?' he asked.

She shook her head. 'No, not since the day before yesterday. He left in an ambulance with a wounded man.'

Armand buttered a piece of bread. 'I expect he is at the hospital. That's why he came, isn't it?'

Nazira made no comment.

Rousseau changed the subject. 'Congratulations, I heard about your front page.'

'Yes, I was lucky. Those pictures I shot in the basement worked very well. They were picked up by *France-Soir*.' She paused and glanced briefly at Rousseau. 'I wondered if you might like to follow up with a story about what has happened to them since.'

Rousseau was interested. 'How would we find her?'

'They all live down there – it's the safest place. There's nowhere else for them to go.'

Rousseau considered it – it would be a natural follow-up. 'Do you think we could find the place all right?'

Armand looked at him incredulously, but said nothing.

'Yes,' she answered, 'no problem. I know where it is.'

Armand butted in. 'Don't you think we ought to have some protection. What about that PLO man we went with before?'

'No. He attracted a good deal of fire because of his uniform. We're safer without him.'

Armand indicated her fatigues. 'Wouldn't you do the same in them?'

175

Nazira contemplated him unblinkingly. The Frenchman found her steady gaze uncomfortable. 'If it worries you, I'll wear something else. But you can't come to a war zone and not expect to be in some danger.' She barely kept the contempt from her voice.

Armand squirmed. 'No, of course not, I realize that. It's just that . . .'

'Yes?'

'Well, there's no point in taking unnecessary risks.' It sounded lame even in his own ears.

Nazira looked directly at Rousseau. 'What about you?'

He knew he had no choice now; besides, the story might be a good one. 'Yes, if you can get us there, I'll come.'

'I can get you there,' she said blandly.

Rousseau shrugged. 'OK, fine, we all go. I'll tell Kemp.' He clapped his hand to his forehead. 'I must be mad.'

They left Yussef in the car at the top of the boulevard that led down to the junction. The only sound of fighting came from the other end of the city, towards the airport. The boulevard was quiet, but no one in the area seemed to be moving about. That was odd, but Nazira didn't comment. Armand was already badly scared.

They stayed close to the buildings, gradually working their way to the junction. Nazira took a quick look round the corner. The street was deserted and a stillness hung over the smashed-up apartment blocks. There was no breeze; the heat haze bounced off the concrete road. Red splashes of earth pockmarked the surface here and there, where a shell had torn it up.

She waved for the others to follow, then ran quickly to the other side of the road, flattening herself against the wall. She could feel the heat; the white concrete was hot against her hand, though it was still early morning. Kemp, Rousseau and Armand joined her, moving as fast as they could with their equipment. She moved along the wall to the entrance to the basement. It was much as before, the drive dipping steeply down below the apartments, the entrance shadowy and menacing in the unnatural stillness.

Kemp looked past her. 'She's there?' Nazira nodded. He

looked at Armand, who was sweating profusely – and it wasn't just the heat.

The Canadian glanced up and down the road. He didn't like it any better than his partner, but they had come this far and they might just as well go through with it. 'Let's go,' he said harshly.

Nazira led the way down the slope. Once inside, away from the sun, it was startlingly cool. She felt the sweat go cold around her neck. She motioned the others to be still, waiting for her eyes to adjust to the gloom. She started to move slowly across the wide, empty car park to where she had last seen the car. Armand's foot kicked against an empty tin – and he swore as it went clattering across the concrete floor.

Suddenly a pair of headlights blazed on from the corner of the car park and bullets began to ricochet wildly from the roof and walls of the building. They flung themselves down, the sound of the automatic reverberating around them.

Armand was shouting, his voice drowned by the magnified sound of the gunfire. Nazira buried her head in her hands. They were totally exposed, they hadn't a chance – she waited for the impact of the bullet, wondering what it would be like. Would it burn, would it tear her flesh, or would it simply extinguish her life without pain? She could hear Armand screaming hysterically. She raised her head. The firing had stopped and a woman's voice was shouting in Arabic. She recognized the voice.

Slowly Nazira raised herself from the ground so that she could be seen clearly in the glare of the car's headlamps. The Lebanese woman started to cry and Nazira moved beyond the circle of light. She found the woman slumped over the driving wheel of the car, clutching an automatic rifle. She was sobbing uncontrollably. Nazira put her arms around the woman's shaking body and tried to comfort her.

Behind them, crouched on the floor, were the two children, their eyes wide with fear, staring at her. She heard a sound and turned. Kemp and Rousseau had followed her and were standing by the open door of the car. Nazira shook her head slightly – she didn't want them to say anything that might terrify the woman still further. Kemp reached into the car, switched off the headlights and picked up the discarded automatic rifle. There was still enough daylight filtering in through the open entrance to see that the car park was empty of all but this single vehicle. Nothing had changed.

Armand walked up behind them and grabbed Rousseau's arm. 'It was the woman who was firing?' His voice was still querulous; he was badly shaken up.

Rousseau nodded. He spoke quietly so that the woman would not hear. 'Yes, she probably thought we were militia, that we would harm her or the children. There is no way of knowing what has been happening to these people.'

'I know.' Nazira had got out of the car. Her eyes challenged him.

'What do you mean?'

'Her husband is dead – he died in the hospital without recovering consciousness.'

Rousseau inclined his head. 'Do you want me to talk to her – see if there is a follow-up story?'

'No, she doesn't speak any English, but she has told me what happened, and I can translate it for you.'

Rousseau wasn't happy with that. Intermediaries always got between him and it . . . His own instinctive responses, as much as anything else, tended to lead him to the heart of the story – if there was one. 'Tell me what you know first.'

Nazira looked at the woman. She had recovered some of her composure now and was talking quietly to her children, trying to calm their fear. She had wrapped them in a blanket and they were no longer shivering.

'Her husband was killed by members of the Damour Brigade.'

Rousseau sat down on an upturned box and began to take some notes. 'Damour?'

'Yes. Damour is a Christian coastal town a few miles south of here. It was sacked during the civil war of '76. Hundreds of people were murdered. The Damour Brigade say it was the Palestinians and they have sworn revenge.'

Kemp butted in. 'How did the woman know it was the Damour Brigade?'

Nazira stared at him coldly. 'They wear black armbands in mourning. If you see them, you know them. They do not disguise their hate.'

Rousseau gestured towards the car. 'What happened here?'
Nazira shrugged. 'What always happens with them. They
come in, searching for Palestinians. They found this family
hiding down here and shot her husband.'
Armand was incredulous. 'But why? They are not Palestinian.'
Nazira began to pace slowly up and down. 'No, they are not.
But he was killed as a warning to others. They believe that there
are many in this area who are sympathetic to the PLO – so he
was shot.'
Rousseau looked up from his notes. 'This Damour Brigade, is
it clear whose side they are on?'
Nazira paused in her pacing, smiling grimly. 'Oh yes, it's
clear. They are part of the power base of Bashir Gemayel and
they work in close collaboration with the Israelis – mostly as
their eyes and ears – reconnaissance. But this Damour Brigade,
they are different. They have modelled themselves on the Israeli
group that went into Entebbe; they want blood.'
Rousseau chewed the end of his pencil thoughtfully. 'How
long have you known about this?'
Nazira stood motionless, her hands behind her back, staring
down at him. 'Two days. I came back as soon as you had all
gone. The woman told me then.'
Rousseau nodded. Now he understood. 'And that's why you
brought us here?'
'Yes. I wanted you to know what was happening. I can only
say so much with photographs – television is needed, too. I
believe I can trust you to tell the truth.'
Rousseau stood up and looked at her reflectively. Her eyes
never left him; she was waiting. For Nazira this was not just
reporting, it was her life. He put the pad in his pocket. 'The
truth . . . What is the truth, Nazira? I have to know more about
this Damour Brigade. I have to confirm what this woman says
– find out, if I can, whether they were in this area when her
husband was killed. I will tape the story, but I need more
information. Will you help me find it. Do you understand?'
Nazira felt nothing. She was neither disappointed nor elated.
Professionally she could understand his caution, but in her
heart was fury. More delay, more muddling of the issue. 'Yes,'
she said tonelessly. 'I understand.' She laughed, though there

179

was no humour in her voice. 'It's curious. This situation, these circumstances, they are so similar. So much like Germany. The Jews kept telling the world about the camps, the atrocities. Yet none believed them until they found Belsen. Maybe no one will believe this until it happens here.'

Kemp watched them. He had no liking for Nazira. Instinctively he distrusted her passion, her obsession with the war. For her, it was a crusade and that offended his professional instincts. He waited to see how Rousseau would respond.

The Frenchman took her arm and guided her back to the woman in the car. 'I will do what I can. We can start here with this Lebanese woman. I can tape an interview. Through you I would like to ask her some questions. But there are other things too – will you help me, Nazira?'

She did not reply. She disengaged her arm and opened the door of the car, asking the women in Arabic to get out. Gently she helped her clamber from the car. They both stood facing him.

'Now,' Nazira said quietly, 'what do you want to know?'

Kemp set up the camera and lights in the basement car park, while Armand tested sound levels. When they were both satisfied, Rousseau began to question the woman on camera, through Nazira. But he learnt little more than Nazira had already told him. Halfway through he paused while a jet thundered overhead, flying low and fast. When it had gone he resumed.

The Lebanese woman could remember nothing about the Damour Brigade, apart from the black armbands, and even to be reminded of their existence distressed her and made the children apprehensive. Rousseau cut the interview; there was no point in going on. The only thing that had emerged was the suffering and degradation of this family, and their despair and fear of the future. That in itself might make compulsive viewing, but would it solve anything? Rousseau doubted it.

He wanted to try and help them, to find a relief organization that could give them some shelter, but Nazira would have none of it. 'Any organization would simply pass them on to one kind of refugee camp or other. They are better off here.' She paused momentarily, her eyes glittering. 'If they survive, at least they

180

will still be a part of a community. If you really want to help, then *give* them something. Money or, better still, valuables. If they have that, at least they can buy food for as long as it lasts.' She turned her back on them and walked away. She would not plead any more; now it was up to them.

The Lebanese woman was unable to understand what Nazira had said. She waited obediently to see if they had finished with her.

Armand switched off the tape recorder and stood up, reaching into his pocket. He found a lighter – it was an expensive one of which he was particularly fond – and gave it to the woman, showing her how it worked. The woman was delighted. She ran to show it to her children. Armand began to pack away his equipment; he didn't look at the others.

Kemp stared at him, surprised and faintly embarrassed by the Frenchman's gesture. It didn't make sense. They couldn't go around giving handouts to every distressed or homeless refugee. And yet, in spite of himself, he had been touched by Armand's action – he knew how much the Frenchman prized that lighter.

'Goddammit!' he exclaimed. He stuck his hand out in front of Rousseau. 'Come on, gimme . . .'

Rousseau shook his head resignedly, but gave him all the cash he had. The Canadian took it and fished around in his own jeans, putting both amounts together. He stared challengingly at Rousseau, daring him to make a remark, but Rousseau contented himself with a shrug.

Kemp turned on his heel and strode across to the Lebanese woman, taking her hand. He placed the money in it and closed her hand over it. 'This is for you,' he said, trying to make her understand.

The woman turned and looked questioningly at Nazira. The Palestinian exchanged a few words with her. She was disbelieving at first, staring at all the money she was holding. When she realized it was true she tried to kiss Kemp's hand.

'No,' he said, stopping her. 'It's all right, it's for you.'

Nazira smiled at him. 'She thanks you.'

Kemp glanced at Rousseau, then at Armand. Both Frenchmen were grinning, delighted at the Canadian's embarrassment. He crossed the basement, busying himself with the arc lamps. 'OK, fine, you have your laugh, but we don't do nothing like this again – understand? Jesus Christ, if the word got round we'd never be able to do our job!'

Rousseau was amused, but he could see the sense in what Kemp said. This was a one-off, not to be repeated. It had only happened because of Nazira's presence. And, even if she was right about giving the woman as much as they could, he still felt as though he had simply bought off his conscience. There was nothing they could really do.

The woman made them some coffee on a primus stove while they packed away their equipment. Gradually the children were tempted from their refuge in the old car as their curiosity got the better of them. They were fascinated by the television camera. Nazira took a few shots of them sipping the coffee in the semi-darkness of the basement, but Armand was anxious to leave. He felt exposed and vulnerable in this part of West Beirut. Nazira's total lack of fear unnerved him, and he had not forgotten Annabel's impression of this woman. Nothing that had happened had changed that view. The Englishwoman was right – Nazira was a fanatic and he felt sure there was a subconscious death wish about her.

Eventually they left. Nazira did not look back. The family had a better chance now, better than when they had arrived. They were independent and whatever decisions had to be made were in their hands and not some faceless committee controlling a camp. That was a start.

Outside, the glare was blinding. The harsh white light reflected from the blasted walls made Rousseau's eyes water. Nazira crouched by the corner of the entrance to the basement and looked up and down the wide, straight road. Still no sign of life. She wondered why. There was no fighting and the shelling was distant. Normally this would be the moment for people to emerge and scavenge whatever they could.

She contemplated going back into the basement to see if the woman knew anything, but Armand wouldn't like that. Psychologically, they were committed to getting back to the car.

Kemp had stationed himself on the other corner. Rousseau exchanged a look with her and they all moved off together, running for the other side of the road. Buildings, shattered by blast, towered above them, sheltering them from the merciless heat of the sun. Already they were sweating – Rousseau's shirt was stained dark, sticking to him. They moved forward one behind the other – Kemp first, followed by Rousseau and Armand, Nazira bringing up the rear. They stayed close to the doorways, moving as quietly as they could. When they reached the junction Kemp poked his head around the corner. Two hundred yards away an overturned military jeep lay half on the pavement, half in a shattered shop window, its exposed under-carriage burnt by blast. It had not been there before.

He motioned Nazira to take a look. 'What do you think?'

She was puzzled. They had heard no nearby explosion while in the basement, unless it had been masked by the low-flying jet.

Kemp indicated the damage. 'Maybe it hit a mine.'

She shook her head. 'No, there's no point in laying mines. These streets can change hands too quickly, and they are just as likely to blow themselves up. A hand grenade is more likely.'

Kemp examined the broken windows along the boulevard carefully. If it was a hand grenade, it must have been thrown from nearby. Nothing moved – no breath of wind so much as stirred a curtain. Their car was waiting at the top of the boulevard and they had to get to it. 'Maybe we should make a detour.'

'If we do that, we have more ground to cover – they could be anywhere.'

Armand had heard enough. 'Look, I thought you said there was no fighting in this area.'

Nazira continued to watch the boulevard, looking for move-ment. 'There wasn't an hour ago. Now there may be – things change.'

Armand decided at that moment that if they got back to the hotel safely he would never venture out with this woman again. She had been looking for trouble – he was convinced of it.

Kemp wished he had kept the automatic rifle he had taken from the car, but it was the only protection the woman had. In any case, if anything happened he could not claim to be a cameraman if he was carrying a weapon. There was nothing for it – they had to take their chances on the boulevard. 'OK?' He glanced at Nazira and the Frenchman; they were ready. 'Keep spread out, but move quickly.'

Armand was already breathing heavily, fear catching him by the throat and making him sweat profusely.

Kemp moved out, staying on the shadowy side of the road, making what use he could of the cover. He ran in little bursts, from doorway to doorway. The others followed. As they neared the overturned jeep on the other side of the boulevard, he could see there was nobody inside. Whoever had been driving had got away. There was no way of knowing if he had been hit or not.

It was Nazira who saw the faint movement in the window above the deserted shop. The short, squat muzzle of a sub-machine-gun poked from between the dirty, frayed curtains. She shouted a warning. Kemp and Rousseau leapt immediately into a doorway, followed by Nazira. Armand froze, paralysed with fear, as the dust spurted up around him.

Rousseau screamed at him to move, but he couldn't – he just stared, terrified, at Rousseau. The Frenchman didn't hesitate. Before Kemp could stop him he leapt out into the street and grabbed his friend's arm, jerking him forward, slamming him into the entrance.

In that instant a bullet smashed into Rousseau's thigh. He screamed with pain and crumpled face down on to the dusty road, his arms outstretched before him, just a few feet from the safety of the doorway.

Kemp dived forward, crawling on his belly until he could grab his wrists. He hauled the Frenchman face down on the ground into the entrance. As he did so the hail of fire from across the road suddenly ceased: the weapon had jammed. They would never know how lucky they had been.

Armand knelt down beside Rousseau. His own fear had disappeared and he felt icy cold in the realization that his panic had precipitated the situation. He took off his jacket and rolled it up, slipping it beneath his friend's head. Rousseau's body was shaking with shock. He gripped his leg, blood spurting from between his fingers. It was clear that the bullet had hit an artery.

Kemp undid his belt and pulled it tight around the top of Rousseau's leg, telling Nazira to hold it firmly. He ripped down the curtain from the shop window, breaking loose the narrow wooden rail. He snapped off about six inches and inserted it into the belt, twisting it round to tighten the makeshift tourniquet until the leg stopped pumping blood. Rousseau's face was waxy and a film of moisture beaded his upper lip.

Kemp looked up at Nazira. 'We have to get him to the hospital before he loses any more blood.' He looked out into the street. There was no more firing; the boulevard was quiet again. Opposite, in the room above the shop, the driver of the jeep who had shot at them was lying slumped by the window, his throat cut, his weapon removed. Warring factions took no prisoners.

Armand lifted Rousseau, slipping his arm beneath his shoulders, pulling him upright. 'Come on, give me a hand.'

Kemp gripped the other arm, taking Rousseau's weight between them. Without comment they moved out of their cover into the street, Nazira leading, expecting to hear the crash of a sub-machine-gun. The street stayed silent, watching, waiting for the real enemy to appear before positions were exposed.

Kemp, the two Frenchmen and Nazira had twice walked through a carefully prepared ambush, their progress monitored by the hidden militia. The decision not to take any action had been a close one. Only their cameras and equipment, plus the prospect of much bigger game, had saved them. The arrival of the jeep had been an unexpected complication.

The war zone was shifting all the time. The Israelis were closing in.

By the time they got Rousseau to the hospital he was drifting in and out of consciousness, his body a dead weight between Kemp and Armand. The ground floor of the entrance hall was crowded with refugees, but Nazira could see no one who looked like medical staff. She spoke to one of the Lebanese. He pointed wearily upstairs, saying nothing.

They struggled up the wide staircase with Rousseau. Few paid them any attention. People sprawled everywhere, occupying whatever space they could find. Twice, Kemp nearly tripped over outspread legs. The second time he kicked the man angrily, cursing him. The offender pulled up his legs beneath him, avoiding Kemp's eyes lest he annoy the Canadian further and risk being ejected from the safety of the hospital.

Kemp glared at Nazira. He sensed her contempt for his action, which he knew was unjustified, but he didn't care any more. He gritted his teeth and adjusted Rousseau's weight, climbing the endless stairs one at a time. He focused all his effort on that – one step at a time. He heard a shout and looked up. Kass was leaning over the well of the staircase looking down at them. At last, someone they knew. Suddenly this dusty, overflowing building did not seem so alien. He swallowed, his throat dry. 'It's Rousseau,' he called out, 'he's been hit.'

Kass's feet came clattering down the uncarpeted stairs as he rushed to help. He took some of the weight and between them they got Rousseau up the final flight. They laid him gently down on the casualty table and Kass quickly cut away the bloodstained leg of his trousers.

Kemp, Armand and Nazira stood exhausted, waiting for the verdict. Kass examined the wound. It was a clean one: the bullet had gone straight through the tissue part of the thigh, without damaging any bones. But the Frenchman had lost a lot of blood. An artery had been severed and without the belt that Kemp had twisted so tightly, Rousseau would have been close to death.

Nurse Setta was already rigging a bottle of blood plasma above Rousseau's head, inserting the needle into his arm. Kass turned and smiled at Armand. 'He'll live, no need to worry, we can look after him.'

The Frenchman didn't say anything, but the relief was plain on his face.

Nazira stared at the American. He was tired, in need of a shave, his clothing bloodstained, but there was a sense of purpose about him. The hesitancy had gone. Here in the hospital, in his own environment, albeit several thousand miles from New York, he was at home.

Rousseau opened his eyes. The bottle of plasma above his head swung lazily, twisting slowly around. The glutinous liquid swirled inside. His arm hurt where the needle had gone in. He raised his hand to touch it and the nurse restrained him. He stared at her blankly.

'It's all right,' he heard her say.

He did not know where he was. The ceiling was chipped, splintered, cracks running through it like tributaries on a map. He twisted his head and saw Nazira . . . suddenly he remembered. The shock made him cry out. Kass turned quickly and leaned over him. 'Rousseau, it's me, Kass. You are in the hospital – you'll be OK.'

Rousseau stared up at him, recognizing the American doctor. He grabbed his hand, his eyes bulging. 'Get her out of here, Kass, please make her go.' He indicated Nazira. 'She did it, she led us into a trap.' He pointed a wavering finger. 'She knew they were there.'

Nazira could see he was close to hysteria. She spoke calmly to the American, trying to hide her own feelings of injustice, of hurt.

The hurt surprised her – she thought that emotion had long since been killed. 'I will go.' She paused. Kass was watching her. She could sense in his look understanding, compassion. She turned abruptly to Armand. 'I hope he recovers soon.'

She brushed past him and Kemp, and ran quickly down the stairs. Something stung hotly behind her eyes. God, no – not tears. She was not going to cry, not for him. She needed to get out – the hospital suddenly seemed to be closing in on her. She rushed outside. The heat was overpowering. She found a tree and leaned against it, glad of the shade. Nazira stared up dry-eyed through the branches, the light diffused by the leaves.

Slowly she regained control of herself. Good, she felt better, though inside she was still shaking. She wondered why.

CHAPTER

NINETEEN

The half-circle of white sand was deserted, just as he had hoped it would be. Not many people knew of this small bay. Forester had discovered it three years earlier, when he had first sailed *Sea Victory* on a leisurely voyage around as much of the coastline as he could. Now they had driven out here in the Morgan. Charlie loved the open-topped sports car, the feeling of speed and the coolness of the slipstream blowing through his hair. He kept asking his father to drive faster, encouraging him to overtake everything on the road. But Forester was not tempted. He'd had enough excitement recently. His eyes felt prickly with tiredness – he was too exhausted to even feel hungry.

Charlie, on the other hand, was full of energy and dashed about the beach, cutting channels in the sand to flood the moat of his castle.

Now, at last, Forester was lying on his back in the warm sand. Yet, strangely, he could not doze off. A thousand thoughts and images made him stir fitfully. He felt Annabel move beside him. Her hand sought his, squeezing it gently. 'Can't sleep?'

He opened his eyes, shading them from the sun. 'No – too much on my mind, I think.'

'Me too.' She paused. 'I was thinking about Leila and her brother.'

'André?'

'Yes.'

They both lay quietly, listening to Charlie's incessant chatter as he explained in lurid detail what was going to happen when he released the water into his castle.

'He'll be in France by now,' Forester said.

'Yes, I suppose so.' Annabel could not lose the memory of his eyes.

'It's strange, but I never really believed he was blind; his eyes were so normal, so luminous. They seemed to see through me.' She shook her head as if trying to shake off the thought. 'Do you think he will ever see again?'

Forester sat up in the sand, holding his knees in his arms. He gazed out over the softly pounding sea, still heavy from the storm of the night before. 'I don't know,' he said. 'I can't believe he is permanently blinded. There was no injury of any kind to his face or head – just the hand. It might have been the shock of the explosion, something of that kind.' He thought about it for a moment. 'They should be able to get the right medical care in France. I don't think money is a problem for them.'

Annabel did not answer, but Forester knew what was on her mind. She had tried to steer the conversation round to it by talking about Leila and André. He did not want to discuss it – not yet – but he knew it had to be faced, it would not go away.

He turned and looked down at his wife. Her eyes were closed, but he knew she was not asleep. Her blonde hair was uncombed, her face without make-up. Every time he looked at her he could see the image of his son.

He leant down and kissed her lips. Her arms came up around him, holding him close. 'Oh darling, what shall we do?'

That was the question. He rolled over on to his back, staring up at the azure sky, empty of clouds. 'I have to go back,' he said. 'I have to, I promised.'

Annabel lifted herself up on her elbow. 'You don't *have* to go, Tom. A promise in those circumstances is hardly one they would hold you to.'

'They?' he said, half to himself. 'Perhaps not, but I will.' He looked up at her. 'I won't force anyone else, of course. I'll ask Rhys and Henshaw if they want to risk it. If not, I'll have to get someone else.'

Annabel tapped him on the chest. 'What about *me*?'

He shook his head. 'No, not this time. Someone has to be with Charlie.'

There it was again – the same choice she had faced once before. But it was still no choice at all. 'I'm coming,' she said firmly.

He started to protest, but she cut him off. 'It's no good, Tom. I'll be on that boat when it sails one way or another.' She put her hand over his mouth to stop any further argument. 'I'm coming.'

He gazed at her. Her eyes never left his face. He reached up slowly, touching her cheek. 'Where did I manage to find you?'

She smiled. 'Oh, I come gift-wrapped with every new boat. It's a kind of incentive scheme.'

He laughed. Charlie shouted with excitement. 'Look, Daddy, look. The sea's rushing into my castle.'

He wanted to make love to her, to tell her how much he loved her. And she knew, instinctively – she had felt the same response herself.

'Mummy, Daddy, quick, come and see.' His voice was shrill, demanding of their love and attention.

They smiled at each other, accepting the impossibility of their desires at that moment. Forester sighed. 'Later, do you think?'

She nodded mischievously. 'Yes, perhaps. If you don't forget and the boat doesn't sink.'

'It won't, and I won't, I promise.'

'I'll hold you to that.'

He grinned. 'I hope so.'

They watched the water gurgle noisily down the channel Charlie had dug laboriously, and cheered. The castle held.

CHAPTER

TWENTY

He picked up the direct-line telephone and recognized the voice instantly.
'Hello, Hank, how are you?'
'I'm fine, sir, making progress slowly.'
The politician laughed. 'Not too slowly, I hope.'
'No, sir. Did you get the report on our operation to Lebanon?'
'Yes, Hank. So far so good – the boat got in all right?'
'Yes, sir, it did, and I've just heard that the return to Cyprus has been accomplished.'
'That's good.'
The director could hear the satisfaction in his voice. 'Yes it is, sir, but it was not as smooth as I would have liked. The Israelis stopped the vessel, as I expected, and searched it from stem to stern. That, too, is normal procedure under the circumstances.'
The politician was quick to agree. 'Of course – there's no way they are going to risk that boat being used as an escape route by the PLO.'
The Director cast his eyes to the ceiling. Already he was preparing his ground for any possible confrontation with Israel – practising the obvious on him. 'Yes, sir,' he said non-committally. 'However,' he continued, 'our ambassador from Beirut was on board and he was taken by the boarding party on to one of the gunboats. It seems they were determined to send Sea Victory back to Jounieh, but he managed to convince them that if all the refugees had dual nationality, there was no problem.'
The politician sighed with relief. 'So they got through OK?'
'That's right. Apparently it was one hell of a night.' The Director chuckled. 'You'll never believe this, sir, but he actually finished up unblocking the lavatory.'

He heard the politician guffaw. 'Well, he needn't expect any more pay for that service.' He thought for a moment. 'Still, it might make good PR. We could use some decent publicity out there right now.'

The Director quickly scotched that idea. 'No, sir, the last thing we need for that boat is publicity, particularly when it comes to any VIP or diplomatic passengers. We have to keep as low a profile as we can on this one.'

The politician swiftly changed his ground. 'Of course, Hank, you're quite right. What do you propose next?'

'I've checked the licensing position with Sea Victory as far as passengers are concerned and, strictly speaking, the vessel is officially allowed to carry only sixteen people out of Cyprus. I've requested, through London, that this is enforced. The fewer people on board, the better.'

The politician chewed the top of his pen. 'What have you arranged?'

'I'd rather not say, sir, not yet. It's a little uncertain at the moment. However, there will be a number of diplomatic and official people to give cover.'

'If you do succeed, are they likely to agree on anything?'

'That's really not my brief, sir . . . but, speaking for myself, I'd say it isn't likely, not first time round. But at least they will be talking, and if we can convince them of the necessity of regular meetings there's always a chance.'

There was a brief silence.

'Hank?'

'Yes, sir.'

'Are they going to be safe on that boat?'

This was the crunch question. The Director paused momentarily. 'As safe as we can make them, sir. Unless it springs a leak and sinks, it should be all right.'

'That's about the only thing we can't take care of, isn't it, Hank?'

'What's that, sir?'

'The weather.'

The Director smiled to himself. 'We're working on it, sir.'

CHAPTER

TWENTY-ONE

Forester shouldered his way into the spacious ground-floor offices of Gemino's Travel Agency. The change in temperature was abrupt, and he was glad of the cool interior after the hot, dusty streets of Larnaca.

He spotted Tony Gemino at once, standing by the open door that led into his office. He beckoned Forester over and greeted him warmly. 'I've been expecting you.'

Forester raised his eyebrows. 'News travels fast. I wasn't even sure myself until a couple of hours ago.'

The Italian waved him into the office and shut the door quietly. 'It does have a way of filtering through in the travel business.'

Forester sat down in the chair facing the desk and grinned at him. 'That must be the understatement of the year.'

Gemino inclined his head deferentially as he moved behind his desk. 'Understatement is not my prerogative.'

The leather swivel chair was expensive and Gemino loved to play his status game. He swung round and faced Forester, watching him closely. They had done a lot of business together since *Sea Victory* had arrived in Larnaca three years before and the two men liked each other. Gemino knew that Forester was deliberately keeping it light, but the banter did not go deep – there was too much at stake.

Forester pulled out a couple of cigars from the pocket of his shirt and offered one to the Italian. Gemino declined, shaking his head regretfully. 'I can't, I'm trying to give it up.'

'They're good, Monte Cristo number ones.' Forester was putting on a brave face, trying to mask his fatigue.

Gemino shook his head again. 'Please don't tempt me; it's difficult enough already.'

Forester shrugged his shoulders. 'Suit yourself . . .' He put one back in his pocket and held the other one up for himself. 'Do you mind?'

'No, just try not to blow the smoke in my direction.'

Forester started to light up. 'Do my best.' He took a deep lungful with slightly exaggerated enjoyment, teasing the Italian. Then he blew the smoke up at the ceiling, away from him. 'You don't know what you're missing.'

Gemino grimaced. 'That's the trouble – I do.' He gazed steadily at the Englishman, wondering how best to broach the subject. 'Look, Tom, I'm worried. The situation out there is deteriorating every day. I've had a telex from Hatan in Jounieh. The port is still choked with refugees, and although he doesn't mention it, they were bombed yesterday for the first time.' He paused. 'It won't be the last.'

Forester held up a hand in protest. 'Just a second. I thought you were supposed to be in the travel business. I know you mean well – I appreciate it – but I'm going back in.'

Gemino stared at the telex in front of him. He looked up suddenly. 'Why?'

Forester drew deeply on the cigar and said with more confidence than he felt, 'Let's just say I need the money.'

Gemino smiled. 'I don't believe you. I just hope you are getting well paid for the risks you are taking.'

Forester said nothing. He had no intention of revealing that all he had asked from each passenger was the price of an air ticket for the same journey. The Italian would think he was mad, if he didn't think so already.

Gemino gave him a jaundiced look. 'You have obviously been here in Cyprus too long. A year ago you would have told me.'

Forester removed the cigar from his mouth. 'A year ago I would not have gone.'

The Italian leaned back in his chair and laughed. 'Well, at least we're having some effect on you.'

There was a brief, comfortable silence between them, then

Gemino leaned forward, serious again. 'Contact Hatan as soon as you get through. I'll let him know of your intentions – there will be people clamouring to get back. Meanwhile I'll arrange your manifest.'

Forester interrupted. 'How many can I take out?'

Gemino shook his head. 'Only sixteen. They just will not allow you to leave with more than you are licensed to carry.'

Forester swore. 'It doesn't worry them if I bring *in* more than sixteen. Oh no, I can land one hundred and twenty refugees with money to spend. They're as welcome as the flowers in May.' He ground his cigar into an ashtray.

Gemino could understand his frustration. But there was no fighting bureaucracy here. In Cyprus they just absorbed resistance and slowed things down even more. The Englishman would learn that eventually. 'Still,' he said, as cheerfully as he could, 'you have an interesting and distinguished group of passengers: the French and Venezuelan ambassadors; a number of staff from their embassies; plus two from the American Embassy. And four businessmen.'

Forester looked up. 'Where from?'

Gemino examined the list. 'Three from Lebanon, and one from the United States.'

Forester stared contemplatively across the desk, but made no comment.

Gemino was curious. 'What do you think?'

Forester glanced at him. 'I think we'll have to lay on some service for our clientele this time. Make sure they are well fed and cared for, unlike those poor bastards we pulled out.' He looked at his watch and stood up suddenly. 'I have to go.'

Gemino came round from behind the desk. 'If anything comes through on the telex before you leave, I'll see you have it immediately. When will you sail?'

'Tonight.'

'Is Annabel going?'

'I couldn't stop her if I tried . . . and I tried.'

Gemino shook his head. 'You're both crazy.' He paused, looking at Forester. 'Do you mind if I ask you something?'

'As long as you don't repeat yourself.'

'Why are you doing this? You don't have to.'

Forester eyed him for a moment. 'That's where you are wrong
– I do.' He smiled self-mockingly. 'Besides, I'll be carrying a
couple of ambassadors . . . What more protection do I need?' He
turned suddenly and left, shutting the door behind him.

Gemino stared expressionlessly at it, then walked over to his
desk and sat down.

Annabel went methodically through her list again, making
sure she had crossed off everything she could think of. Medical
supplies, food and fresh water were their most urgent require-
ments. She had a sudden thought. 'Darling, why don't we get
some champagne?'

Forester didn't answer. She looked up. He was staring
moodily out of the wheelhouse window, watching preparations
on the dock below.

'Tom?'

'What?' He didn't turn round.

She crossed to him. 'What's wrong?'

'Nothing,' he said shortly. 'Get as much champagne as you
like.'

She knew this mood: something was worrying him. When
that happened he tended to get short-tempered about details.
She touched his arm. 'What is it?'

He looked round at her. Her eyes were concerned. Christ! she
had a right to know. He glanced behind him and slid the door
shut, cutting out most of the noise from the dock below. 'Listen,
there are two things that don't quite add up. First, why are we
only being allowed to take sixteen passengers? I know that's our
licensed figure, but there are lots of people stuck here who want
to get back to their relatives. And secondly, why no journalists
on this trip? Who put the embargo on them?'

Annabel had not really considered it – she had been so busy
organizing their supplies. She had simply assumed that politicians took precedence over media. It did seem odd that in the
circumstances they should insist on the licensed number of
passengers. She remembered something. 'Yes, and last time,
you had that sudden gift of war insurance for *Sea Victory*.'

Forester started to pace up and down the wheelhouse. He
stopped. 'And when we went in and when we came out we

196

carried diplomatic and political passengers.' He stared out of the window again. 'It may be nothing,' he said, half to himself, 'but keep your eyes open. If anything is going on, I would sooner know about it.' He grinned suddenly.

Annabel was puzzled. 'What?'

'I just thought – it might be like that old joke about the man who kept going through customs with an empty wheelbarrow. In the end the customs man was so frustrated he promised not to prosecute, if he would tell him what he was smuggling.'

Annabel smiled.

'And he said, wheelbarrows.'

'That's right. We may just be moving a lot of politicians about.'

He remembered something. 'What was that you said about champagne?'

Annabel shrugged. 'I just thought that since we have all these distinguished passengers we might as well turn it into a luxury cruise – it's going to be hard enough for all of us once we get there.'

Forester liked the idea. 'Why not? Give them a good dinner. We have video films they can see if they want to. By the way, did you order those sea-sick pills?'

'Yes, a thousand Dramamin.'

'Fresh water? We ran out last time.'

'A ton. There's plenty of medical supplies as well. I've got more blankets and foam mattresses. Sleep and food is what they need most of all coming back.'

Henshaw slid back the wheelhouse door and poked his head round. 'Looks like they're coming, Skipper.'

Annabel and Forester joined him at the rail. Three limousines carrying diplomatic insignia were drawing up on the dockside. The French and Venezuelan ambassadors had clearly decided to arrive together, and a third car contained the two staff members from the US Embassy in Beirut, and one American civilian.

Forester gazed down on them with some displeasure. He was not looking forward to playing host on this trip. There were more doubts in his mind. Several unanswered questions were beginning to trouble him. He did not like being kept in the dark, and if *Sea Victory* were being used in some way . . . what

197

then? Did he just pack it in and leave those people he had promised to return to on the quay in Jounieh? They would wait for him to come back until hell froze over – he knew that. They had nowhere else to go.

He really had no choice – though he found it hard to reconcile those desperate faces and pleading eyes with his own motives and ambitions. He could still not admit, even to himself, that now they were the real reason for his return to Jounieh. The money had ceased to matter.

During the next few hours prior to departure, diplomatic bags for most of the foreign embassies in Beirut were loaded, together with several crates of medical supplies and equipment.

Last to come on board, and most disturbing, was the arrival of the three Lebanese businessmen. They came separately, each one with an 'assistant'. Forester had seen enough hard cases to recognize security when he saw it. The three 'assistants' moved cautiously, watching every possible source of danger, screening their charges as much as possible. The businessmen and their 'assistants' disappeared below. They would not be seen again until after *Sea Victory* had sailed.

There were no problems this time with the Cypriot authorities. Two ambassadors, some embassy staff, and the success of the first voyage were too much for the Chief of Police to disregard. Dimitri Xydias did nothing. The word from the top was to leave well alone. He waited; his time would come, sooner or later. If *Sea Victory* survived another voyage into Jounieh, then it would need the port facilities of Larnaca to continue to charter around the coast of Cyprus. And Xydias could make things very difficult indeed.

Rhys took the helm, sailed the vessel into the small bay outside the port area and dropped anchor. A steady ship in the lee of the land was a much better base for Annabel to serve dinner from. Eight people sat down that evening: the two ambassadors and their aids; three Lebanese businessmen and the American; while the other two staff from the US Embassy in Beirut decided to belly up against the bar in the saloon.

Forester served them drinks, while Henshaw helped Annabel. She had laid dinner on the long table in the stern, under the canopy. The weather was perfect, on its best behaviour for the

198

VIPs on board, unlike the hazardous and nauseating crossing they had made with the refugees.

As Forester contemplated the fine show of food and cutlery for his exalted passengers, he could not help but reflect sourly that there seemed to be not only one rule for the rich and another for the poor, but also a different weather system. It was nonsense, of course; bad weather could blow up at any time. It was just bad luck – but how much bad luck did you have to have before you got obsessional about it?

The three 'assistants' – mentally, Forester had dubbed them Curly, Larry and Moe – had stationed themselves in the stern, where they constantly scanned the inky waters around the boat, and also kept an eye on the brightly lit seafront that glittered in the dark behind them. Larnaca twinkled in the soft Mediterranean night which disguised its dusty streets and the ugly Western advertising that clutched at every café and bar. In the dark, Larnaca looked magical.

Forester plied the two young Americans with long, cool brandy sours. As the evening wore on and they relaxed, he learnt a little more. They seemed to believe that soon there would be a mass pull-out from Beirut. He also learnt that the US Sixth Fleet was now in the area, and that the 61,000-ton carrier *Kennedy* was already lying somewhere off the Lebanese coast, ready for an evacuation of all diplomatic personnel. One of them seemed convinced that the PLO would turn West Beirut into another Stalingrad rather than surrender, and try to gain as much public sympathy for defeat as possible. Their hold over that part of the city was total.

For Annabel, the dinner was an extremely difficult experience. Normally, after a little wine and food, the formal barriers would begin to disintegrate. But, while the two ambassadors seemed happy in each other's company, the three Lebanese remained coldly aloof, conversing as little as possible with her, and hardly at all with each other. It was clear there was more than the usual stiffness with strangers between them. She sensed a deep underlying hostility.

Only the lone American at the table seemed willing to talk. He tried valiantly to break down the barriers, but to little effect. Annabel was glad when her duties came to an end with the brandy and cigars. They seemed to be waiting for something, though what, she had no way of knowing.

Later, after she had taken a breather at the bar with Forester, they were joined by the two ambassadors. Forester glanced at his watch. It was nearly ten o'clock, and time to get under way. He was about to leave for the wheelhouse when Annabel took his arm and squeezed it. He followed her glance: the three Lebanese and the American were still at the table in the stern, but now they were deep in discussion. She smiled at him. 'That's what they were waiting for. They wanted to be alone,' she said in mock Garbo.

His smile lacked amusement. Inside alarm bells were ringing and his suspicions crowding back. He didn't like it one little bit.

Forester had the wheelhouse to himself. He held the wheel loosely, listening to the steady throb of the engines, as the vessel made its way through the flat, calm sea. The more he thought about it, the more uneasy he became. He tried to put the jigsaw together. All the pieces were there now, and they were beginning to form a pattern, but just where did *Sea Victory* fit into all this? Was it a pawn in a much wider political game, or did the vessel fulfil some definite purpose, of which he was unaware?

He glanced at the green scope of the radar – then looked again, more closely. All around *Sea Victory*, moving steadily in the same direction, were a number of large and small blips. He watched them, fascinated, but they did not come any closer, or move away. They stayed right with him. He strained his eyes, peering out into the black, moonless night. There was nothing to be seen. But the radar did not lie. He was surrounded, in the middle of a large fleet. Whose fleet?

They were everywhere, out there in the darkness, watching him on radar as carefully as he was watching them. 'Jesus,' he whispered softly to himself, 'I hope to God they're on our side.'

CHAPTER
TWENTY-TWO

David Kass gripped the iron stanchion that supported the stretcher rack, and held on grimly as the ambulance bucketed through streets littered with the debris of war. The driver kept the vehicle moving as fast as he dared, dodging broken glass and the sharp edges of shattered paving stones which would have blown his tyres instantly.

Trying to get an ambulance through what passed for roads in Beirut was a lottery, with only one macabre prize if you lost. The red crosses were often ignored – sometimes deliberately, more often by mistake. The various military factions were fighting a bitter guerrilla war from street to street. If you got caught in the middle, that was tough, and usually fatal.

Ambulance was hardly an apt name for this vehicle, not any more. Blood wagon was better. Inside, Kass could smell it, sweet and heavy in the baking heat. It stained the canvas stretchers rattling in their racks.

The two medics hung perilously out of the back of the vehicle, unarmed, in white uniforms, displaying as prominently as they could their mission.

Kass sat stoically in the back, numb to the danger, waiting for whatever might happen next. He wondered idly about his reaction, or the lack of it. Medically, it might be put down to stress, or shock; more likely it was just exhaustion. He was too tired to feel any fear – he'd grown used to the dangers, and a certain philosophical fatalism had crept in. If he was going to die, then so be it.

He had not ventured out of the hospital before – it hadn't

been necessary. He did not have to look for patients; they overwhelmed the hospital and its staff. The fact that he was still there had roused a little ironic surprise from the remaining members of the regular staff. Many had already quit as the hospital became more and more isolated in West Beirut.

They were all vulnerable. The military factions in this bloody religious and political confrontation observed few niceties. And the hospital retained its precarious safety only for as long as it suited all concerned.

Kass had welcomed this opportunity to get out. His existence in the hospital was becoming increasingly confined. It seemed he had spent half a lifetime stitching flesh wounds, staunching the flow of blood – trying to save life. Each day had merged into the next, broken only by the darkness of night, and a snatched meal. Sleep was taken whenever the flow of wounded ceased, wherever a bed or a chair could be found.

He had been asked to deal with this outside emergency because he was an American, and it was felt that he had a better chance than the others of dealing with a confused situation: a school had been hit – there were casualties, and there was doubt as to who was responsible.

The driver swept into a paved courtyard, through a set of high, iron gates, and brought the vehicle to a stop in front of some steps that led up to wide double doors. Kass climbed stiffly from the back and gazed up at the building. It appeared to be undamaged. Palm trees fringed the courtyard, providing a welcome shade from the blinding heat. Then he noticed that the windows were covered in wire mesh. He wondered for a moment if it were to prevent them shattering from blast – but he rejected that idea. It was not a method he had seen employed elsewhere. He climbed slowly up the white stone steps and was about to press a buzzer when the door opened partially. He could see the woman was a nun, her face framed by a heavy black veil. She appeared to be looking at him, but he had the strangest feeling she was looking *through* him. She did not speak.

He leaned forward – she was quite small. 'I'm sorry to trouble you – do you speak English?'

Her eyes focused on him, as if seeing him for the first time. She inclined her head. 'Yes.' Her voice was almost inaudible.

Kass indicated the ambulance in the courtyard behind him, and the two medics who were waiting at the foot of the steps. 'We are from the hospital, we have come to help.'

A look crossed her face. It was as if something inside her, something fearful, constraining her, had been released. 'You have come to help?' There was the barest trace of hope in her voice, as if hoping was too much to bear – a tempting of providence.

He nodded. 'Can we come in?' he said gently.

She swallowed, trying to speak, but said nothing. Silently she opened the door and beckoned them inside.

He noticed that her habit was torn and covered in white dust. He turned and motioned the two medics to follow. The small figure of the nun led them through the cool central hallway into a long, white corridor. Immediately he was aware of a sharp rise in the temperature. The warm, stifling air carried faint traces of white dust as it blew gently past them, seeking the colder air of the hall. Once again he smelt the familiar odour of blood.

They passed a large room on their left. There were a number of young children inside, some sitting on the floor, others just standing . . . waiting. They stared mutely at them as they went by. The nun hurried on ahead.

There were a number of rooms that branched off on either side of the passageway. Some were clearly used as classrooms, others were playrooms. They were all empty but for toys littering the floor – as still and mute as the children they had just passed.

Kass could see bright sunlight at the end of the corridor flooding in, outlining the black-clad figure of the nun in front of him. He hurried after her. She had stopped, and as he drew closer he slowed down. He could see now why she had halted. The end of the passageway had disappeared. He stood beside her.

Three of the old walls were still standing, bare and gaunt, the stained-glass windows in one of them not even cracked. The rest of the chapel had collapsed inwards under the impact of an explosion. The roof had completely disintegrated, burying the pews and the religious ceremonial artefacts. The figure of Christ still hung from one wall, eyes cast down on the devastation around him.

Kass turned to the nun beside him. Tears were rolling slowly down her face through the film of dust that had settled on her. 'What happened?'

'I don't know. I was with the younger children you saw in the other room. It was a bomb or a shell.' She swallowed hard, her voice breaking. She turned to look at him. She pointed to the remains of the chapel. 'They are all there . . . everyone. The children, Mother Theresa . . .' She began to sob. Deep agonized grief, shaking her whole body. Tenderly, Kass put his arm around her. She rested her head on his shoulder, unconscious of the contact she was making with a man in her need for the simple, human relief of his presence.

Kass stared at the mass of wreckage, looking for signs of life. He began to see death, the torn, crushed bodies of women and children mangled beneath the debris. He gazed, horrified, at the carnage as he held the nun, stunned by this total annihilation.

He did not know how long he had worked amongst the devastation, the smashed masonry and splintered woodwork of the roof. Time had lost its meaning in the utter desolation of the ruined chapel. With the two Lebanese medics and the driver, he laboured to find some sign of life, tearing at the blocks of stone, removing the broken timbers. All they uncovered was death. And already the obscene clouds of flies, attracted by the smell of blood, buzzed around them.

Kass spoke to one of the medics. 'Find some sheets and cover them up.' He indicated the pathetic row of the bodies they had dug out. Silently the medic left, glad to get away from the dreadful slaughter. Hardened as they all were by the fragility of life in a war zone that made no distinction between soldiers or civilians, men or women – still, the sickening, mindless killing of innocents affected them all. It was impossible to close one's mind, to blot out the horror.

Kass wrapped his handkerchief around his nose and mouth, more to protect himself from the flies than anything else. He moved continuously over the wreckage, unwilling to give up hope of finding some life – one life. The sun had shifted from directly overhead now, its rays lighting up one of the corners of the chapel, and something caught his attention. Something bright, flickering, reflecting the sun. He picked his way carefully towards it, keeping his eyes on the spot. As he moved the reflection disappeared, because his angle had altered, but he had it pinpointed, and as he reached the place he was sure he was right.

He knelt down and eased away one of the heavy timbers, pushing it to one side. There it was again, flickering brightly in the shaft of sunlight, diffused now by the powdery white dust he had disturbed. He lay flat on his stomach and reached down, trying to touch whatever it was, but it stayed tantalizingly out of his grasp. He sat up and rolled away a huge piece of granite. Now he was able to burrow deeper and pull out a broken joist. Once more he lay flat and reached down into the darkness beneath the rubble.

His hand touched something soft. Gingerly he moved his fingers slowly along it, tracing its outline. He stopped. There was something else. Something holding on to the object. He could feel another human hand grasping it. Suddenly he knew what it was. The hand was clutching a doll. No, not a doll; a bear, a furry bear.

He tried to move it, but the hand held it tightly, for dear life. Life! It was alive! He felt the fingers tighten on the bear. He shouted, his voice hoarse with excitement. 'Quick, here – I've found someone!'

They stared at him idiotically. He screamed, tearing at the wreckage. 'Come on, he's alive, he's alive!'

Kass didn't know why he'd said 'he's alive'. Maybe he associated the bear with his own childhood. In fact it was a girl of about seven. She'd been protected from the debris and falling masonry by two wooden pews that had formed a tunnel into which she had ducked on impact. Too shocked and frightened to cry out, she had lain there, clutching her teddy. It was the bear's single remaining eye that had reflected the sunlight and led Kass to her.

As the last piece of wreckage was removed Kass lowered himself down into the cavity between the two pews. She watched him, her eyes wide, curious, but strangely unfrightened. He examined her briefly. As far as he could tell there

205

were no major bones broken. He signalled up to one of the medics. 'I'm going to lift her out.'

He knelt down beside the child, placing an arm under her shoulders, the other under her legs. Tenderly he lifted her up, raising her as high as he could. The two medics took her weight from him, placing her on a stretcher. Then they reached down and helped him scramble clear. He walked alongside the stretcher as she was lifted over the mountain of rubble towards the passageway. She lay quite still on her back, shielding her eyes from the sun, the bear still held tightly in her other hand.

As they came to the entrance of the corridor, Kass became aware that there were two figures standing in the shadows, waiting: the black-clad figure of the nun, and someone else using a camera. It was Nazira.

He looked at her once but her eyes were on the child. She continued to use the camera, the flashes of light etching the grim faces of the three men in the comparative darkness of the passage. Kass ignored her; he had work to do.

The nun led the way into a private room where there was a couch. The medics gently laid the child down upon it, then waited by the door for Kass to complete his examination.

Nazira had seen enough of the devastated chapel and mutilated bodies to realize that this was a major story. She wanted to hear what the Sister had to say. She moved over to the corner by the window.

Kass was hardly aware of her presence. The child lay passively while he carried out the usual checks. There were no broken bones, no sign of internal injury, not even an abrasion. It was remarkable. Where everyone else had perished, this one child had survived, apparently unscathed. But Kass was worried. She had still not spoken, nor had she cried out while they had burrowed amongst the wreckage to get to her. He turned to the nun who was waiting anxiously. 'I'm sorry, I don't know your name . . .'

Her eyes never left the child. 'Sister Christina. How is she?'

Kass turned back to the girl. 'As far as I can tell, she's fine. There are no injuries I can detect.'

The nun glanced at him, sensing his uncertainty. 'What is it?'

He wiped away the sweat that was trickling down the side of

his face. 'I'm not sure . . . she doesn't say anything, and I don't think she is reacting normally. She may be in shock.'

Sister Christina stared at the child for a moment, then took him by the arm and led him gently away from her. 'Melissa is always like this, Doctor. I don't know how much she has been affected, but you cannot take her away unless she is physically hurt.'

Kass tried to explain. 'As far as I can see, there is no physical injury, Sister. It's her mental condition I am worried about.'

She interrupted him. 'Then you must leave her here with us, Doctor' – she hesitated and corrected herself – 'with me. That is what I am here for.'

He stared at her, puzzled. 'What do you mean?'

'This is a home, Doctor, not just a school. We look after children who are mentally disturbed.'

She watched him, her face framed by the white coif. 'Do you understand?'

Through the blur of his exhaustion, he was beginning to. The wire mesh on the outside windows, the blank incomprehension on the faces of the children they had passed on their way in. It added another sickening dimension to this appalling tragedy.

He heard Nazira's voice behind him. 'You mean, Sister Christina, that *all* the children here are mentally handicapped?'

The nun turned to look at her directly. 'Yes.'

The room fell silent. The simple, pathetic statement of fact reverberated soundlessly in the quiet room, as each one of them absorbed the implications.

Kass felt a growing sense of anger, a bitter frustration that there was nothing he could do, nothing anyone seemed to want to do, in this web of killing – each atrocity sparking off another. An endless, mindless cycle of death. He stared bitterly at Sister Christina. 'Who did this?'

She lowered her eyes away from his. She could see in them the anger, the lust for revenge which she had seen too often before. 'I don't know,' she said simply.

'I do.' It was Nazira. The Palestinian studied David Kass, wondering how he would react. 'It was the Israelis,' she said tonelessly. 'The area came under attack. They systematically pounded each block with artillery fire.'

Kass stared at her balefully. 'How do you know?'

'I have a contact; he told me that this convent had been hit.'

Kass remembered the militiaman she had spoken to at the checkpoint. 'Did your PLO contact also tell you it was Israeli shellfire that was responsible for this?'

'Who else would have done it?' she said savagely. 'Who else has that kind of artillery or aircraft to bomb civilian targets? Not the PLO.'

The taut knot of anger inside him suddenly snapped. Something about her cold stream of invective, the constant haranguing, was too much for him. His normal tolerance and understanding had been eroded, sapped by the stress of trying to cope with streams of injured. His presence was too little and too late. Her self-righteousness made him want to lash out, strike back.

'And you, what about you – what do you do? You come here with your camera and your carefully prepared ideology. You take pictures of the dead children to plaster the front pages. All you see is through a dead eye – the eye of a machine. What about your eyes, your feelings? Look at this child, see her . . .' He grabbed Nazira's arm and pulled her close to the couch on which Melissa was lying. 'Why don't you help instead of just churning out your propaganda with that.' He gestured contemptuously at the camera round her neck. 'What's inside you, Nazira? Don't you *feel* anything any more? Is there no pity for these people, for their suffering? Don't you want to help instead of merely recording their pain?'

He looked into her eyes. They were dark, unfathomable, telling him nothing. He laughed harshly, without humour. 'No, you don't really care about what happens to them. Just as long as you can feed it into this . . .' He jerked the leather strap savagely. 'They are just fodder for your camera. Feed them in, chew them up, spit them out. Make your readers feel a comfortable sense of guilt. But to actually help a child who has been buried beneath that mess out there, that's too much for you, isn't it, Nazira? You might just begin to feel something.'

He waited for some reaction, but it didn't come. He turned away, disgusted, and spoke quietly to Sister Christina. 'Can I leave Melissa with you? I must go back, there may be others. Will you be all right?'

The nun acquiesced. 'Of course, don't worry about me. I'll look after the child.'

He turned to go, and she touched his arm shyly. 'Doctor?' He paused, looking at her. Her face was grave. 'Thank you for Melissa.' Her eyes were soft, tender. He placed his hand on hers and squeezed it gently, then left the room. The two medics waiting by the door followed him.

Nazira had not moved. She felt drained, weak. Her hands were gripping the camera to prevent them from shaking. Camera fodder! Was it true? Was she using the sick and the maimed for her own ends, in much the same way as her people had been used? The thought shook her. Was she as guilty as them? She rejected that, but was it true that in her desire to give her people a chance, she was using the refugees, the innocents, the pain of Beirut, simply for her own ends? In her heart she knew that was so. She had not cared . . .

She felt a hand on her arm and her eyes focused on Sister Christina.

'I am going back to the other children. Would you mind staying here with Melissa for a while? I shall not be long.'

Nazira looked at the child, still clinging to her one-eyed teddy – the eye that had saved her life. She knelt down by Melissa and tenderly brushed some of the white, powdery dust from its furry coat.

The child smiled. 'He's got a dirty face, too.' It was the first time she had spoken.

Nazira agreed. 'Yes, he has, but I think we can clean him up.' She took a handkerchief from her pocket. 'Shall I wipe his face with this?'

Melissa shyly handed her the teddy, relinquishing the bear at last.

Nazira took it. 'Thank you.' She dabbed the corner of her hanky on her tongue, and wiped the bear's face carefully, just as if it were a child. It was an instinctive action, not approved of by Sister Christina who was standing behind her, but one that Nazira's mother had often employed when water was not available.

Melissa was delighted. 'Can I do that?'

Nazira smiled. 'Yes.' She gave her the handkerchief.

Melissa dabbed it on her tongue and very slowly rubbed the dust from round the bear's single eye. 'There!' she said triumphantly. 'He'll be able to see better now.'

Nazira brushed the damp hair from the child's face. 'Shall I do yours?'

Obediently Melissa gave her the hanky and held up her face, screwing her eyes shut, waiting.

Nazira looked down at the child's trusting face. The grey powder from the chapel was streaked with sweat. One eye opened, studying her gravely. 'Aren't you going to do it?'

Nazira swallowed the lump rising in her throat. It would do no good for this child to see her cry. Such sentimentality was out of place here. She clamped down on her emotions, businesslike again. 'Yes, see . . .' She touched the corner of the hanky with her tongue. 'Here we go, close your eyes.'

The eye shut, and gently Nazira wiped away the marks of Melissa's entombment.

Sister Christina left the room. She had seen enough. The woman and the child were happy with each other. She sensed that it was a breakthrough for Nazira, that in some way the hard shell she kept around her emotions was cracking. The doctor had been cruel, but his harsh words had forced a reaction. Quietly she closed the door.

Kass worked on through the heat of the afternoon, pulling aside wreckage wherever he could, always looking for any sign of life beneath the mountain of rubble. Gradually, more people arrived, joining in the search. At regular intervals a shout would be heard, and they would all converge on the spot, and gently ease away a layer of wreckage until the body could be examined. Not one more remained alive.

As afternoon wore on into evening and the shadows grew longer, the pathetic line of bodies increased.

Kass found himself going over and over what Nazira had said. He could not believe it was true – he *would* not believe it – and yet, he knew there had been regular bombardments, indiscriminate shelling of Beirut. But that had been as much a part of the defenders' tactics as the attackers'. The situation was so confused now, splits widening between the various factions. It was impossible to apportion blame accurately.

Even as he thought it, Kass knew it was a rationalization – it would not do. Wherever the ultimate responsibility lay for this dreadful slaughter, it could not bring these innocent victims back to life. He closed his mind, and found relief in the unremitting physical slog. It became a kind of waking nightmare, blurred by fatigue, and punctuated by each brief moment of hope as another body was found. Then the search resumed.

Kass did not know how long she had been watching him. He straightened up, trying to ease the pain from his breaking back. He wiped the sweat away from his eyes. Then he saw the familiar green and khaki fatigues. She was standing at the bottom of a hill of rubble, looking up at him. She beckoned.

He stared at her blankly and she waved again. Slowly he began to descend, picking his way tiredly down the mountain of debris. He stopped in front of her, swaying slightly. Nazira examined him.

Sweat and dust stained his shirt and his trousers were ripped at the knee. His damp hair stuck to his face, which was streaked with grime where he had constantly wiped away the perspiration.

'Come,' she said, 'Sister Christina has made some food and drink.'

He waved an arm at the men still working behind him. 'There may still be more . . .'

She cut across him. 'If there are, Doctor, they will be dead. You can always come back if they need you.' She took his arm and pulled him in the direction of the corridor. 'Come on,' she said firmly, 'or you'll be no good for anything.'

He allowed her to guide him across the uneven surface. He felt a wave of sheer exhaustion pass through him and he stumbled to one knee. He would have fallen if Nazira had not steadied him. He knelt, head bowed. He did not think he would ever get up again. His legs were like rubber – he just wanted to lie down.

Nazira leaned down beside him and spoke quietly. 'It's no good, David, you must get up.'

She tried to haul him to his feet, but he didn't move; his body seemed to weigh a ton. Kass jerked his arm away angrily. 'Leave me alone, goddammit!' His voice echoed harshly back from the three remaining walls of the chapel. The last word, the profanity, seemed to hang in the still, choking air.

Work stopped. The tired men looked down at the American doctor on his knees in the dirt, mirroring their own feelings of utter hopelessness: the deadly backbreaking work was pointless. Why go on if the doctor was quitting?

Kass looked up wearily. Nazira stood before him, her hands on her hips, smiling, veiling her contempt. *This* was the woman he remembered. He gritted his teeth. 'Jesus Christ, don't you ever give in?'

She made no reply, but stood there, waiting for him to give up.

He shook his head. 'Oh no, no, not this time . . .' His clenched fist pounded his knee then, with the last shred of his strength, he pushed himself upright and stood facing her, swaying. He stared at her, his eyes half shut, blinking away the sweat that rolled down his face and rubbed the back of his hand across his eyes, trying to get her into focus. Her face told him nothing.

He turned, and slowly started to force his way back up the hill. She called him. 'David!'

He stopped, his back to her.

She called again. 'We need you in the school, David. Sister Christina wants you to examine some of the children.'

He didn't move.

'Please, David, for the children.'

Kass closed his eyes, holding his face up to the darkening sky. For the children. Oh God, he prayed to himself . . . give me the strength. He turned once more and came back down. He stopped beside her, and gestured for her to go. She looked anxiously at him, then picked her way ahead.

She had lied about the children, but she did not know how else she could have got him out. His presence had become crucial to the work. But now, knowing he was needed elsewhere, the men would not stop until it was too dark to continue.

In her heart Nazira knew that there was no one else alive in the ruins of the chapel. And Kass had to be protected from his own boundless commitment if he was still to function as a doctor.

Kass slumped into the hard-backed chair and stared blankly down at the polished wooden blocks of the floor. He felt an incredible sense of relief at being simply off his feet. The coolness of the inner, private room dried the sweat on his back.

Sister Christina came in carrying a tray with a pot of tea and some sandwiches. Nazira watched as the nun poured out a cup and gave it to him. He drank quickly, swallowing it in almost one gulp, then handed the cup back to the Sister. 'How is Melissa?'

The nun busied herself with the pot of tea, pouring out another cup for him. 'Melissa is well; there are no problems. Your colleague helped enormously. She got her talking again. Melissa is quite taken with her.'

Kass stared at Nazira. He was confused – he found it hard to take in . . . he pushed the confusion to one side. 'And the others?'

Sister Christina glanced quickly at Nazira, aware of the subterfuge that she had used to bring the doctor inside. 'Oh, drink your tea first; you can see them later.'

The tea was good. It was hot and sweet and it sparked off his appetite. He took one of the sandwiches and ate it quickly. He began to feel more human.

Nazira was sitting behind a heavy desk that must have belonged to Mother Theresa. She was jotting down some notes on a pad. He watched her for a moment. 'I thought you would have been gone by now.'

She stopped, now looking at him. 'No, there was work to do.'

He didn't say anything at first, and she was uncomfortably aware of his eyes upon her. She tried to continue with her notes.

'Sister Christina said you got the girl to talk.'

Nazira looked up. 'Yes. It wasn't difficult. I helped her clean up the teddy, and she responded quite naturally. I don't think there's much wrong with her, anyway. Sister says she was left

213

here. She may simply have been abandoned. It would not be surprising under the circumstances . . .' Her voice trailed off. She had not wanted to get on to anything political.

'Did you spend some time with her?'

'Yes, she's a good kid, very bright once you can get through to her, unlike some of the others.'

'The others?'

She looked down at the desk in front of her. 'They need a lot of attention, I think. There's a blankness in their eyes; they do not react easily.'

'But you tried?'

'Yes,' she said quietly, 'I did try.'

There was a silence between them, and Nazira began to work on her notes again.

Sister Christina came back into the room and began to clear away the remains of the small meal. Kass thanked her. 'That was good. I was hungrier than I thought.' He stood up shakily. 'Now, perhaps I could look at the children.'

Sister Christina put down the tray, looked quickly at Nazira, then turned and faced the American. 'I'm sorry, Doctor, you cannot see them now – they are all fast asleep and there is no need – I think they will be all right.'

Kass frowned, trying to concentrate. 'Are you sure?'

'Yes.' She smiled up at him. 'It is time for you to go. You and your colleague have done more than enough.'

Kass tried to absorb this, but he knew he was not thinking clearly. He needed to sleep for about a week. 'OK, if you're sure, Sister.'

'I'm sure.'

He half-turned, looking back at Nazira. 'I'm just going back for a moment.' He paused, thinking, 'They might have . . .' He stopped, letting the thought hang there. He knew, and they knew, there was no one left alive. But he must be sure. 'I shan't be long.' He left the room, his footsteps receding down the corridor.

Nazira rose from behind the desk. 'I think I'd better go with him.'

Sister Christina nodded her agreement. 'Yes, you must stay with him, get him back to his hotel.'

'I will.'

The nun reached out to take Nazira's hand. 'Thank you for what you have done.'

The Palestinian looked down at the small, slight figure. 'I'd like to come back some time, to see Melissa.'

'Of course, she has a new friend now. I will tell her in the morning.'

Nazira leant down and kissed the nun on the cheek, then left quickly, following Kass along the passageway.

He stood by the jagged end of the corridor. Darkness cloaked the jumbled piles of debris. It was empty; the rescue teams had gone, taking the dead with them, leaving the ruins to the night creatures who would soon find nooks and crannies to make their new hiding places.

A half-moon was rising slowly, bathing the three remaining walls in ghastly white, their pale shadows falling softly across the pulverized wreckage of the chapel. It seemed strangely peaceful after the turmoil and heat of the day, as though the chapel were reclaiming its own, filling the empty spaces with tranquillity, holding the dead peacefully at rest.

Kass became aware that she was standing beside him. They didn't speak; words were superfluous. The stark nature of the tragedy that had been enacted here had etched itself deep into their minds and emotions. They were grateful for the darkness that cloaked the havoc; the silence that gave it some dignity. He looked curiously at Nazira. Her face was drawn, her eyes shining luminously in the dark. She knew he was looking at her and met his gaze. It was a moment of understanding, of shared experience.

'Come,' she said, her voice quiet, almost a whisper, 'I'll take you back to the hotel.'

They turned and left.

The drive through the empty, silent streets had been a strange, frightening experience. The sound of the car's engine had been deafeningly loud in her ears, loud enough to attract some attention. But, oddly, she had seen nothing; better still, had heard nothing: no fusillades, no explosions. There was only the usual problem of negotiating a way around the obstacles strewn in their path.

Kass had slept through it all, his head lolling against her shoulder, out to the world. He would never have known what hit him if they had been attacked. As it was, they reached the dirty, narrow street that fronted the Commodore Hotel.

Nazira turned off the engine and breathed a long sigh of relief. She shook his arm, but he didn't stir; his exhaustion was complete. She contemplated leaving him in the car, but that was impossible – there were dangers here, too. Lightly, she slapped his face, calling to him urgently. Still no movement. She gritted her teeth. It seemed she was always going to be hurting this American. She slapped him hard, twice.

Kass grunted and opened his eyes wide, startled. He sat upright and looked around, trying to discover where they were in the dark. 'Sorry, I must have dozed off.'

Nazira smiled. 'It's all right – nothing to worry about. We're at the hotel.'

He relaxed. 'Thank God for that. I thought we had got stopped.'

'No, nothing. We had the roads to ourselves.'

He opened the door, and climbed stiffly out. 'Let's see if we can get a drink.'

The entrance doors were securely shut, but after a little while a sleepy-eyed porter, who had obviously been napping, opened up. The lounge and bar were deserted, and the porter refused to serve them anything. He was only interested in getting back to his sleep. Even the Reuters wire machine had given up for the night. It stood mute and frozen, waiting for its signal to spill out more paper and information.

The parrot, taking its cue from everything else, had also shut up shop and slept beneath its canopy.

They had drawn a blank. Kass shrugged disconsolately. 'Seems we've run out of luck.'

'I've got a flask of coffee in my room.'

He glanced at her. There was a defensiveness in her remark . . . She was waiting to see if he would refuse. Kass knew the invitation had cost her dearly. A barrier between them had finally been broken. He accepted gratefully. 'Thank you.'

216

Her room was the same as his own, as far as he could remember. He'd only slept in it on the first night. There were two single beds; shuttered verandah windows leading out on to a minuscule balcony – bolted for security reasons; a small bathroom with a shower; and a single telephone on a stand between the beds. He stood awkwardly for a moment, just inside the door. She indicated the armchair in the corner. 'Sit down.'

She reached down into the drawer inside the stand, and pulled out a large flask. She tossed it to him. 'Do you mind helping yourself while I wash? It should be full.'

He unscrewed the cap and, using the top as a cup, poured himself some of the coffee. It was white, sweet and delicious. He sat down on the bed.

The water in the tap was not cold, but at least it was cool and fresh. Nazira washed her face and body, removing the grime and the last of the powdered grey dust from the chapel. She quickly towelled herself dry, feeling refreshed and human for the first time that day. She gazed at her battle fatigues lying on the bathroom floor. They were filthy, and her clean change of clothes was in the other room. She took her dressing gown from behind the bathroom door and put it on. Nazira glanced in the mirror. It was respectable, she concluded, if a little warm. She opened the bathroom door, then stopped in mid-stride halfway into the bedroom. Kass was slumped in a half-sitting position at the head of one of the beds, the empty top of the flask still clenched in his hand. He was fast asleep.

Nazira could not resist a smile. At the back of her mind she had been aware of the possibilities in this situation. It was as if she had been challenging herself to risk them. Now there was no need. Physical exhaustion – nature itself – had removed the risk. The joke was on her.

Carefully, she took the top of the flask from his hand, then pulled back the sheet. She lifted his legs up on to the bed and eased his body down until his head was on the pillow. He hadn't stirred; he lay flat on his back.

She removed his battered, dusty boots, then took off his socks. She carried them gingerly into the bathroom, dumping them in the sink. The smell was appalling. Quickly she put in the plug

217

and filled it with hot water. At least it took the sting out of the smell. She went back.

His trousers were ripped, his shirt stained with dried blood. Gently she began to undo the shirt. It was difficult to get off – his body was heavy and well muscled. Eventually, by rolling him on to his side, she managed it. His trousers were easier. She took them to the bathroom and hung them behind the door.

Nazira gazed down at him. She had not seen a naked man for a long time. He was beautiful, she thought, his body well proportioned, his long legs covered in a fine black hair. But he wasn't too hairy, she decided; some on his chest, grading down to a point on his stomach, and disappearing beneath the waistband of his underpants. They were stained and dirty, too, from his exertions, but she wasn't taking those off. No way, she reprimanded herself.

She pulled the sheet quickly over him and took off her dressing gown, sliding in between the sheets of the other bed. She raised herself on one elbow and glanced at him. He was inert – fast asleep. She switched off the light and slid down on her back, feeling the tiredness in her legs and the exquisite pleasure of lying down, knowing that sleep would soon come.

She thought about Melissa, how she had responded to something in the child. She would go back to the convent to see her; there might be something she could do – she didn't know what, but she wanted to help. She thought about David Kass in the bed next to her. Oddly, it never crossed her mind that he was a Jew, but she did think of him as a man. She found her hand on her breast, her nipple hard between her thumb and forefinger. She groaned and rolled over, pushing the erotic image from her mind.

Eventually she slept, tiredness claiming her body from desire. They both slept.

Kass sat bolt upright, staring into the darkness of the room. The noise of the explosion still reverberated in his ears. He could feel the bed shaking, the sound of falling debris. The bed . . . what bed? Where was he? He heard something roll, then crash to the floor. He threw back the sheet as a sudden blinding light was switched on. He sat up, blinking the sleep from his eyes. Nazira was in the bed opposite, her hand on the light.

'It's all right,' she said. She reached down and picked up the flask that had rolled on to the floor, shaken from the stand by the nearby explosion. 'It was probably a rocket – there's always one or two round here.'

He felt foolish and confused, suddenly realizing that he was sitting on the edge of the bed and that all he was wearing were his underpants. He pulled the sheet over his knees. 'We didn't get that many at the hospital, at least not at night.'

'You're lucky.'

'I suppose so.' He looked down at his bare legs. 'Did you put me to bed?'

'Yes. By the time I'd finished in the bathroom, you were fast asleep.'

'I'm sorry.'

'No need – it was my fault for taking so long. You must have been shattered.'

He grinned. 'I was.' He glanced at his watch. 'It's only four o'clock.'

She snuggled down under the sheet. He could see the clear outline of her body underneath. 'You'd better get back to bed then,' she said, 'and turn the light off.'

He leaned over and pressed the switch, plunging the room into darkness, then pulled the sheet over him, lying on his back, thinking. Remembering the chapel.

'Nazira?'

'Yes.'

There was a silence, then, 'Why did you stay in the convent?'

She stared above her head at the faint white of the ceiling. 'I don't know really. Maybe some of the things you said about me were true.'

He shook his head. 'I had no right to talk to you like that. You've got your job to do, I've got mine.'

Nazira didn't answer.

He waited, listening to her breathing. 'Are you asleep?'

'No.'

'I'm glad you stayed.'

She smiled in the darkness. 'So am I.'

She heard him yawn tiredly. 'That girl you found – Melissa?'

'Mmmmmm . . .'

'We got to know each other quite well. She's a nice child. I'd like to see her again, David.'

'No reason why you shouldn't. I'm sure Sister Christina wouldn't mind.' The room fell silent again. He tried to fathom Nazira. The change in her attitude had been so abrupt, it was difficult to assess. It had happened in the convent, some time after he had left her and returned to the chapel. Maybe his anger had sparked off a kind of challenge. Daring her to care for someone, to find a response. Perhaps it was as simple as that.

He heard her bed creak, then a sudden rush of cool air as his sheet was lifted. He felt her body warm beside him, her hand sliding across his chest. 'Nazira,' he said.

'Don't speak.' Her fingers touched his face, rubbing the stubble on his chin. 'You need a shave.'

'I know.'

She leaned over him, kissing his lips, her breasts lightly touching his chest. She could feel his erection hard against her thigh. His hands slid down the small of her back, grasping her buttocks, pulling her towards him. She buried her face against his, the rough stubble scratching her face, kissing his neck, his ear.

She felt his hand go down on to his penis, pushing it between her legs. She wrapped herself around him, feeling it plunge into her. His back arched, forcing her over, on to her back.

They made love to each other with a kind of wild desperation. The total physical consummation blotted out the images of the day, removing the horrors that lurked, waiting to fill their dreams, giving to each other the only reality that made any sense in Beirut: a primitive, simple life force, an instinctual response to the threat of extinction in a city where life had little value.

TWENTY-THREE

The crowded radar scope had started to empty shortly before dawn, the dots spreading away from *Sea Victory* as mysteriously as they had arrived. By first light they had gone completely. Only Rhys and Forester were aware of their presence; there was no point in alarming anyone. There was no way of knowing if they were a source of danger or not. In any case, they had come and gone without any direct visual or audio contact. Their disappearance before first light and his subsequent arrival in Lebanese coastal waters could not be coincidental – he was sure of that.

Sea Victory nosed slowly into the harbour outside the port of Jounieh. It was empty – no water skiers or paddle boats this early in the morning. A grey, tenuous mist hung just above the water, enveloping the ship as it slid through flat waters towards the channel entrance of the port.

The Turkish cattle boat in the harbour had gone, finally released by the blockading gunboats to carry its wretched cargo of Egyptian refugees to Alexandria. A stench still hung over the area. Dozens of black plastic bags, swollen with rubbish, had been dumped in the harbour as the refuse collection had entirely broken down.

Forester steered his vessel carefully through the polluted water and up the channel to the port proper, cruising past the long blockhouse of the naval barracks. A cattle boat was unloading protesting livestock. This was done by attaching a cable to one of the unfortunate animals' legs, and simply winching it off its feet. The manoeuvre was cruel and barbarous by European standards, but common practice in the Middle East. He watched as six goats were hauled up together from the hold, each attached to the cable by one leg. Once clear of the deck, the winchman jammed on the drum brake; the jolt was wicked enough to dislocate their joints. The goats bleated pathetically as they were swung haphazardly to the waiting truck on the quay. The winchman tried to load them quickly – too quickly. They crashed into the side of the lorry, until by dint of trial and error, he finally got it right. The squealing animals were dumped unceremoniously, on their heads, into the truck. Forester was glad to see they all regained their feet without apparent injury, once they had been released.

He didn't know quite what he expected to see once he rounded the end of the naval barracks: more of what he'd seen before, probably. But Jounieh had another surprise waiting for him.

Tied up almost opposite the berth *Sea Victory* had occupied, was the huge white hull of the West German hospital ship, *Flora*. He was familiar with the craft. He'd seen it in Larnaca two days previously, but he had not expected to see it here. Forester did not know whether to be pleased or annoyed. That it had got in at all was a plus, but berthed here in Jounieh it was a sitting duck, an open invitation for any trigger-happy militia faction that wanted to make a name for itself. That made it a danger to *Sea Victory*.

Hospital ships were not normally considered targets in a war. Their presence was usually respected by friend and foe alike. But this war was not normal – if war was ever normal. It was a filthy, bloody confrontation, a civil war in which there were no boundaries of any kind. Enemies were hard to distinguish. The lines were blurred, split and counter split into various religious and political factions and further complicated by the interests of the USA and, through Syria, Russia. And now there were the invading armies of the Israelis de-stabilizing the country still further. Forester decided he didn't like the hospital ship at all.

He edged *Sea Victory* slowly in as Rhys joined him. The crowd on the quay began to thicken, waving and shouting encouragement to Henshaw, who was standing by the bows with the line. He grinned and waved back good-naturedly. The mood was joyous, untroubled by the muffled, distant explosions in Beirut. People were glad that *Sea Victory* was back, that they still had a chance to escape.

Makarion came into his office and quietly locked the door behind him. He took a pair of binoculars from his drawer and watched the vessel as it tied up. There were a number of limousines drawn up, waiting on the dock. Two of them carried the diplomatic insignia of France and Venezuela.

He could see Forester in the wheelhouse, Rhys beside him, and Henshaw who was tying up at the bows. But there appeared to be few passengers apart from two men leaning over the rails near the stern. He quartered the upper deck slowly with his glasses. He stopped. He'd seen something move on the upper superstructure close to the bridge. Makarion drew back into the shadow of the curtains and watched. The man was obviously a bodyguard, or security of some sort. His attitude more than anything else betrayed his role. Then Makarion saw another man near the stern: again the same wariness, his hand never far from the weapon concealed by the well-padded jacket.

Makarion wondered if they were part of the diplomatic entourage. It would have been unusual – they didn't usually employ local muscle.

Eventually the two ambassadors emerged from the saloon, chatting amiably. They seemed relaxed, enjoying the welcome given by the refugees crowding the dock. The French ambassador left first, bidding adieu to his Venezuelan counterpart. Accompanied by his aide, he carefully negotiated the gangplank and, escorted by some Phalange militiamen, made his way to his car. He waved once before getting inside and Makarion saw Forester return the gesture. The Venezuelan diplomat left a moment later with his aide, followed by the two staff from the American Embassy, and the US businessman. The bodyguards had still not moved. Makarion waited.

When all but three of the cars had gone, a security man he had not spotted before emerged from the shadows of the galley door and gave a signal to the officer in charge of the militia on the dock. Makarion kept his glasses trained on the stern deck, close to the gangplank. He saw the security man come out, scan the deck briefly and nod to someone inside. A small, slight figure emerged and made his way quickly off the vessel, followed by his bodyguard. Both were immediately surrounded by Christian Phalange militia and escorted to one of the cars. It drove off immediately.

Makarion had recognized him at once. He was one of the leading figures of the Christian Phalange movement.

Another one of the security men in the stern motioned his charge to come out and the same procedure followed. It was repeated once more for the last Lebanese.

Makarion waited, but no one else left the vessel. All the cars had gone, together with their passengers. He put the glasses down and moved over to unlock the door. Then he slumped into his chair behind the desk and gazed blankly out of the window. What did it all mean?

Why were leading members of the three main political groupings in Lebanon travelling on board a neutral British vessel? And what was the significance of the Americans on board? There was only one conclusion: they were trying to come to some arrangement.

Forester went alone to the offices of Inter-Travel. This time the short walk was less hazardous. The crowds parted, slapping him on his back, greeting him like a saviour. He smiled and waved, responding to their optimism, but he knew he could not carry them all out, and this time he made no promises. In spite of their cheerful faces, the tension was stronger, and the sense of approaching danger hung above them like a physical force, bearing down upon the port – waiting in the wings. Retribution was expected from the PLO.

Elements of the Christian Phalange militia were actively helping the Israelis as they advanced through the outer suburbs of West Beirut. And, while Jounieh had so far received only the occasional hit in the barrage of fire, it could not expect to remain inviolate for long. They knew this; he could see the fear behind their eyes.

Albert Hatan had already arranged a manifest for him: just over a hundred passengers – slightly fewer this time. Forester made no comment. It gave him some leeway to pick up a few of the refugees he'd seen on the dock and in the shipping office. They were relatives of those he had shipped out the first time. Husbands and parents he'd been forced to split up. He intended to make good his promise to them, if he could.

Makarion stood quietly and respectfully behind Hatan as the arrangements were discussed. Forester waited to see if either of them would make any comment on the passengers he'd brought in, but they didn't. 'When did the hospital ship berth?' he asked.

Hatan looked enquiringly at Makarion, who answered, 'Yesterday evening, Captain, at about six. They have been unloading medical supplies ever since.'

Forester chewed uncomfortably on that for a while. 'How much control have the Israelis got now?'

Hatan pursed his lips. 'The PLO still occupy the west of the city, but the Israelis appear to have the rest. They cut off water and electricity supplies for the first time this morning.'

'Trying to squeeze them out?'

'Yes, but also to demonstrate their power to us, and to the USA. The PLO have said they are willing to withdraw from Beirut, but only after the arrival of a peace-keeping force. The Americans are the only ones capable of mounting it.'

Forester didn't mention his own suspicions, or the presence of the fleet of radar blips that had escorted him the night before. It could be American ships and, if they were about to order a complete US evacuation as the Embassy staff had suggested, this could only de-stabilize the area still further. 'Have you got permission from the Israelis to allow us out?'

Hatan shook his head. 'Not yet, but I am hopeful. The fact is they have allowed the Egyptians to leave for Alexandria. This hospital ship has got in and, of course, you have already set a precedent yourself.'

Forester sighed. It was what he had expected. 'OK. I'm going back to the ship now. I want to give the crew a break before we sail. I'll speak to you later.'

Hatan levered himself up out of the chair. 'I'll be in touch shortly.'

Forester rose also, and Makarion stepped forward politely. 'Would you like me to accompany you back to *Sea Victory*, Captain?'

Forester smiled wryly. 'No, there's no problem any more. The people down on the dock seem to have got used to me – maybe that's a good sign.'

Makarion inclined his head. 'I'm sure it is, Captain.'

Forester glanced at him. There was something about the inflexion in his voice . . . Faintly mocking? Makarion smiled blandly back at him. There was nothing in his eyes, nothing Forester could see. But there was *something*. As he walked back along the quay to his ship it nagged away at the back of his mind, worrying him.

He found Annabel in the galley. She was leaning over a work top, preparing for the trip back. She hadn't heard him. He crossed the space between them swiftly and wrapped his arms tightly around her waist. She squealed with fright, then relaxed as she recognized the feel of him.

'How would you like to have some breakfast in the best place I can find?'

She twisted round in his arms, looking up into his eyes. 'Now that sounds like a very good idea.'

'OK,' he said, 'it's a date. But only if I can walk you home afterwards.' He squeezed her again, pressing his body against hers.

Annabel sighed mockingly. 'How can I resist such a sophisticated invitation?'

Forester laughed and smacked her bottom. 'Quite so – now get a move on before something turns up to stop us . . .'

She slipped from his arms. 'For once you're right, Captain, you are absolutely right. I shall be but a moment.' She paused in the doorway. 'Don't go away.'

They found a small restaurant that was open in the old part of the town. It never ceased to amaze Annabel that a degree of normality should continue in spite of the proximity of the war nine miles down the coast road in Beirut. The restaurant was full: waiters buzzed around, dispatching and taking orders; there were some businessmen, a few soldiers. Trade was thriving, whatever the conditions – perhaps because of the conditions. De-stabilization had become a way of life. Lebanon had been a war zone since the civil war of 1976. Meanwhile, things went on as best they could. In spite of the deprivation in Beirut, here, in this restaurant, it was possible to eat well.

Annabel's thoughts must have betrayed themselves to Forester.

'Feeling guilty?'

She looked up quickly from the menu, surprised. 'No, it's just that . . .' She stopped, realizing that he had intuitively guessed right.

'Look, darling, I know this place . . . that menu seems wrong, somehow. Maybe it is wrong, I don't know.' He leaned across the table and took her hands. 'What I *do* know is that no one could have done more, worked harder, than you on that last trip back to Cyprus.' He smiled to take the edge off his words. 'And you, madam, are going to sit there, relax, and enjoy someone looking after you for a change. You'll have plenty of time to be noble later on.'

She shook her head apologetically. 'I'm sorry. I didn't mean to spoil it.'

'You're not spoiling it for me.' He squeezed her hands. 'I think I like you almost as much as I love you.'

Annabel gulped. She was touched by his tenderness. She slipped her hands from his. 'Look, you'd better stop talking like that or you'll make me cry – and I'll embarrass us both . . . Now, where's the menu?'

He grinned. 'In front of you.'

They were relaxed and happy together, glad to be able to forget the war – deaf to its distant rumbles. Like the Lebanese, they were getting used to it.

They both had a fresh grapefruit, then a full English breakfast of eggs, bacon, sausages and fried bread, washed down with hot, sweet tea. Forester helped himself to some toast and marmalade afterwards – he was ravenous. Annabel was almost tempted to do the same. Then she saw Albert Hatan making his way across the restaurant. He bowed a little stiffly to her, and turned to Forester. 'I'm sorry to interrupt your breakfast, Captain, but there is something I wish to talk to you about.'

Forester stood up. 'I'm sure we don't mind.' He glanced apologetically at Annabel and she picked it up immediately.

227

'No, of course not. We were just about to have some more tea; perhaps you'd like some.' She smiled encouragingly.

Forester pulled back one of the spare chairs at the table. 'Why don't you sit down?'

Hatan inclined his head gratefully. 'Thank you.' He lowered himself carefully into it.

Forester called for an extra cup and saucer. The waiter had anticipated his request, and laid it on the table. Annabel began to pour. 'Milk and sugar?'

Hatan nodded. 'Please.'

Forester settled down and looked curiously at the old man. 'What is it?'

The Lebanese was not to be brought to the point that quickly. 'I hope your meal was satisfactory.'

Forester smiled. 'So far.' He was puzzled. 'How did you know we were here?'

Hatan cupped his hands together. 'There is not a lot that goes on in Jounieh I do not know about, Captain,' he said sagely.

Forester didn't doubt it. He buttered some toast and looked at Annabel, who had changed her mind and was munching some, too. 'Nice?'

'Mmmmmmm.' She looked at Hatan. 'You should try an English breakfast.'

He declined. 'No, it's a little too much for an old man.'

Annabel and Forester continued to demolish the toast. Hatan watched without envy. He decided to broach the subject that had brought him here. 'I take it, Captain, you have no fundamental objections to riches?'

Forester put down his knife and sat back in his chair. The discussion had finally begun. He smiled. 'No, other than the fact that they have so far eluded me.'

Hatan chuckled. 'Quite so – me too.'

Forester did not believe him.

Hatan continued, 'To take the point a little further. Would you have any objection to carrying out gold bullion to Cyprus?'

Forester licked some marmalade from his sticky fingers. 'Depends . . .'

'On what?'

'On where it's coming from, and who it's going to.'

228

Hatan waved a deprecating hand. 'It's a straightforward business transfer from a bank in Beirut to another in Cyprus. Understandably, they want to get out the bullion before it is too late.'

'It's already too late, if they want complete security. I cannot guarantee that on *Sea Victory.*'

Hatan accepted that. 'Of course, they understand that, and they would be foolish if it did not concern them. But the situation in Beirut concerns them more . . .'

Forester interrupted. 'And there is no other way out?'

The old man raised his shoulders. 'Precisely.'

Forester glanced at Annabel, then back at Hatan. 'How much?'

'About twenty-five million dollars.'

Annabel looked incredulously at him. 'Twenty-five million?'

Hatan replied, speaking softly. 'Yes. Each bar weighs four hundred ounces and is worth in excess of twenty-five thousand dollars. Six bars to a case, and there are sixteen cases.'

Forester remembered something. 'Why didn't you tell me this when I was in your office?'

Hatan surveyed him shrewdly. 'I wondered if you would ask me that.' He scratched the side of his nose reflectively. 'The answer is, I don't really know . . . Let's just say I like to be careful.' He paused. 'Will you do it?'

Forester didn't hesitate. They could put the packing cases in the bathroom next to his own cabin – it would not affect the passengers in any way. 'Yes. When will you want to load? We sail this evening.'

Hatan took a sip of the tea. He raised an eyebrow appreciatively. 'It's good – just how I like it.'

Forester knew he was stalling. 'Fine . . . when?'

Hatan coughed, clearing his throat. 'There is a slight problem. Today is Sunday, and the vault is time-locked until tomorrow – you might not be able to sail until Monday evening.'

Forester sighed; the fee was slipping away again. 'Sorry, I can't hang around here for twenty-four hours. Anything might happen. It's getting very tight.'

Hatan agreed. 'I know. That is why the bank wants to move reserves out. There is a substantial fee.'

'What is it?'

'A quarter of one per cent.'

Forester shook his head. 'I'm no good at arithmetic. How much?'

Hatan smiled. 'It comes to about sixty-three thousand dollars.'

That sounded better. Forester knew they needed it. If he was ever going to get *Sea Victory* across to the West Indies, he would need every penny he could raise. He looked questioningly at Annabel. 'What do you think?'

She shook her head. 'It makes no difference to me. You decide.'

Forester was tempted . . . but it wasn't just him. There were the refugees on the dock – some had already been there for days. There was also the safety of his crew. They hadn't hesitated when he'd asked them to come back. The longer they were in these waters, the more dangerous it was. Not least, there was Charlie. He remembered his son as they had left, his blond head bobbing up and down as he waved. 'No, it's too risky.'

Hatan sat quietly for a moment, contemplating the tablecloth in front of him. He looked up. 'Before you finally decide, there is something I think you ought to consider.'

'What?'

'You remember last time that you had on board the American ambassador?'

'That's right. We were about to sail when you heard the transmission on the VHF.'

'Exactly. That transmission was clearly for the Israelis' benefit. In effect the Americans were saying "hands off".'

'Well?'

'Well, Captain, there is no such message this time, and I doubt that they will let you through.'

'What are you saying?'

'I'm saying that this bullion is from an American bank.'

The implication was clear: wait for the US money or no passage through the blockade. Forester remembered that they had still been stopped by the gunboats, even with the ambassador on board. Possibly *because* he was on board. Maybe they had a deal. But the Americans and the Israelis had always had a deal – they were allies. Most of Israel's military and financial support was derived from the US – so why? Why would they have to put on board an ambassador, or gold bullion from an American bank, to get *Sea Victory* passage? More importantly, why did the Americans want his ship to ply between Lebanon and Cyprus? Questions, questions, but no answers.

Forester didn't look at his wife, or at Hatan. 'It seems I've got no choice,' he said savagely. He sawed at his toast, cutting it up into tiny pieces, then left it on his plate. He wasn't hungry any more.

CHAPTER
TWENTY-FOUR

The Commander was a short, stocky man, his hair now permanently white, cropped close to his head. His face was deeply lined by the sun and years of command in the open, desert regions. The report from Makarion lay upon his desk before him. It was explosive, and it required action. The crucial importance of Jounieh had long been foreseen: Makarion's presence was no accident; it had been planned years ahead. Strategically, the small port was vital once Beirut was cut off. And with the many and varied opposing factions, that had been inevitable – as, indeed, was the Israeli blockade.

However, it was crucial to have someone in there who could be relied upon, and Makarion was a good agent. He, too, clearly saw the significance of the neutral British craft, and it had not been difficult for him to keep a check on it.

Now the real purpose was clear. The Americans wanted to try to find some rapport between the warring factions. The men Makarion had seen leaving the vessel in Jounieh were all leaders of the various groupings. Sea Victory was being used not only to get refugees out of Lebanon, but as a secure negotiating venue on its way in. But for Makarion's presence in the shipping offices, the Commander would have been none the wiser.

So, the Americans were trying to bring the factions together. That did not suit the Commander at all; nor did it suit his country – not yet, not until they had gained full control themselves. Sea Victory would have to be eliminated, but it would have to be done cleverly, perhaps under the cover of something else. It was a neutral, civilian ship and he did not want the finger levelled at him. That could be arranged. The number of armies, different militias, the confusion in Jounieh, could be *put to good use. He would use the Special Strike Unit. It would have to be done quickly. The vessel was due to leave within twenty-four hours. He wanted it destroyed before it left port. That would accomplish two ends. The vessel could no longer be used by the Americans, and the gold would stay in the country.*

The code had been broken. The Director read the report, then read it again – he could not believe it. It was in Hebrew. An Israeli code?

They now knew where the signals were emanating from in Jounieh. But it was the order that had come from the other end of the line that had been impossible to trace as yet. The content of that order was as incredible as its Israeli connection: 'Destroy Sea Victory*'!*

Was it conceivable that the Israelis would go that far to eliminate the negotiations his department had so secretly set up on the British vessel? The Director found it hard to believe. He knew the consternation this information would cause when he passed it up.

Sea Victory *had to be protected. It was his responsibility to see that it was. Using a neutral vessel was one thing; allowing it to be destroyed was another. Britain was a valuable ally and the fact that this ship had been set up without the knowledge of any of those concerned could rebound on him personally, as well as on his government.*

But there was also his government's relationship with Israel to consider. An American strike on an Israeli force would damage that irreparably. He was grateful that he did not have to decide. He picked up the telephone.

CHAPTER

TWENTY-FIVE

They had breakfast together for the first time since the morning on the boat, when Nazira had confiscated some bandages for him. He reminded her of that.

She laughed.

'Why did you do it?' he asked.

'I don't know. You were so unprepared.'

He sipped his coffee. 'Did you despise me?'

She looked away. 'I don't know – I think I suspected you.'

'Of what – carnal desire?'

'No, not that,' she said quickly, then added, 'but it was nice when it did happen.' She eyed him provocatively across the table.

He glanced quickly around the breakfast room. 'You'd better keep your voice down, otherwise we'll get slung out for lowering the moral fibre of the country.'

She looked round as well. 'There's no one here except us. It's early – the world's press and all the media are still fast asleep.' She was right, it was empty and quiet. No bombs or explosions, apart from the odd imitation from Drake's parrot by the pool. It was as if they had the hotel to themselves. He looked at her, puzzled. 'Why is it so quiet?'

Nazira finished off her scrambled eggs. 'I don't know. Maybe because it's Sunday.'

He was startled. 'Is it Sunday?'

She looked at him, realizing that he'd completely lost track. 'Yes it is . . .'

The tiredness was still around his eyes, although a night's sleep and a shave had improved his appearance considerably. He might have looked even better, she thought mischievously, if she hadn't interrupted it. 'Why don't you get Yussef to take us down to the promenade?'

He looked surprised. 'Is it still there?'

'Yes . . . well, most of it. Besides, the sea air might do you some good.'

He declined. 'I've got to get back to the hospital.'

She felt a flash of annoyance. 'Oh, for heaven's sake, stop being so goddamn noble. You've not emerged from that place until now. You're entitled to a day off.'

She was right, maybe he did see it as a way of paying back – atoning. 'I'm sorry, I didn't mean to sound sanctimonious, but I must go. You've seen them, Nazira – they've got no chance. There are just not enough doctors.'

She lowered her head and picked at her food. 'I suppose so. It was bloody stupid of me to think we could do anything enjoyable in this place.'

He tried to cheer her up. 'Come on, don't be so gloomy – last night was pretty enjoyable . . .'

She looked at him and he grinned. 'Tell you what, why don't we go to the promenade, then Yussef can take me on to the hospital?'

Nazira smiled. 'Well, that's almost as enjoyable.'

The parrot by the pool went into his dive-bombing routine again. It was weird – funny and weird at the same time; but they laughed.

They left Yussef in the big Buick and she led him towards the sea. It was still early enough to be reasonably cool by Beirut standards, yet already people were out. Not just out, but promenading. Families dressed in their Sunday best strolled down the seafront. Some were elegant and assured, others on family outings with kids who ran screaming with delight down the steps, flung off their clothes, and leapt into the sea. How polluted that water was, Kass was not prepared to guess. Psychologically, it was doing them a lot of good, lifting their morale – another breath of normality in this tattered, battered city. He just hoped that the kids didn't swallow any of that sea water.

There were bars or, more correctly, the remains of bars, night clubs. Their fronts were open and exposed to the elements; most had no roofs, some no walls. All had exotic names and smart décor hanging forlornly from their walls. Somehow, behind all this devastation, he could see why the city had once been dubbed the Paris of the Middle East. He looked at a couple strolling just in front of them – in their middle thirties, he would guess. What were they thinking about? What were their memories of this Sunday promenade?

Nazira had said something. He looked at her enquiringly. 'I'm sorry, what was that?'

She sighed. 'I said, a penny for them.'

He laughed. 'My thoughts.' Then, more seriously, 'I don't know really – it's just that I feel close to these people. They have such strength and resilience. Yet this . . .' He indicated the passers-by.

'You mean the dressing-up, the promenading?'

He didn't answer. She continued, 'Ah, you'd have to live ten years in a continuous war zone to understand that.'

He took her hand. 'Oh, I *understand* it, Nazira. I understand it is a fragile hold on what they once had. A way of staying sane, if you like.'

'But?'

'It just makes me feel so helpless.'

They walked on in silence for a while, enjoying the breeze blowing in off the sea, the children laughing.

Nazira turned to him suddenly. 'When can I go to see Melissa?'

He held out his hands expansively. 'Any time – I'll fix it for you, if you like.'

'Would you do it today?'

'You want to go today?'

She nodded, pleased. 'Yes, yes I'd like that; after you've gone back to your hospital.'

'OK,' he said, 'I'll do it.'

She thrust her arm through his and they walked some more.

He broke the comfortable silence between them.' 'You like the girl, don't you?'

'Melissa?'

'Yes.'

'I do.' She paused, thinking about her feelings. 'I think I'd like to take her out of here when we go.' She looked at him anxiously. 'Would that be possible?'

He considered it. 'I don't know, Nazira. She is in a convent for mentally disturbed children.'

She pulled her arm angrily from his. 'There's nothing wrong with her – I understand Melissa . . .'

He took her by the shoulders and turned her towards him. 'Hey, wait a minute . . .' He looked down into her eyes. 'I didn't say you couldn't take her. I understand how you feel. But there may be formalities. It may not be that simple.'

She shook her head, still angry. 'I want to take her out, give her a chance. She deserves that, at least.' Her voice was muffled by emotion.

He held her close. 'I'll try, Nazira. Maybe, as a doctor, I can suggest that I know where she can get the right kind of medical treatment.'

She jerked back in his arms, staring at him. 'No, *I* want her, David. She's not going to some medical centre.'

He shook her gently. 'Of course not, but if we *both* take her . . .' He smiled. 'Get it?'

'You mean an arrangement?'

It was the first time he had seen her hesitant. 'No, I mean *we* take her out, you and me both.'

She was delighted. She took his face in both of her hands and kissed both cheeks – then squeezed him so tightly he could hardly draw breath.

'Here, hold on,' he said, looking round, slightly embarrassed – but no one took the slightest notice. He pulled her to him and they kissed.

A geyser of water sprang up in the sea about ten metres from the promenade, followed instantly by the muffled boom of an explosion. They sprang apart, guiltily, as though it were their fault. Two men were standing on the other side of the seafront rails, hanging on to prevent themselves from falling in. They were PLO. One yelled something at the other and pointed at the spot where the explosion had occurred. He dived into the sea, fully clothed, and swam rapidly. When he reached the place, he stuck his hand just below the surface and pulled out a stunned fish. He laughed, holding it aloft triumphantly.

The war was back again, if it had ever been away.

They sat quietly in the back of Yussef's cab. There was plenty of room this time, but she snuggled down in his arms in the corner. She felt a deep sense of contentment. Their intimacy required no physical act; just being close, being with him, was enough. How odd that she should fall in love with an American, a Jew.

She had thought about that when she lay in his arms, when he'd made love to her, wondering if it made any difference. There was a difference, but it had nothing to do with his sexuality — it was *because* she loved him. She knew that. Instinctively, deep within herself, she had known it since the night on the boat when he had tried so gently, so sweetly, to reach her.

It was his tenderness, his caring — not just for her, but for the children in the convent and the wretched people in the hospital — that had changed her. There was nothing excessively masculine about him — she knew he had been badly scared on the way into Beirut in the taxi. She had been tempted to sneer then, for she herself had no fear of death. She had lived with it all around her, all her life. Growing up in a Palestinian refugee camp, she had quickly sorted out her priorities: first, survival; then revenge. And now, ironically, she loved a Jew.

Perhaps this had always been her fate. Amongst the sophisticates and cynics of Paris, she had become aware of a strong sense of fatalism in herself. Some had mocked her for it, which only served to strengthen her resolve to help her people, but none had ever got close to her. Men had made love to her many times; they had often used her crudely; they had tried to crush her spirit, to degrade her physically.

David had not tried to take her. She, in a sense, had taken him; she had needed him. His gentleness concealed an incredible strength. She had seen it in the chapel as he worked and sweated amid the carnage, trying to find the living – laying out the dead. Nazira lifted her head, placing her hand on his cheek; it was smooth now, he smelt nice. He kissed her, and she closed her eyes. Oh God, she ached for him. Her insides seemed to be breaking – tearing her apart as the pain she had locked within her flooded away.

Kass felt the wetness on his cheek. He kissed it away, quietly trying to comfort her as the sobs racked her body, easing the hurt she had suffered.

Yussef could hear the desperation in her muffled sobs. He drove slowly back along the seafront, giving them time. It was Sunday – there was all the time in the world.

Slowly her cries died away. Kass took a handkerchief from his pocket and dabbed the dampness round her eyes and mouth. She suddenly pulled away from him, taking the handkerchief and wiping her eyes. 'Don't be so nice to me, David, please.' She looked out of the window. 'Where are we?'

Kass sat up. 'Still on the prom. Yussef has driven up and down it at least three times.'

She saw him glance at his watch. Her strong sense of practicality reasserted itself. 'You must get back to the hospital. What time is it?'

'Just after ten.'

She leaned forward and spoke to Yussef. 'Take us to the hospital.'

Yussef was glad she had recovered. Women always seemed so much stronger after crying. He wondered if it would work for him – he doubted it. He'd cried enough when his business had been demolished, and that had only made him more miserable. But he still had the car, and he enjoyed ferrying these people around. It made him feel a part of things, gave him back his self-respect.

The courtyard in front of the hospital was as hot and as crowded as ever. Seeing it again turned Kass's stomach to water. He didn't want to go back; he would have given a lot

239

simply to order Yussef to drive them back to the hotel; and then take Nazira to bed. But he couldn't, he knew that. He swallowed, trying to keep his voice as normal as possible. 'Will you be there this evening?'

'Yes.'

The car stopped and Yussef switched off the engine.

'I'll try to get back as soon as I can.' He knew the promise was an empty one. There was no way of knowing when he could afford to leave.

Nazira knew it, too. She looked at him penetratingly. 'If I don't see you tonight, I'll come here tomorrow.'

'OK.' He remembered something. 'I'll let Sister Christina know you are coming to see Melissa.'

He kissed her, then opened the door and got out. An ambulance swung noisily into the courtyard, stopping behind the cab. Yussef started the engine, checking to see if the American doctor had got out. Kass shut the door and stepped back as Yussef drove the Buick in a semicircle back to the open gates of the courtyard. Kass watched until it disappeared around the corner. He turned and started to walk up the steps into the main entrance. Two medics pushed past him carrying a stretcher. He was about to follow them when he heard the whine of an approaching shell.

For one stupid moment he thought it was the parrot doing his impression. Then he saw people flinging themselves to the floor. A woman screamed.

The blast tossed him against a door. He staggered upright as the sound of shattered glass falling to the floor filled his ears. He wiped the dust from his eyes, looking for the point of impact. Through the open doors he could see a pall of smoke rising from the street beyond. He froze – his mind running into a kind of breakneck speed. Images, thoughts – searing, awful fear coursed through his body. He found himself running through the courtyard. He didn't remember coming down the steps. His body took over, responding to the sickening, blood-pumping terror in his heart.

He cleared the gates and stopped. The Buick was on its back, tossed there by the blast, wheels still spinning foolishly. A hole had appeared in the side of the street where a moment before had stood a busy shop.

Dust spurted from beneath his feet as he raced to the overturned vehicle. Sounds rushed through his head, hardly registering. He could hear agonized screams coming from the debris of the shop but he didn't pause for an instant; they were meaningless to him. All his fibre was concentrated on that silly, sad, overturned car.

He tore at the door handle, but it wouldn't budge. He grabbed the front door and jerked it frantically open. Yussef fell from his upturned seat, his head lolling at an angle. His neck was broken; he was dead.

Kass whimpered like an animal, crying out in fear and anguish, and climbed into the rear of the car. He wanted to hold her, grab her to him and cradle her body; only his instinct as a doctor prevented him from breaking down completely. He steadied himself. She was unconscious. There was blood on the side of her dress. He tore it away. Blood pumped from a shrapnel wound in her side – she was alive!

Quickly he examined her. There were no other wounds apart from a severe bruise appearing just under her hairline, where her head had struck the roof. He ripped the dress into a temporary dressing and held it tightly against the wound to stem the flow of blood. Then, holding her in his arms, he leaned back and kicked at the door with all his strength. It sprang open and he slowly eased himself out until he was able to get on to his knees, clear of the cab.

He lifted her up and carried her through the gates into the hospital. Nurse Setta saw him struggling up the winding staircase and cleared a way for him as best she could until they reached casualty.

Within half an hour he had operated on her himself, removing the small, jagged piece of shrapnel from her side, just beneath her ribs. He stitched her up and walked beside her as Nurse Setta wheeled her along a passage and into a small room where he sometimes slept. She helped him get Nazira on to the bed, then covered her with a sheet, tucking the ends in firmly. She left, shutting the door gently behind her.

241

Kass sat down beside Nazira. Her face was pale, the dark hair matted against her forehead. He brushed it lightly away, wiping a streak of dirt until her face was clean. Her eyes were closed. She would be unconscious for at least another half-hour. But she would live.

He waited, and thanked his God.

CHAPTER
TWENTY-SIX

There were four vehicles: a tank, an armoured personnel-carrier and two rocket-launchers, all of them tracked: this was vital, as for much of the operation they were crossing harsh, desert terrain. It was necessary to avoid roads if they were to achieve the surprise they required.

The Commander occupied the turret position in the tank, which led the small column. They were making good progress on the hard, rocky surface of the wadi. The sun was rising behind them in the east. It cast their long shadows before them, elongating the shape of the tank and twisting it into peculiar forms as it danced ahead over the broken ground. Soon the sun would be rising swiftly in the sky, blazing down on the heavy armour of the tank until the surface would be too hot to touch, turning the interior into an oven. The Commander would have preferred to make this crossing under cover of darkness, but that was impossible if they were to reach the heights above Jounieh before the ship sailed next day.

It was essential that Sea Victory was sunk in the port. The bullion would be a useful prize if they could lay their hands on it. Makarion had received his instructions, and a back-up operation was in hand to ensure the attack would not fail in its objectives. They continued to trek westwards, towards the distant mountains. The squad had been handpicked; they were the best of his available men. They were beginning to suffer in the appalling heat; the interior of the armoured personnel-carrier behind him must have been well over a hundred by now. But his men were used to difficult conditions. This was not the first time they had slogged their way across a desert in the heat of the day.

With luck they should be into the mountains by nightfall, and reach the coastal region by early morning. When they got to the mountains *they would be entering Christian Phalange territory. The Phalange were strongly pro-Israel. The route they were taking made it unlikely that they would be seen, but should they be spotted, it would rouse no surprise. Israeli hardware was expected in the mountains — the encirclement of Beirut was almost complete.*

Sunday hung heavily. Jounieh was now the only way out of Lebanon from Beirut. The road to Damascus had been blocked again by heavy fighting and Jounieh bore the brunt of the refugees' flight. There was nowhere else to go.

It was not just the docks that were crowded. People infiltrated wherever they could find an open space, a place to sit down. Flies had become a problem because of the mounting piles of refuse. They hung in swarms above the refugees.

Forester and Annabel were glad to be back on board ship. The enforced delay gave them a chance to prepare more thoroughly for the passage to Cyprus next day. Forester crawled about below, checking to see how the timber-framed vessel was standing up to the heavy loads and constant pounding of the sea. She was as sound as a nut. The old girl was taking the strain and, as far as Forester could see, there were no problems. He counted his blessings and kept his fingers crossed.

It was a strange afternoon. All of them were wrapped up in their respective tasks, Rhys inspecting the engines, Annabel and Henshaw making certain they had all the supplies they would need. Yet, over it all, in the hot, steamy port, there was an unnatural silence that contrasted starkly with the increased sounds of conflict from Beirut.

Late in the afternoon a young Englishwoman arrived on the dock. She clutched the hands of two of her sons; the third stood immediately behind her, holding her skirt. None of the boys was more than five years old. From the saloon window Annabel could see the woman was exhausted, broken, and she ran to the stern. The woman saw her. She held tightly on to her children, shepherding them towards the gangplank. Annabel descended it and helped her and the children up on to the deck.

The sight of another Englishwoman, the sound of her voice, was too much. The tired woman started to cry, her arms hanging limply by her side. Long, shuddering sobs rose from deep inside

244

her. Annabel did the only thing she could, and held the woman in her arms, trying to give her some comfort.

The children remained silent. Dazed and confused, they stayed close to their mother, clutching her round the legs, instinctively pressing themselves to her, making her aware of their presence. It acted as a recovery mechanism, causing the woman to put her arms around them. She wiped her eyes with her hand, dabbing away the tears, unwilling to distress them still further. 'I'm sorry,' she said to Annabel, stepping back a pace.

Annabel gave her a handkerchief. 'That's all right.' She knelt down in front of one of the boys. 'Would you like a drink?'

He was too shocked to respond normally and looked up to his mother for her reaction. The woman nodded gratefully. 'Thank you, that would be nice.'

Annabel led the way into the saloon and quickly prepared three long, cool lemonades and a weak brandy sour for the woman.

They sat down on the bench seats opposite the bar and Annabel joined them, handing the drinks round. She waited quietly, knowing that an explanation would come in time.

The woman sipped reluctantly at the drink, as if unwilling to take anything. Then, as she began to taste it, she swallowed it more quickly, realizing how thirsty she was. She emptied the glass.

'Shall I refill that for you?' Annabel asked.

'Please . . .'

Annabel took the glass and went behind the bar. The woman watched her silently as she poured another drink, waiting for her to come back.

'We were trying to get out by road.' Her voice was low, strained, the breaking point not far away. 'We took the Damascus road – my husband had been there many times. It seemed the best way; we have friends there.' She stopped, her eyes blank, thinking about the past.

Annabel prompted her gently. 'Yes . . .?'

She looked at Annabel as though surprised by her presence. Then she remembered. She cleared her throat and continued, 'At first we made good time, then . . .' Her voice faltered, she hesitated, looking distractedly at Annabel.

245

Annabel took her hand, holding it tightly.

'It was a patrol . . . Syrian, I think. They stopped the car and made my husband get out.' Her voice had grown fainter – she was almost whispering. 'They took him to one side, asking him questions. I couldn't hear what they were saying, but it seemed OK. He looked at us once and waved, as if to say everything was all right, then –' Her hand tightened involuntarily on Annabel's, her eyes gazed at Annabel horrified. 'There was an . . . an explosion.'

Her voice was tight with fear. She swallowed, then seemed to separate herself from what she was saying, her voice toneless. 'There was another, and another, on either side of the car – missing us completely. They were shells, you see – they were being shelled. But my husband was with them . . . We crouched in the car until it stopped. I got out – I made the children stay. My eldest, Tony, looked after them. I tried to find him, but they had all gone – there was nothing there, just a hole and . . . and . . .'

She tried to continue, but it was impossible. Annabel put her arms around the woman, trying desperately not to cry herself. It was horrible; she would always carry with her the memory of the images the woman had conjured up, the feeling of sickening desolation – and then the harrowing flight, driving the children back through the desert until she reached Jounieh. Until she reached *Sea Victory*.

Yet, even here, she was still not secure – but she must not know that. Annabel wiped away the woman's tears. 'Come with me,' she said, matter-of-factly, 'you're safe now. There is a cabin below where you and the children can have a wash and some rest. Come on, children.'

She stood up, and obediently the woman followed, the boys trailing behind. Annabel took them to her cabin and reassured them once again, fussing around, showing the woman where the towels were, inviting her to use the bed. She made normal, hospitable chit-chat, trying to begin the process of filming over the dreadful horror, relegating it to the past, where it would have to live – where it might be possible for the woman to live with it. She paused by the door before leaving. 'Oh, by the way,

246

my name's Annabel.' She nearly added that her husband's name was Tom. She stopped, just in time.

The woman seemed calmer. She looked gratefully at Annabel. 'I'm Mrs Dawson.'

Annabel smiled reassuringly. 'I'll be back soon with some food.'

Mrs Dawson nodded. The door closed behind Annabel and Mrs Dawson stared at its blank surface unseeingly. She was alone again. She heard a voice behind her. 'Mummy, where is the toilet?'

She turned, pushing the thoughts out of her head, finding some relief in dealing with the physical needs of her children.

CHAPTER
TWENTY-SEVEN

The hospital was quiet – or as quiet as hospitals ever are. This one had more than its fair share of the sick and the wounded. Their cries of pain continually broke the stillness of a heavy, humid night.

Kass was sitting in the staff room, while Nurse Setta prepared some coffee. He was glad of her company. Nazira was sleeping peacefully after the op. They had spent some time together when she had recovered consciousness. She was going to be all right, and sleep was the best medicine she could get.

Setta handed him the mug. The coffee was hot and sweet, and he began to feel hungry. 'Have we got any biscuits?'

'I think so.' She went to a cupboard and found a packet of digestives. He dunked his and drank some of the coffee. Setta watched him, amused by the ritual. 'How is it?'

He put the mug down. 'It's fine, just what I needed.' He thought of something. 'I didn't get a chance to see Rousseau. What did he want?'

She raised her eyebrows. 'Well, what it all boiled down to was a release so that he could go back to the hotel.'

Kass shook his head. 'Not with a thigh wound like that. He needs more time before he can move about.'

'I've told him that, Doctor, but he just doesn't listen. I think he's been trying to walk.'

'What! How do you know?'

'His feet were dirty – dust from the floor.'

Kass took another sip of the coffee. 'I'll speak to him in the morning.' He glanced at Setta. She looked worn out. 'Why don't you get off to bed? I'll wash these dishes.'

'No, I'm all right,' she protested; but there was no conviction in her voice.

'You go to bed, Nurse – that's an order.'

She sighed. 'If you say so.'

'I do.'

She finished off the last of her coffee, stood up and walked to the door. 'Don't forget to put the biscuits back or they'll just go. We have a lot of non-staff round here.'

'I will. Goodnight.'

The nurse left and he sat with the warm mug clasped between his hands. Since his arrival in the hospital Nurse Setta had been a godsend, helping him to find his feet, sticking to him when they were overrun. They'd formed a pretty good partnership.

He put the mug down on the table and it quivered strangely. He could feel the vibration in the floor beneath his feet. The mug began to slide across the table. Then he heard a series of muffled explosions. They seemed to be coming from the lower floors of the hospital. He stood up and threw back the door.

Suddenly he heard screaming – people screaming in panic and fear. He began to run towards the stairway. As he reached the well, Nurse Setta turned away from the banisters, facing him. She was pale. He gripped her arms. 'What is it, what's happened?'

She stared at him, her eyes glazed with fear. 'The Damour Brigade – they are in the hospital.'

'How do you know?'

'I saw one of them on the stairs below. They'll kill us all.'

Kass knew about the brigade. Their vow to kill all Palestinians and all who helped them haunted the refugees who crowded the hospital . . . Nazira! Oh God, not Nazira! She was two floors down, close to where Setta had seen the militiaman. He began to run down the stairs, three at a time. He didn't hear Setta screaming for him to come back. Only one thought pulsated through him as he descended. Nazira. She couldn't die, not now, not now . . .

The circular staircase undulated downwards before him,

always moving like a strange misshapen serpent, humping insidiously through the sand, trying to escape from him, it rolled away beneath his flying feet. His body seemed to be separated from his mind. His feet leapt down the stairs in giant slow-motion strides, while his mind raced on to Nazira's room.

People rushed by him up the stairs, running away. Their faces were contorted. He heard gunfire. It boomed in his head, sounding more like someone hitting a huge kettledrum than gunshots.

Now he was on the right floor. He raced silently along the passage towards her room. He stopped. A militiaman wearing a black armband stood in her doorway. He was grinning, his eyes fixed on something inside. Kass walked slowly towards him. The militiaman saw him and swung his automatic rifle round, pointing it at his stomach.

Kass spoke. His voice sounded peculiar in his ears. 'It's all right,' he said, spreading his hands to indicate he was unarmed. 'I'm a doctor.'

Then he heard Nazira scream. 'David!!' Her voice was twisted with fear. It reverberated piteously in his head.

'What are you doing?' He moved forward. 'She is my patient.'

The militiaman would have killed him on the spot, but he realized he was an American. He glanced inside the room, then back at Kass. The fixed smile never left his face. He beckoned to him. 'Come here and look, Doctor, you might be able to help.'

Kass advanced slowly towards the door. He could hear the bed moving, and strange little cries, like an animal in pain. He reached the door.

One man, his trousers down around his ankles, lay on top of her, his buttocks clenching tightly as he pumped up and down on her body. Another stood by the bed, watching, holding her legs apart, his trousers bulging from his erection.

Nazira had been stripped. Her bandages were already deeply bloodstained. Her eyes wide, staring at Kass, imploring him. She screamed suddenly. 'Please, David, kill me . . .'

He bought his elbow viciously back into the militiaman beside him, and ran into the room, grabbing at the half-naked man lying on top of her. His limbs seemed to have acquired the strength of ten men. He flung the man across the room and turned to leap at the other, who was levelling his rifle at him. He was not going to get to him in time – he knew that. Instinctively, even as he prepared to leap, his stomach muscles braced themselves for the awful, tearing impact of the bullet.

The blow, when it came an instant later, was on the back of his head. A blinding, flashing blow that removed all control from his body, and sent him sprawling unconscious to the floor.

The militiaman who had been standing by the door lowered the butt of his rifle. He looked down at Nazira's body, her legs spread wide, the blood from her wound beginning to stain the sheets red. He grinned obscenely. It was going to be his turn . . .

He could see two eyes, a nose and a mouth. It was a man's face, but not the one who had levelled the rifle at him. This one had a funny, square beard, and he wasn't moving. He was peculiarly still, like a snapshot. He blinked and tried to move, but the pain began to pound in his head. It made him feel sick and dizzy. He closed his eyes.

When he opened them the man's face had gone, resolving itself into a patterned square tile on the floor. He lifted his head a little more, trying not to jerk it, and more tiles defined themselves on the floor of the room.

He remembered now. As consciousness crept back the realization of what had happened struck him like a blow in the stomach. He lifted himself on to his knees and looked around the room. It was empty. The Damour militia had gone. On the floor, twisted round his leg, was a bloodstained sheet. He turned sharply to look at the bed and a blinding pain struck him behind the eyes. He groaned and steadied himself, opening his eyes again, frightened of what he might see. At first he saw nothing – his eyeline was just below that of the raised bed. He stood up slowly.

Her body was naked, curled up on her side as though she were trying to keep warm. Beneath her was a wide, deep red stain that was slowly congealing. He knew she was dead; he had seen death too many times.

He turned her over to examine the wound in her side. They had plunged a knife into the original wound, killing her instantly. He laid her gently on her back and picked up the sheet from the floor, covering her up. He did not cover her face, not yet. He wanted to look at her.

Death for Nazira had come as a welcome release. Her eyes were closed, masking the pain, and her face had relaxed. The dark lashes of her eyes were clear against her pale face. She was utterly beautiful, and he could feel the despair inside him breaking loose, filling his body. He sat on the bed and looked down at her. Dazed, he picked at her hair, arranging it around her face the way he had seen it when she slept.

He did not know how long he sat with her – his mind was not really functioning. He was shocked, mourning his loss, unaware of the passage of time. Not until the first yellow streaks of light began to throw their shadows across the floor was he conscious of his whereabouts. He stared at the tiny finger of sunlight sliding across the tiled floor. And then looked up at its source. The sun was rising at an angle to the window, casting its beam into just one corner of the room. But it was getting stronger, the room was warmer and another day was beginning as though nothing had happened.

He laughed harshly, the sound echoing back from the bare walls of the room. Lucky old sun, lucky old day. It comes and goes and feels no pain; unaffected by the horrors it illuminates, or the beauty it may discover.

What beauty? he thought, savagely. Was there anything left worth illuminating? Then he remembered their walk on the promenade – was that only yesterday? The hard knot of grief started to rise in him again. He remembered how they had enjoyed yesterday. Just one morning ago they had woken to that same warm sun, basked in its glow, holding each other close. He remembered the people on the promenade, how they had dressed up for a Sunday in the middle of a war. He remembered how she had clung to him and what she had said. And then he knew what he had to do.

He stood up and went to a cupboard. Inside there were several blankets. He selected a red one and returned to the bed. He placed it down on the bed beside her and rolled her cold body on to it, wrapping it round her tightly. He could still not bear to cover her face. He lifted her up easily and carried her from the room. The long, narrow passage was empty. He walked along it

252

unhurriedly until he came to the stairwell. Still he had seen no one. As he descended the circular stairs he passed a body lying awkwardly, twisted, against the wall, then another. He did not look at them, nor did he hesitate. His work here was finished.

As he came down to the ground floor, a medic and a nurse were examining a body lying behind the reception desk. Nurse Setta didn't see him at first, not until his feet crunched on a piece of broken glass. She stood up as he walked towards the wide, double front doors.

She could see that the Palestinian was dead. She looked up at Kass. His face was drawn, dark stubble on his chin, his eyes still bloodshot from weeping. He looked neither right nor left, staring straight ahead at the daylight beyond the doors of the hospital. He did not see Setta.

She made as if to say something, then stopped, realizing there was nothing to say, nothing that made any sense. This was a private grief that could not be shared or eased. Setta knew then that the doctor was leaving, that she would not see him again. She walked quietly to the open doors and watched him place the body tenderly on a stretcher in the back of one of the parked ambulances.

He got into the driver's seat and drove away. He did not look back.

Kass didn't use the siren. There was no need – he wasn't in a hurry. The streets were empty this early in the morning. No one was venturing out until they were sure that the lull of the night would continue.

Kass drove easily. He was getting used to the debris strewn around the roads, and automatically took evasive action to avoid it. The narrow streets were not, as yet, receiving the sun. Not until later in the day when it was overhead would it penetrate down into these dirty, rubbish-strewn areas. The acrid smell of burning rubbish assailed his nostrils as he negotiated his way towards his destination. Then it cleared as he once more drove down a wide street. He turned into a familiar courtyard and drew quickly up outside the doors of the convent. He switched off the engine and sat still in the driving seat, listening. There was nothing – no sounds of conflict yet, this Monday morning, just some birds in the bushes close to the railings. They chirped loudly, welcoming the warmth of the day.

Kass felt disconnected from it all. He could hear the sounds and see his surroundings, but he was isolated from them, inhabiting a strange world that tunnelled his reactions solely down to what he was physically doing. He saw a curtain move behind one of the windows, and he got out of the ambulance and walked around to the back. He lifted Nazira's body from the stretcher and carried her up the steps to the front door. As he reached it, it opened. Sister Christina stared, shocked at his haggard face.

Kass stood quietly before her, holding Nazira's body. He didn't speak – he wanted to, but somehow he could not articulate the words in his head. In the event, they were not necessary.

Sister Christina looked at Nazira's face and, realizing instantly that the American was close to complete collapse, she opened wide the door and led him once again to the small room where he had earlier carried Melissa. He placed Nazira on the same couch, then stood, his arms limp by his sides as the nun came in and closed the door behind her. She pushed a chair forward and took Kass by the arm, seating him in it. He didn't protest.

Sister Christina went to a small table in the corner and poured some water into a glass. She gave it to him and he drank it in one swallow. She refilled the glass and passed it back to him. He thanked her. It was the first thing he had said since he regained consciousness.

The nun stood close to him and examined the wound in his head. The blood had dried hard where it had run down his neck, and the collar of his shirt was bloodstained. She left the room for a moment, then came back with a basin of warm water and some cotton wool. Gently, she began to wipe away the coagulated blood, until she could see the place where the blow had struck. The cut on his scalp, though long, was superficial. He had been lucky. Sister Christina stuck a piece of plaster over it, then wiped away the blood from round his neck.

Through all this Kass did not speak. He just sat quietly, staring at the wooden blocks of the polished floor, thinking about the man's face he had distorted from the pattern of the tiles in Nazira's room. He looked across at her, still wrapped in the red

254

blanket on the couch. She appeared to be asleep. His professional eye was blinded. He could not see the slow setting of her features, the stiffening of her limbs. He could only see what he wanted to see. Instinctively, his mind was protecting him, helping him to survive.

He thanked the nun again, watching her tidy away the basin and the bloodstained cotton wool. 'She died this morning,' he said suddenly.

Sister Christina crossed the room slowly and stood in front of him.

'It was the Damour Brigade – they killed her in the hospital.' She waited quietly. It was not the time to speak yet.

'I brought her here – I couldn't leave her in the hospital, you see. I want her to be buried here . . .' He stopped, thinking of something. 'I don't know what religion she is. If there are any problems . . .' He stumbled to a halt.

Sister Christina shook her head. 'There are no problems, doctor. She helped us when we needed . . .'

They buried her in the small garden behind the shell of the chapel. Both of them dug the grave. Sister Christina abandoning her veil and one of her outer garments as the heat of the day increased.

The hard physical activity gradually lifted Kass out of his mental oblivion. When the nun tired he insisted she rest. Instead, she returned with cold drinks and sandwiches. Amazingly, he found he could eat. The worst part was having to fill the earth in on top of her body. Each thud as it fell on her made him feel sick with grief. Only the presence of the nun, toiling away beside him, prevented him from breaking down. Then, at last, it was done.

Sister Christina said a prayer. Kass did not hear it. He could only see Nazira's face, feel her body pressed against him. He stared at the mound of earth sightlessly, and slowly became aware that the nun had stopped. He looked to her, and she inclined her head slightly.

'I think we ought to go inside now.'

She led him around the chapel to the cool passage, and back to the room. There was only one thing left for him to do. He asked the nun if it would be possible. There was not a lot to say. Sister Christina understood full well his reasons for the request, and he made it clear that it was his intention to go home now.

Normally such a request would have to receive dispensation from a much higher authority. But for the moment, here in this convent, Sister Christina was the sole representative of her Church. No one would know. As far as the Church was concerned, Melissa would have died in the atrocity of the chapel.

Kass drove away with the child in the seat beside him. He waved once to Sister Christina as he steered the ambulance through the gates. Then she was gone, a small, black-clad figure, standing in an open doorway.

Kass looked down at the child beside him, and smiled to reassure her. 'We're going for a ride on a boat,' he said.

Rousseau had decided on Sunday, when Kass had not come to his bedside, that he was going to get out of the hospital next day, one way or another. He had tried to walk while the screen had been around his bed and, although his leg was stiff and painful, he could manage it – not well, not easily, but he could move. It was to save his life: events precipitated his departure.

When the explosions occurred downstairs he had lain quite still, listening. He heard the screams, the panic spreading through the hospital like a virus. He guessed what was happening.

The ward was silent. It had emptied of everyone except those who could not move. Rousseau knew that he couldn't run and that if he tried to he would only be caught, and probably murdered. He swung his legs out of the bed. The floor was cold, as cold as the sweat trickling down beneath his armpits. Quickly he removed the screen. It was bound to attract attention. He looked up and down the ward. Only the night light shone dimly over the abandoned beds. Two badly wounded PLO men lay terrified in their cots – they knew what to expect.

Rousseau could hear boots thumping closer down the corridor. He did the only thing he could: he crawled under the bed and prayed. He heard the doors of the ward crash back against the wall. He saw the boots thud down the aisle between the beds.

Then the screams of the PLO men as they pleaded for their lives. They were butchered, bayoneted to death, then shot to be sure there was no flicker of life left in their bodies.

Rousseau hardly breathed. He clung to the floor, sweating with fear, his smell strong in his own nostrils, certain that it would betray him.

They ransacked the staff room further down the passage, looking for anything of value. When they found nothing, they smashed the furniture with their rifle butts and sprayed ammunition haphazardly round the room. Suddenly the ward was full of ricocheting bullets as they shot out the windows in an orgy of fury. Rousseau expected to die as one of the bullets buried itself in the wooden floor, half an inch from his head. Still he didn't move or make a sound.

He heard their raucous laughter grow fainter as they moved down the corridor to find another ward. He remained beneath the bed all night, not venturing from his simple hiding place until light began to grey the floor around his bed.

He crawled out and slowly, with infinite care, made his way down the staircase to the lower floor. The lobby was now a hive of activity. He was half an hour behind Kass.

Medics were carrying out bodies from the wards, and placing them in long rows on the dusty forecourt. Nurses helped where they could; there was not much they could do. No one, as yet, had been found alive.

At first the Frenchman was unnoticed as he limped down the winding staircase in his pyjamas – perhaps because he was not Lebanese, or perhaps because no one expected him to be alive. It was Nurse Setta who saw him first. She rushed up to him as he reached the bottom step, but before she could put an arm around him, he held up his hands and yelled at her, 'Leave me!'

His voice echoed up the empty stairwell and Setta stopped dead in her tracks. The lobby was suddenly still and quiet; eyes watched him.

Rousseau was breathing heavily from the exertion and the pain in his leg. But no one here was going to touch him. He had to get across that lobby himself – he had to get to the hotel. He looked at Setta. 'I'm OK, just leave me. Is that clear?'

Setta nodded. She understood well enough the stress he was under. Her own escape had been a matter of pure luck. The Damour had not put a guard on the emergency stairs and exit. She had managed to get out and hide in the grounds until they left. She moved aside, waving the others back too, until there was a clear passage to the doors for the Frenchman.

Gingerly he stepped down the last step and stopped, swaying slightly on the floor. One of the medics made as if to help, and Setta called out sharply, 'Leave him.'

Rousseau looked at her, his eyes glittering with determination. He started to limp slowly across the lobby; no one moved to stop him. His pyjamas were torn and stained – stubble dark on his chin. He looked a faintly ridiculous figure, slightly overweight, but nobody in the hospital was laughing.

He reached the steps outside and began to descend them painfully. He heard a shout and stopped, looking towards the entrance of the courtyard. Armand was standing beside the open door of a car with Kemp. They both started to run towards him.

He waited, swaying, as they dashed up the steps – then sat down abruptly as they reached him. He glanced up at their anxious faces. He smiled suddenly. 'So where's the equipment? How are we going to cover this without camera and audio?'

Kemp stared at him in amazement. 'Are you kidding?' He looked up at the hospital. 'What happened here last night?'

Armand knelt down beside Rousseau. 'Are you OK? We heard that there had been a massacre . . .'

Rousseau was not prepared to talk about it, not yet – not if he was going to get through this ordeal. He would do his report on camera. 'Armand, get the equipment from the car, we are going to shoot this.'

They looked at him disbelievingly. Kemp waved an arm in exasperation. 'You can't do a front job, not in your condition.'

Rousseau stared at him without expression. 'Get the camera, Jack – I want to do it. I must.'

There was a stubborn determination about him that brooked no argument. And the Canadian could see the possibilities . . . Rousseau could be one of the few survivors. An interview now, exactly the way he was, would be dynamite. His instincts as a cameraman overwhelmed any objections he might have made on humanitarian grounds. 'OK, but don't move, we'll do it right here on the steps, just as you are. You stay with him, Armand. I'll bring your stuff as well.'

And that's how it was done. Rousseau sat on the steps in his pyjamas and told the world what had happened to him, and to those less lucky than himself in the hospital. The strain around his eyes, the monotone in his voice, said more than any words about the horrors he had witnessed. And as he talked, the medical staff were still carrying out the bodies behind him. They were to get worldwide exposure of the hospital atrocity. It was to become the top news item for all of twenty-four hours. Then the media moved on, hungry for the next item.

After they had taped Rousseau's report, they put him in a taxi and sent him back to the hotel. Kemp and Armand then moved inside the hospital. They taped the ward where he had hidden beneath the bed, and the remains of the PLO soldiers who had been slaughtered. Kemp knew they really didn't need the footage. Rousseau's distressed report had said it all.

Even the staff at the Commodore, who had seen practically everything, were mildly surprised at Rousseau's condition. He was limping badly and his heavily bandaged leg could be seen through his ripped pyjamas. The reception manager insisted on accompanying the Frenchman up to his room.

Rousseau accepted the unwanted assistance with as much grace as he could muster. Then, at last, he closed the door to his room. He was alone.

He moved immediately to the telephone and called the American Embassy. They were relieved to hear from him at last, and gave him his instructions. They were quite explicit.

He washed, shaved and changed, checking the wound in his thigh. As far as he could tell it had not reopened – it was stiff and painful, but he could operate. From a small compartment beneath one of the lighting boxes he took a Beretta 9-millimetre hand gun, and a shoulder holster. He checked the magazine: twenty rounds – it was full. He slammed it in with the palm of his hand, then strapped the holster on carefully and put on his jacket. He glanced in the mirror. He looked a hundred per cent better, hardly recognizable as the wreck who had come into the hotel half an hour before.

He took the elevator down to the lobby and wrote a note for Kemp and Armand, which he left with reception. There were plenty of cabs outside in the narrow street. The ride to the checkpoint was uneventful. The usual barrage of shellfire was falling somewhere on the battered city – but it *was* usual, it had become the norm.

He paid off the driver and walked painfully down to the green line crossing. No one was swimming in the bomb crater today, though it was just as inviting as the sun rose hot and unremitting above the mountains behind Beirut.

There were two men at the checkpoint. One of them was Elias Mourad, the man they had seen on their arrival and who had subsequently taken them to the area where they found the Lebanese woman in the basement.

Mourad and Rousseau recognized each other instantly.

'I'm glad to see you,' Rousseau said. 'We thought you might have been hit when you disappeared that day.'

The PLO man stared at him unblinkingly. 'Where are you going?'

Rousseau shifted his weight slightly, wincing.

Mourad pointed to his leg. 'What happened?'

The Frenchman waved a hand dismissively. 'Nothing, just a minor injury – a scratch.' He didn't like these questions, and he didn't want to be held up.

The PLO man eyed him suspiciously. 'Pull up your trouser. I want to see.'

Reluctantly Rousseau did so. The heavy bandaging was now slightly stained with his blood.

Mourad examined it briefly. 'Just a scratch?'

Rousseau didn't reply. He adjusted his trousers, covering the bandages.

Mourad made up his mind. 'You are coming with me.'

Rousseau protested. 'Why? I've got to get to Jounieh, there's a deadline.'

'It can wait,' Mourad said shortly. The Frenchman was the

second person from the original party to leave West Beirut this morning. He wanted to know more. 'Come on,' he said.

Rousseau had no choice. The sub-machine-gun the PLO man was holding loosely would have cut him down before he could do anything. And there was his leg. He cursed roundly in French and followed Mourad back up the road, then across the battle-scarred terrain behind the makeshift swimming pool to a half-demolished building.

Inside it was cooler. Some PLO men were lounging around, reading magazines or eating. They watched curiously as the Frenchman was led to a small room. Mourad threw back the door and motioned him inside. Rousseau hesitated.

'It's all right, there are no locks. I want you to answer a few questions, that's all.'

Rousseau went in. There was a table and two chairs, nothing else. He sat down, glad to take the weight off his leg. The PLO man sat opposite. He tossed his hat to the floor. 'Now tell me about your wound.'

Rousseau explained what had happened. How they had gone back to see the woman in the basement a second time at Nazira's insistence – and how they had come under fire on their return.

The PLO man nodded. 'And were you taken to the hospital?'

'Yes – I was unconscious for some of the time.'

'Who treated you?'

'The American, Doctor Kass. You remember he came in with us.'

Mourad remembered all right. 'When did you leave the hospital?'

'This morning. I told you I had to get to Jounieh.'

'That's right, you did.'

The PLO man studied him from behind his dark glasses. Kass had driven through the checkpoint earlier in an ambulance with a small child. Mourad had asked him about Nazira, and the American had reacted strangely. There had been a look in his eyes that he found difficult to understand. He had said he hadn't seen her. It was only after Kass had driven off with the child that Mourad had identified the look. It was despair.

He repeated the question to the Frenchman. 'Have you seen Nazira?'

Now Rousseau understood. This was the reason he had been brought here. How much did Mourad know?

'You heard about the hospital?'

Mourad nodded. 'Yes . . . you were very lucky to get out.'

'They murdered everybody – I saw no one else alive.'

'It was the Damour,' Mourad said. 'We knew what they would do if they got the chance.'

Rousseau looked steadily at the PLO man, wondering how he would react. 'Nazira was in the hospital. Nurse Setta told me. She had been hit by shrapnel, but she was all right. Then . . .'

The PLO man was sitting very still. 'Then?'

'Yesterday evening . . .'

Mourad didn't speak. She was dead; he knew that now. He thought about the American doctor – that explained the look. He had known, but hadn't told him. He'd guessed that he would not let him through. At least, not until he'd extracted all the information. He took off his glasses and stared down at the floor. He heard the Frenchman speak. 'I'm sorry.'

Mourad looked up. 'Yes . . .' Rousseau's eyes were sympathetic. 'Yes, perhaps you are. She is a loss, I will remember her.'

He remembered how it had been in the hotel room. He had not enjoyed having his balls cut off by a woman, particularly a Palestinian woman. But he understood why she was the way she was – she was a product of the camps. But they needed women like her, and now she was dead. Strangely, he felt relieved. He didn't know why, nor did he analyse it. But, instinctively, he had regarded Nazira as a threat. He needed to know more – what had been her relationship with the American?

Mourad sat quietly, unmoving. The Frenchman waited a decent interval, then coughed, and looked at his watch. 'I have to go.'

Mourad looked up sharply. 'I'm sorry, that will not be possible, not yet.'

Rousseau sat quite still. He had to get out – reach Jounieh. It was imperative. He thought about the gun in his holster, but he knew that with his injury he'd never make it. He would have to bide his time.

Mourad watched him, surprised he had not protested further – perhaps there was nothing. He would see. He reached out and picked his hat up off the floor, jamming it on his head, then he put on his dark glasses. His image was back in place. 'This will not take long,' he said.

CHAPTER
TWENTY-EIGHT

Morning came brightly over Jounieh. The early half-light quickly dissipated and the foggy tendrils that had gathered in the harbour, stretching their grey fingers into the port area, soon disappeared as the sun rose high enough over the mountains to burn off the vapour.

The four vehicles were almost impossible to see unless viewed directly. The Commander was satisfied. His men had done a good job digging them into position at the base of a steep slope that totally commanded a wide sweep of the port and harbour, which was in a direct line, just two miles away, and nearly 2,000 feet below.

The weeks of training on camouflage and field cover had paid off. They had made excellent progress, reaching the coastal area in the early hours of the morning, which gave them the time they needed to seek and find the right position for the attack on the port. That would come later in the day, once he was sure the bullion was on board.

Distance lent charm to the port. It looked bright and pretty, nestling in the protection of a natural dip in the coastline. The heat and the dust, the flies and the smells were all blown away on the wind. From this height the two vessels looked like toys, their white hulls standing out clearly in the Mediterranean sun – the hospital ship fat and squat, Sea Victory much smaller. Both were well within range.

The tank, a Merkava, built in Israel, was being used for the first time this year. The M68, rifled barrel of the gun could project an armour-piercing 120-millimetre shell a distance of well over two miles. The two BM24 multiple rocket systems could fire twelve rounds apiece. Their range was better, nearly seven miles. The steep slope of the hill gave him the angle he required for the tank's weapon system. The rear, elevated on the slope, lowered the barrel, giving him the right projection *for hitting his targets in the port below. The logistics and ammunition had already been checked. The gun and rocket-launchers were trained on the two ships, waiting for the order.*

The signal from Makarion would come in morse, and in the code it had always done. Voice transmissions would not be used – they could betray their presence.

Everything was ready.

Forester was bending over the chart table, trying to work out what routes the Israelis would be using as they spread out from their encirclement of Beirut. There was a light knock on the door. He turned. It was Makarion, carrying a small briefcase. 'Good morning, Captain.'

Forester stood upright. 'Morning.'

'I thought you ought to know the bullion is on its way from Beirut. It should be here soon.'

'How is it coming?'

'By car.'

'Car?'

Makarion was unconcerned. 'Three, to be precise. It was necessary for safety. If it came in a security van, it would be an obvious target.'

Forester was dubious. 'Let's hope they make it.'

Makarion smiled. 'They will.'

Forester rolled up the chart and put it back in its case. 'Right, I must warn my crew.'

Makarion shifted the briefcase from one hand to another. 'Yes, of course. I'll stay here if it's all right, Captain.' He stepped out of the wheelhouse and stood by the rail.

Forester passed him and started to climb down the companionway. He looked up. 'If you see them coming, give me a yell.'

Makarion waited until he was sure Forester was gone. He moved into the wheelhouse and placed the briefcase carefully on the chart table. He opened it and began to work swiftly and efficiently. He had practised this exercise many times and knew exactly what he had to do. He paused from time to time, listening carefully, but no one came in and no one disturbed him.

When he had finished he quietly closed the briefcase and

looked around the wheelhouse, examining it minutely. It looked undisturbed; nothing betrayed his task – everything was in place, as it should be.

He walked back out to the rail and leaned on it casually, watching the narrow road that wound its way down into the port area – waiting for the arrival of the bullion.

Forester leaned across the bar in the saloon and addressed himself to the others. 'You know what to expect. There will be sixteen cases, each weighing between one hundred and fifty and one hundred and sixty pounds. We've decided that the best place for them is in the bathroom, next to the main cabin.'

He glanced at Annabel. 'Are Mrs Dawson and the children still asleep?'

Annabel shook her head. 'I don't know, I imagine so. I haven't heard anything yet. I expect they're dog tired.'

'Right. Well, we'll try to get it into the bathroom without disturbing them – the fewer who know of its existence the better. Which means' – he turned to Rhys and Henshaw – 'that we get it on board as fast and with as little fuss as possible. Is that clear?'

Rhys scratched the stubble on his chin. 'Might be a good idea if we used the trolley to wheel it up the gangplank.'

Forester agreed. 'Yes, it should take it – and it'll be a lot quicker than trying to lug it on board . . .'

Henshaw butted in. 'I'll organize that, Skipper. I know where it is.'

'Fine . . .' Forester paused. 'Once we have it aboard I want to get out as quickly as we can. But there is a problem . . .'

They waited for him to continue.

'If we try to leave before our normal evening departure, we may get held up by the gunboats.'

Rhys looked sceptical. 'There's no guarantee they won't stop us anyway, just for the hell of it.'

Forester accepted that. 'Yes, I know. But it might be better to follow normal procedures. Remember, this time we have no diplomats or ambassadors on board.'

'Just the gold,' Henshaw said sardonically.

Forester eased himself up from the bar. 'That's right, *just* the gold.'

Rhys caught the emphasis. He looked at him curiously. 'Do you mean that it's cause and effect? No politicians *because* we are carrying bullion?'

Forester took a cigar from his shirt pocket, and unwrapped it thoughtfully. 'Yes, that's right. It could also mean that there are no politicians this trip because we don't need them. Instead, we have the gold.'

Henshaw was puzzled. 'Wait a minute. Are you saying that we only got through before because we carried some bigwigs from the embassies?'

Forester knew there was no going back now. Annabel had heard what Hatan had said in the restaurant about the bullion coming from an American bank. She knew as much as he did. But the others had a right to know what was on his mind. Their lives were at stake too. 'Yes, I think that's true. I've a feeling that this ship has been used in some way – that we were meant to get through the blockade.'

Rhys glanced at Annabel and Henshaw, then back to Forester. 'Why? What's the reason? What makes you think that?'

Forester surveyed them all, trying to put it all together – all the niggling little worries and suspicions. 'OK,' he said finally, 'this is how I see it. The first thing that happened was the business of the war insurance. That came right out of the blue. We were given cover which is practically unobtainable for a civilian craft working in these waters.

'Two: until now, we have always carried some diplomatic people, particularly US diplomats, on our trips, either in or out. They were never sought by us, but they were always made available. Remember how the American ambassador suddenly arrived when we could make no contact with the gunboats to get clearance on our first voyage out.

'Three: on the last trip into Jounieh we had a trio of so-called businessmen on board. They were not businessmen, not unless businessmen always travel with heavily armed bodyguards these days. They stayed firmly apart. Even at dinner they would not talk to each other until the two ambassadors left the table.'

He paused, thinking about the next part. 'Then, later that night, when I was at the wheel, I did a routine radar check, and we were *surrounded* by a fleet of ships – some of them mighty big ones. By dawn, when we came into Lebanese waters, they'd gone. I think they were protection.'

Henshaw was incredulous. 'Who for – the businessmen?'

'That's right, only they were not businessmen.'

Annabel sat down on one of the stools. 'They didn't like each other very much. They could be involved in the political situation here.'

Forester nodded. 'That's right, and there was also an American with them.' He let that sink in for a while. 'And now we have this bullion going out. This time, no politicians, but the gold is from a US bank.'

Rhys shook his head. 'What does it all add up to?'

'I'm not sure. I don't know if the Americans and the Israelis are working together or not. But I don't like being used – not by anybody, and once we get back . . .' He let it hang there.

The silence was broken by Rhys. 'Meanwhile, do we take on the bullion?'

'That's right. If it means protection, and if that is all we have, we'd be stupid to turn it away.'

Makarion climbed noisily down the companionway and poked his head around the corner of the saloon door. He smiled at Forester. 'The cars are coming.'

Forester eyed him reflectively. He'd forgotten about Makarion.

Kemp and Armand carried their equipment wearily into the lobby of the Commodore. It was busy: a couple of journalists were standing by the Reuters wire machine, checking the news that spewed constantly from its chattering mouth. The Commodore was popular because it had the only wire service in and the only telex out. Word had it that the owner paid a high price to keep the privilege. But it clearly paid off in satisfied customers.

Associated Press, across the alley next door, slung a line between the rooftops and through one of the windows, to tie in with the hotel's machine. They paid dearly for that privilege, too.

The parrot was adding to the real sounds of war out by the empty pool – empty of water, but full of debris. The bird's realistic impression of a bomb screaming down upon them added to the general air of stress and tension.

Armand went across to the wire machine, while Kemp picked up their keys. The man behind the reception desk pulled out a note and gave it to the Canadian. 'Philippe Rousseau left this for you, Mr Kemp.'

He took it, puzzled. Left it? Why? Where had he gone? He should be in bed. He read the note, then walked irritably across to Armand. He waved the note. 'Rousseau has gone to Jounieh.'

Armand was shocked. 'What for? Does he say why?'

Kemp glared at the note again. 'He says he wants to check out the hospital ship there, and would we follow as soon as possible.' He handed the note to Armand. 'Here, read it.'

Armand skimmed through it, then shrugged. 'Maybe he thinks there's a good story there.'

Kemp was annoyed. 'Maybe, but he's in no condition to cover anything at the moment.'

Armand wavered uneasily. 'What shall we do?'

Kemp snatched at a piece of ticker tape and tore it angrily. 'We grab a quick cup of coffee and follow the silly bastard.'

Forester was sitting in a bath of gold. Gold bars, to be precise. He was surrounded by them. Heavy gold bricks weighing 400 ounces a time, six to a case, sixteen cases in all, worth more than twenty-five million dollars.

He had to sit in the bath – there was nowhere else to sit. Two of the packing cases had burst, ruptured by the weight and the difficulty they'd had lowering them below decks. Henshaw was perched on one of the cases, fingering a bar of gold, rolling it slowly round in his hands. He'd been doing it for some time.

Forester watched him. 'I know it feels nice, Henshaw, but you can't take it with you.'

The Australian grinned wickedly. 'I'm not too sure about that, Skipper. You see, if I do this long enough, I may get some of it under my fingernails.' He rubbed his forefinger and thumb together expressively. 'That could be worth something.'

Forester had to smile. 'I hope you make it, but don't rub that thing out of existence. It's supposed to weigh exactly four hundred ounces.'

The Aussie looked pensive. 'Do you think they'd notice half an ounce a bar?'

'They'd notice even a fraction of that. Now, help me repack this stuff. It's not good for my morale.'

Henshaw showed his teeth. 'I like it.'

The truth was that they were both a little dazed by the amount of instant wealth that surrounded them. Neither of them had ever seen so much gold in one place, or were likely to again. Forester's attitude was probably the healthier. It did no good to dwell on what this represented: how it could completely alter *all* their lives and bring the kind of wealth that most people only dreamed about. Gold lust was not a figment of the imagination. Too many normally level-headed people had succumbed to its lure.

Forester felt almost trapped by the shimmering, heavy bars he was handling. He was glad when he and Henshaw had finally got it safely repacked. He shut the bathroom door behind him and clipped the padlock shut.

It was quite ridiculous. Twenty-five million dollars! Normally, it was held deep below ground in huge time-locked rooms, and here it was now, shut in the bathroom of his cabin on *Sea Victory*, protected only by a padlock. The irony was, it was here for its safety!

It did not take much imagination to see how easy it would be for all of them to be hijacked at sea. Unless . . . Forester considered it. Was it possible he was about to be escorted back to Larnaca? He didn't really know – he was just guessing. But the thought made him feel a little less vulnerable.

Kass was surprised to see the West German hospital ship in Jounieh. He'd almost forgotten its existence. Someone had told him about it, but where and when? It must have been in the hospital. Then he remembered Nurse Setta mentioning that fresh supplies of medical equipment had arrived on the *Flora*. Was that yesterday or the day before? He found it difficult to concentrate his mind on anything.

But what had happened to Setta? Had she survived? He didn't know. He could remember very little about what had happened after he had recovered consciousness. All that stuck in his mind was the face on the tile. Two eyes and a little square beard that had disappeared as he tried to get up. Strange how the mind could be so selective about what it remembered, what it wanted to remember. He realized, wryly, that he was, in a way, discovering a few, neat medical and psychological truths about himself. But these were the kind of tests he could have done without.

Melissa bounced excitedly up and down beside him, pointing at the big hospital ship and the harbour. There was a healthy normality about her reactions that was reassuring.

Once again he caught himself thinking like a doctor. Perhaps it wasn't a bad thing: at least he was thinking. Until now he'd done things automatically, his mind like a tunnel, seeing only what was immediately in front of it.

He drove slowly along the stone quay, avoiding the small groups of refugees huddled into family units with their luggage and possessions. He stopped the ambulance close to the gangplank, and climbed wearily out of the cab. Melissa jumped out her side and made as if to rush to the edge of the quay. Kass called her to him and took her hand, leading her up the gangplank on to the stern deck.

As he did so Annabel came rushing out of the saloon. 'David!' She held out her arms and embraced him. He looked terrible, his face drawn and haggard, his eyes red-rimmed, a dark stubble of beard on his face. He seemed to have aged ten years since she had last seen him leaving the vessel here in Jounieh.

Melissa ran to the stern rail and was peering over the side at the murky waters of the port.

Kass squeezed Annabel's arm. 'Let me fetch her.'

He crossed the deck and took Melissa's hand. 'I'd like you to meet someone.'

As he led her towards Annabel, she began to resist, pulling away from him. Kass held on to her hand, but stopped. He leant down. 'What's wrong, Melissa?'

She glanced uneasily at the blonde Englishwoman and half hid herself behind Kass, holding on to his trousers.

He squatted down beside her. 'It's all right, that is Annabel. She's my friend.'

271

The child shook her head vigorously, not speaking.

Annabel called out softly to Kass. 'I'll be back in a minute. She may be thirsty.'

He nodded gratefully.

Annabel went back into the saloon and called down below, 'Tom, Henshaw, are you there?' She started to prepare a cold lemonade for the child.

Forester came up the ladder. 'What is it?'

She indicated the stern. 'Kass is back. He has a little girl with him.'

Forester started towards the stern. She called to him quietly. 'Wait . . .' She gestured for him to come closer.

Forester looked at her curiously. 'Yes?'

'He looks awful, Tom. And he has a little Lebanese girl with him. Something's wrong. I think the girl is frightened . . . be careful.'

Forester nodded understandingly. They'd had enough badly shocked people on *Sea Victory* to recognize the symptoms. He strolled casually through to the stern.

Kass was sitting on a seat, holding the child on his knee. He looked up as Forester appeared. 'Hello, Tom.'

Forester smiled, disguising his reaction at the American's appearance. He stuck out his hand. 'David, how are you?'

'I'm fine, I guess.' There was a terrible strain about him, a tension like a coiled spring held grimly in place.

Forester changed tack, turning his attention to the little girl. He pulled up a chair and sat opposite. 'Who's this?' He smiled at her. Melissa stared at him confidently, secure now she was in Kass's arms.

The American looked at him. 'This is Melissa. We met at Sister Christina's, didn't we?'

The child nodded brightly, and turned to Kass. 'Yes . . . you came with a lady.'

Kass's eyes went blank, he closed them. A hole had appeared inside him. He could feel his guts draining away until he was hollow – a shell. He could see her face, white against the sheet, a red stain spreading from beneath her side. He didn't know it, but he cried out.

He felt someone tugging at his shirt sleeve. Melissa's voice, alarmed in his ear. 'Wake up, wake up . . .' He opened his eyes suddenly. The child was gazing up at him, her eyes frightened.

Forester had stood up and Annabel was beside him. She put her hand on Forester's arm, signalling him to leave this to her. She proffered the American a tall, frosty glass. 'Drink this,' she ordered.

He took it automatically and sipped a mouthful. It was delicious, and he remembered the taste instantly. The boat ride across, the long cool night. The brandy sours . . .

Annabel offered the other drink to Melissa. The child looked at her doubtfully. Annabel smiled, trying to instil some confidence. 'It's lemonade, try some.'

Kass did not interfere. He realized it was important to build up trust between the child and Annabel.

Melissa looked up at him enquiringly.

'Yes,' he said, 'it's nice. I've got one.' He indicated his glass.

She reached out and slowly took the drink, holding it to her lips for a second before sipping it. She got the taste and her eyes brightened. She swallowed some more, then looked at Kass, repeating what he had said. 'It's nice.' She glanced at Annabel, and said it again, delightedly. 'It's nice.'

Forester smiled, too, feeling the tension relax. But he was deeply concerned about the American doctor. He was under stress, holding something back, and it was tearing him apart.

CHAPTER

TWENTY-NINE

The signal from Makarion came in loud and clear, corroborating what the Commander had already observed through his binoculars: the bullion was on board, stored amidships in the bathroom.

Makarion had overheard the discussion in the saloon between Forester and his crew. Forester's suspicions confirmed what the Commander knew already: they were not just carrying out refugees, and in this instance, bullion; the boat was also being used, under US protection, to provide a safe debating platform. Makarion also confirmed that the back-up operation was now in place. All that remained was the timing.

The attack on Jounieh was set for 1200 hours. At noon the port would be busy, and maximum impact would be obtained.

In his office on the top floor, Makarion packed his transmitter into its battered suitcase and hid it in the ventilation shaft for the last time. After this operation he was to fade. Jounieh was getting too hot.

Melissa was fast asleep, bedded down on Henshaw's bunk. She had grown drowsy after eating a late breakfast. Annabel had been surprised and delighted by her healthy appetite, and the child had enjoyed helping prepare the food in the galley. It was a good sign that she was sleeping so peacefully.

Kass was a different matter. Both Forester and Annabel were worried about him. He had seemed to regress once he had passed the responsibility of Melissa over to them. He sat silently in one corner of the saloon, staring blankly down at the deck between his feet. He hadn't moved or spoken, except monosyllabically to direct questions, and it was Annabel who had suggested that Forester get him off the boat for a while. There was plenty of time before they were due to sail that evening and perhaps, if the two were alone together, Forester might be able to loosen him up – find out what had happened.

Forester had driven off in the ambulance, taking the American with him up into the mountains above the town. The port was claustrophobic and jammed with people – up there it would be cooler and peaceful. It might work.

Annabel, Henshaw and Rhys started to board some of the early arrivals soon after Forester and the American had departed. They checked each name against the manifest Hatan had prepared. In addition to Mrs Dawson and her three sons, and now Kass and Melissa, they were carrying just over a hundred refugees, all of them Lebanese; no diplomats or politicians on this trip. But not all of them were ready to come on board yet. They were getting used to the process and, traditionally, the Lebanese were not good seafarers. Since departure was not until seven that evening, many who had their authorization preferred to stay on dry land until later.

A small crowd of people without the necessary papers were hanging around the dock, waiting to see if some did not turn up. It was a forlorn hope, but Annabel had taken their names in strict rotation so that, should a space become available, it would be taken fairly. The processing was the most heartbreaking task of all. Some still offered bribes, others simply begged Annabel to take their children, not caring if they were left behind. All she could promise was to take as many of them as she could, once the manifest was full. There might be some leeway, but not much.

She had just finished listing the names and was climbing the gangplank back to the stern, when she heard a car draw up on the dock behind her. She looked round. Jack Kemp and Armand were climbing out of a battered taxi. The Canadian saw her and waved, then paid off the driver. Annabel ran back down the gangplank and through a small crowd of Lebanese. They stared curiously, some resentfully, as she greeted them, fearing that some spaces were going to be taken. But they need

275

not have worried. Kemp and the Frenchman were looking for Rousseau, not seeking to get back to Cyprus.

Armand dumped his heavy tape recorder on the stone quay and kissed Annabel on both cheeks, smiling broadly. He liked the blonde Englishwoman; they both did.

Kemp took her hand a little more formally. 'How are you?'

Annabel was delighted to see them.

'We're fine – it's a bit like old home week today.'

Kemp glanced at Armand. 'Why . . . have you seen Rousseau?'

Annabel shook her head. 'No, but David Kass turned up here earlier. Where is Philippe?'

The two men picked up their equipment and began to walk towards the vessel. Armand was worried. 'We don't know. He left a note at the hotel to say he was coming up here, to see if there was a story on the hospital ship. We've checked there and they haven't seen him either.'

They climbed the gangplank, Annabel leading. She waited until they were safely on deck. 'Well, he's not been here. Does he usually go on ahead?'

Kemp was puzzled. 'No, he doesn't – we usually cover everything together. But today was different.'

'In what way?'

'There was a massacre at the hospital in West Beirut. Rousseau was there when it happened – he was receiving treatment for a wound in the leg. But they didn't find him, he got out all right.'

'They?'

'The Damour Brigade.' Kemp looked at her curiously. 'Didn't Kass tell you about it?'

'No, he didn't. He had a little girl with him from a convent. He wants to try and get her back to America, I think. He didn't even mention the hospital.'

Kemp glanced at the Frenchman, then back at Annabel. He took a deep breath. 'You recall the Palestinian photographer who came out with us?'

'Nazira?'

'That's right . . .' He paused, remembering how Nurse Setta had shown them the room where she had been. 'She's dead.

The Damour killed her. She was in the hospital when they took over. She had a shrapnel wound, and Kass was treating it. The nurse told us she saw Kass carrying her out. He drove off with her body in an ambulance.'

Armand butted in, 'Where is he now?'

'Tom took him off in the ambulance . . .' She stopped, suddenly realizing. 'You don't think . . .?'

Kemp and Armand exchanged a look. The Canadian spoke. 'I don't know. He must have gone to that convent to pick up the girl; maybe he took Nazira there. He would have kept the ambulance because he could drive across the green line in that.'

Annabel was still uncertain, horrified at the thought of Nazira's body still being in the ambulance. She indicated the saloon. 'Let's go inside; I'll get you something.'

As she took the large flagon of brandy sour from the freezer, she told them how strangely Kass had been behaving. The reason was clear now.

Kemp sipped the cold drink. 'Do you think we could interview Kass when he gets back?'

Annabel was doubtful. 'No, no I don't. He's in a very bad way.'

Armand stood up and stared moodily out of the window towards the hospital ship. 'Besides, we have to find Rousseau first.'

Annabel filled another glass for herself – she needed it. She tried to keep her mind off what might be in the ambulance. 'Where do you suppose Philippe is now?'

Kemp held the cold glass to his forehead. He was worried. Maybe Rousseau hadn't made it across the green line – maybe something had happened. He didn't like it.

The old ambulance rattled its way out of Jounieh and began to climb, protestingly, up the dusty road that led into the eastern mountains. Forester was driving. Kass sat beside him, gazing blankly through the windscreen as the road twisted and turned up the steeper inclines.

Forester was glad to get away from the overcrowded, stinking port. The heat he could take, but the garbage piled high in

277

every street and the clouds of flies sickened him. Even that was not the real reason; in his heart he knew he couldn't take the selection – who was to go, and who must stay. It was cowardly, but he'd been relieved to hand that over to Annabel. She was a better God than he.

Forester glanced at the American. He hadn't moved. 'Did you work in the hospital?'

At first he thought Kass wasn't going to reply and looked at him sharply; then Kass mumbled, 'Yes . . . I was in the hospital.' He stopped, then seemed to remember something. 'With Nurse Setta.'

'Setta?'

Kass stared at him as if slightly confused by the question. 'Yes, that's right; Nurse Setta. I don't know if she got away.'

Forester let that hang there for a while. The ambulance continued to toil up the road, a billowing cloud of dust rising behind it. It wasn't too difficult to see that whatever had happened at the hospital was affecting Kass deeply. Forester prompted him again. 'You mean, got out of the hospital?'

Kass nodded, but didn't enlarge.

'Was the hospital bombed?'

The American looked surprised. 'No, it wasn't bombed. The Damour Brigade came.'

Forester knew of the massacre in Damour during the civil war; he also knew about the Damour Brigade. Their fame had spread. In Jounieh, in Christian Phalange-held territory, they were respected. Their ruthlessness worried some, but not many. It posed another question. 'Is the hospital in West Beirut?'

'Yes.'

That made it clear. A hospital in a part of Beirut occupied by the PLO, raided by the Damour.

'They killed everybody, you know . . .'

The remark was shattering – all the more so for being so unexpected. Forester glanced at him, worried. He decided that it would be better if they were not in the ambulance – the road was hairy enough, without any loss of concentration. 'I'm going to pull in,' he said.

Kass stared past Forester at the coastline below them – he

could just see the road into Beirut. It all looked so peaceful from up here, the sea glittering under the sun like a thousand diamonds.

Forester found a track leading off the road. He pulled into that and switched off the engine. It was suddenly very quiet. They sat there for a moment. Forester threw open his door – it was baking hot in the metal box of the ambulance. 'Shall we walk?'

Kass did not answer, but he clambered out and they began to walk slowly, side by side along the track.

'Do you want to talk about it?' Forester waited without looking at Kass.

'They came last night . . .' Kass stopped, thinking of how his mug had shivered over the table when the grenades went off downstairs. 'I was in the staff room,' he said. His voice sounded hollow, empty. He found it hard to articulate . . . it had to be forced. 'Nurse Setta was with me.'

They stared out at the sea. The view was magnificent. Behind them, in the dried undergrowth and bushes, Forester could hear birds chirping loudly, calling to each other as the morning wore on and the sun got hotter. Forester bided his time. He sensed that Kass wanted to talk – but let him choose the moment.

'I ran down the stairs to the second floor . . .' He glanced at the Englishman. 'That's where Nazira was.'

'Nazira? The Palestinian lady?'

There must have been something in his voice. Kass turned to look at him. 'Yes, that's right. She had been wounded; there was shelling. I took her into the hospital myself.'

Forester shook his head. In a way he had been half expecting it. He remembered what Annabel had said about her.

The American must have guessed what was going through his mind. 'She was all right – I fixed the wound.' He looked at Forester, trying to find the right words. 'She'd changed, you see, she was very happy – we both were.' Then suddenly, 'It was her idea, you know, to try to get Melissa out.'

Forester was beginning to glimpse the truth, that Kass loved Nazira. Everything about his attitude, his defence of her, indicated that. 'Melissa will be all right, David.'

Kass accepted that. 'Yes, I know, I'm going to look after her.'
They resumed their stroll along the track.

'Nazira was still alive when I got there.'

The starkness of the remark, emerging from Kass's thoughts, and without any lead up, jolted Forester. He continued to walk contemplatively, keeping in step with the American.

'There were three of them, one on top, raping her. She was naked. The wound in her side had reopened.' The words came swiftly now, tumbling over each other. The dam had been broken, the horror poured out. 'There was blood all over the sheets beneath her; she was lying in it. She saw me standing in the doorway and she screamed at me.' He stopped and stared at Forester, his face contorted, trying not to cry. 'She asked me to kill her – she wanted to die . . .'

Forester faced him, there was nothing he could say. All he could do was be there, and listen.

Kass turned and began to walk faster. 'I tried to stop them. I didn't care if they killed me, too – I just wanted to stop them doing that to her. I dragged him off.' He fingered the cut in his scalp that Sister Christina had cleaned up. 'I don't remember anything after that . . .'

It wasn't true – he did. He remembered the man's face in the tile on the floor, then Nazira's face. He could see it, her dark hair spread out on the bloodstained sheet. He stopped and turned to Forester, his eyes tortured. 'She was dead . . . they'd killed her, left her lying on the bed.'

Forester saw the horror in his eyes. Kass sank slowly to his knees on the track, covering his face with his hands. His whole body shook with grief. He bent forward as racking sobs tore at him, releasing him from the pain.

Forester knelt down beside him and gently lifted him up, holding him in his arms until, slowly, he began to get control of himself.

Kass stepped back and Forester reached into his pocket and gave him his handkerchief. He started to walk along the track again, rubbing the tears from his face. 'I'm sorry,' he said.

'Nothing to be sorry for; I liked her, too.'

Kass looked at him, surprised. 'Did you?'

'Yes . . . That night on the boat, after we'd left Cyprus, I

280

found her lying asleep on the bench in the saloon.' He paused, remembering how she had looked. 'Her face was relaxed, like a child's. All that hardness had gone. I covered her with a blanket – she didn't wake up.'

Kass smiled to himself. 'She wasn't hard at all, really. It was just a shell, a protective thing. I expect she needed it, coming from one of those camps.'

A comfortable silence grew between them as they walked along the twisting track. The sea disappeared from view as they got into some wild scrub trees, which cut off the sun. Then, as they rounded a bend, it opened out again into a small clearing near the foot of a hill. They both stopped and stared.

A stone monument stood in front of a cemetery. The cemetery was not large: about fifty white marble crosses dotted the sightly sloping ground. Around it was a low stone wall. But it was what was on the crosses that transfixed them. Men were sitting down, leaning on them, asleep – about twenty of them, wearing the usual militiaman's uniform: green camouflage combats, some with dark glasses, some with hats. Oddly, they appeared to be unarmed.

Kass and Forester started to walk closer. It was only then that the Englishman realized that they were not sleeping. They were dead. The stench of death pervaded the air around them. Their bodies were draped over the white marble crosses – one of them still had a cigarette between his fingers, as though he had sat down casually for a smoke.

They stopped by the stone wall. The graveyard was well tended, the graves themselves free of weeds or shrubbery; only the dead militia seemed strangely out of place. Some of the bodies were already bloating, the life juices draining away into the dry soil, their clothing tight around them. Kass climbed over the wall and began to examine one of the bodies. Forester was so sickened by the smell that he moved away to the foot of the cemetery and stood in front of the commemorative stone at the entrance. It was a British military cemetery dating back to the Second World War. How or why they were here Forester wasn't sure, the stone did not make it clear, and he was hazy about Britain's role in this part of the world during the war.

Of one thing he was certain: he was getting no closer. He felt like throwing up and he marvelled at the American's clinical disregard of the smell. He waited for him to come back and checked the surroundings to see if there were any more bodies outside the cemetery . . . He froze for an instant, then looked casually away, directing his attention elsewhere. He'd seen something move. The uniform was camouflaged, but because of the quick change of position, he had been able to distinguish the soldier. He gazed up at the hill, trying not to appear as if he were looking for anything, keeping his body relaxed, when every instinct in him was urging him to run. If he did, he knew he would not get ten yards.

There was something up there, dug into the hill behind the graveyard. He turned away and began to stroll around the stone wall to where Kass was standing. He called out, trying to keep his voice as normal as possible. 'What do you make of it.'

The American gazed round at the other bodies. 'They're all Christian Phalange,' he said. 'And they have not been stripped of their possessions; only the weapons have been taken away.' He started to walk back to the wall. 'I think whoever put them here did so because this is consecrated ground. They had no time to bury them, and they knew they would not be disturbed here.'

He climbed over the wall and Forester began to walk slowly back towards the track. Kass fell in alongside him. As unhurriedly as he could, Forester asked the next question. 'How long have they been there, do you think?'

Kass shrugged. 'A few days – a week at most.'

'Do you think anyone will come back to bury them properly?'

'They might, eventually.'

By now they were almost within the shade of the trees. Forester spoke as quietly as he dared. 'Look, David, don't react, just keep walking back with me. I saw a soldier back there, a live one.'

Kass glanced at him quickly, aware of the sudden danger.

Forester continued, 'He was hiding behind some scrub up near the hill. There may have been others.'

Now they were under the trees, the shadows giving an

illusion of cover after the glaring sunlight, but they were still in full view of the hill behind them. Forester's flesh crawled as he waited for the impact of a bullet in his back. He tried not to think about it, concentrating his attention on getting the information across to the American. Kass wanted to turn and look back; the urge was almost irresistible. He controlled it. 'Did you see any others?'

Forester shook his head. 'No, but I did see a tank and what looked like a rocket-launcher dug in on the hill.'

They were beginning to approach a bend in the track.

Kass's voice rose an octave. 'What!'

'For Christ's sake, keep your voice down!'

'What do you mean you saw a tank?'

'There was one, and a rocket-launcher. They were both hidden and well camouflaged, but it was heavy armour all right.' He paused, glancing left and right into the scrub. 'And the soldier was an Israeli.'

Kass stared at him incredulously. 'Are you sure?'

'I think so – he moved pretty quickly, but I've seen that uniform before, in Haifa. He was certainly not militia.'

Now they were rounding the bend; still no one had opened fire. They didn't speak, continuing to walk as unhurriedly as they could, until they figured they were on safe ground. They stopped and looked back. The hill was out of sight, hidden by the bend.

Kass gripped the Englishman's arm. 'Why would the Israelis have hardware up here?'

Forester stared thoughtfully back the way they had come. 'I don't know. There are no PLO targets in this area. The Israelis control it anyway through the Phalange.' He turned and looked out, down the side of the mountain at Jounieh, nestling in its harbour below them. 'That's the only target they have – that's what their armour was lined up on.'

Kass stared down at the port. *Sea Victory* and the hospital ship stood out clearly in the harsh light. The thought occurred to both of them at precisely the same moment. The bullion! Maybe the Israelis wanted to sink *Sea Victory* and claim the bullion for themselves . . .

Forester began to run as fast as he could down the track,

towards the ambulance. He had to get back. Get his ship out to sea and out of range of that armour dug into the hillside behind them. He ran grimly, silently, concentrating every effort into moving as swiftly as he could. He didn't know how much time he had. Kass was right behind him. It was 11.41.

CHAPTER
THIRTY

The radio transmissions between Makarion and the Commander's Strike Force above Jounieh had been monitored and decoded. The messages lay on the Director's desk in front of him. Copies had already been sent to the Vice-President's office at the Pentagon, and the Israelis had been contacted. They had denied all knowledge of the Strike Force. Whether this was true or not remained a matter of speculation. If it was an Israeli force, they had certainly not received any instructions to countermand their operation. Everything coming in or going out of that area was on twenty-four-hour surveillance; nothing could slip through the net.

It was clear the Strike Force intended to begin its attack at twelve noon, local time. It was now for his superiors to decide whether they could risk action to prevent the attack and protect Sea Victory and the hospital ship in Jounieh.

The stakes were high. If they were Israelis — and everything indicated that was the case — then the rift if they were taken out would be enormous. The Israelis, as far as his department could tell, knew nothing of the real reason for the neutral vessel's voyages in and out of the Lebanon. Yet here was an Israeli Strike Force, set to begin an attack on the port of Jounieh that would destroy the ship and end the negotiations they had so painstakingly set up on Sea Victory.

On the other hand, if they allowed the attack to proceed and the truth about the US role ever emerged, that too would be politically unacceptable. The debate was taking place now. He had put in his recommendation as strongly as he could: Sea Victory had to be protected.

The decision was not in his hands, but he could deal with Makarion. Wherever his loyalties lay, he could be eliminated, and the order had been given. His operative was already in Jounieh.

There was precious little time left for the major decision to be made. Carrier aircraft were on stand-by, but still the order had not come. The politicians would have to make their move within minutes. It was 11.45 Middle East time.

The countdown had begun. Tension in the Strike Force rose as the time approached. Watches had been synchronized, the missiles loaded into the rocket-launchers. The main weapon of the tank was mounted to fire its armour-piercing shells directly down into the hospital ship. The more destruction they caused, the greater the impact they would have on world opinion.

On board Sea Victory *the bomb Makarion had hidden in the wheelhouse was ready to be fired at noon. Makarion himself would trigger the weapon by radio from his position in the shipping offices. He would wait for the bombardment to begin to camouflage the explosion. No chances were being taken.* Sea Victory *would be blown apart at noon.*

It was 11.50 hours local time.

The old ambulance, with its high chassis, tipped crazily on the sharp, corkscrew bend, threatening to overturn and cartwheel down the mountainside. For one terrifying moment Forester thought he had pushed it too far, but then the heavy rear pulled around in a wide arc, skidding sideways on the red dust of the unmetalled road, and he was able to compensate enough at the wheel to regain balance and steering. He kept his foot hard down on the accelerator, while Kass hung grimly on to the open window frame, trying to keep himself steady.

The ambulance bucketed and roared its way down the lower slopes towards the outskirts of the town. The road was too narrow to take more than one vehicle at a time, but they were lucky – nothing came up. Not that Forester had any thought of slowing down. His mind was fixed on one objective – his ship.

The cloud of dust rising behind them would be seen by whoever commanded those heights above him. He prayed that it would not trigger an immediate response. He needed ten minutes to get her away from the dock – please God, give him ten minutes.

They were into the town now, but Forester didn't slow down. He screamed at Kass, 'The siren! For Christ's sake, switch on the bloody siren.' The American searched frantically along the dashboard, looking for a switch. He pressed everything he could find – levers, buttons, switches. The light above the cab began to flash, then the siren started to hee-haw.

Forester had his fist hard down on the horn, and people scattered before them. Some chickens scratching for grain were not so lucky: feathers and fowl were flung brutally aside. He roared down the causeway that led to the dock. A taxi emerged from round the corner of the naval barracks, climbing the road. Forester and the cab driver both swerved to avoid each other, but they had no chance.

The front offside wing of the ambulance crashed into the taxi, flinging it sideways. The ambulance went out of control, smashing through a pile of garbage and coming to a halt, the front end hanging perilously over the edge of the causeway. Forester and Kass leapt from the smashed vehicle and ran along the cobbled, raised road. They heard a huge splash behind them as the ambulance toppled into the sea. They neither stopped nor turned round. The corner of the naval barracks blocked their view of the quay where *Sea Victory* was berthed. They kept on running.

Kass felt the air being sucked from his ears. It was as if he were in a train, with the window open as it entered a tunnel. He heard a strange whistling sound and, for a split second, he wondered foolishly if it were the parrot from the hotel imitating a shell.

It was no imitation. It went over their heads and into the dock, while a salvo of rockets hit the road in front of them, tracing a pattern of explosions across the barracks and beyond. The blast wave flung both men bodily sideways to the ground. Kass knew he had been hit. His leg was numb and he could smell cordite on his clothing. He looked down. The right leg of his trousers was torn and bloodied. He tried to tear open the material, then the pain hit him. He groaned, arching his back.

Forester was dazed. He could hear the explosions in the port area and a cloud of acrid, burning smoke rose above the roof of the barracks. He could hear people screaming. Kass was lying beside him, blood pumping from a wound in his leg. The temptation to leave him and run to the corner to see what had happened was almost overwhelming. He thrust it from his mind.

The wound was in the calf. It looked a mess, but he could see no bone splinters. He tore a strip from the trousers and tied it tightly round the wound. Kass groaned again. 'For God's sake leave me, get back to the boat.'

Forester didn't answer him. He gripped him under the arm and lifted him to his feet. Kass cried out. Forester grabbed his arm and put it round his shoulder. 'Come on, Doc, we've got some walking to do.'

Rockets and shells continued to plaster the area, hitting the town behind them as well as the docks. Forester half-carried, half-dragged Kass down the remainder of the causeway. They reached the corner of the barracks and staggered round it.

The hospital ship was smoking. They learned later that she had been hit directly by two shells, one in the wheelhouse and another exploding in her open hold. One had died there, and eight more were injured. Smoke and flames were billowing from a warehouse next to *Sea Victory*, enveloping her from their view. A sheet of flame shot up from the warehouse, dispersing the smoke for an instant and, in that brief moment, Forester saw his ship. Incredibly, she appeared to be undamaged, lying close to the quay, gouts of spray rising sporadically from the churning water of the harbour as rockets continued to zero in.

Forester gripped the American tightly. 'Come on,' he screamed, 'come on!'

At 11.55 Philippe Rousseau ordered the cab to stop beneath the shadows of the naval barracks, a hundred yards from the entrance to the shipping offices of Inter-Travel. He paid the driver, who had made good time after the hold-up at the checkpoint crossing.

Elias Mourad had continued to question him for nearly an hour before he decided to release him. Mourad knew that the PLO could not afford to antagonize the media; they needed all the support they could get. He had accompanied Rousseau back to the checkpoint and apologized for the delay. If Rousseau hadn't been so conscious of the passage of time, he could have sympathized with Mourad about Nazira's death. As it was, he bid the Palestinian goodbye as quickly as he could, picking up a cab on the other side of the green line.

The driver thanked him profusely for the big tip and pointed to the quay where *Sea Victory* was berthed. 'Is that the boat that goes to Cyprus, sir?' he asked.

Rousseau put his wallet back in his pocket. 'Yes, they sail between Larnaca and here.'

The driver looked up at him quizzically. 'Are there any others?'

Rousseau didn't know. 'There may be, I can't say.'

The driver stared at the dock stretching away beyond the British vessel. 'I think I'll go and have a look.'

Rousseau was becoming irritated; there was work to do. 'Please yourself.' He began to walk slowly, favouring the injured leg. He stayed close to the barracks, keeping to the dark shadow cast by the long building. The taxi drove past him towards the docks.

Rousseau stopped, and waited until it was out of sight. Then he resumed his slow progress towards Inter-Travel. He reached the entrance as a dejected Lebanese family emerged. They did not see him, and he slipped inside before the door closed. It was cool. The air-conditioning made the two large circular fans in the ceiling redundant – they served an almost decorative purpose. Although it was Monday the reception area downstairs was busy. Clerks behind desks were constantly having to repeat the same heartbreaking news: that the manifest was full and so was the waiting list.

No one noticed Rousseau slip from the main offices into the tiled passage that led to Albert Hatan's office. Rousseau moved silently, his rubber-soled shoes making no sound on the hard, shiny surface. He stopped outside Hatan's office and listened. At first he heard nothing, then he began to pick up the background noise from the VHF radio as the wavelength was changed.

Rousseau looked quickly up and down the passage. It was empty. He pulled the Beretta hand gun from its holster and screwed on a silencer, making sure it was tight, then he gripped the handle of the door. He eased it open very slowly until he could see inside the room. Hatan had his back to him. The old man was fiddling with the receiver waveband, grumbling quietly to himself; otherwise the room was empty.

Rousseau closed the door again without attracting Hatan's attention. He moved down the passage, still limping from the wound in his leg. He tried to relieve the pressure by moving the bandage slightly. It helped a little, but it still throbbed painfully. He came to the well of the staircase and looked up as it circled its way to the top floor. He started to climb. It was 11.58.

His leg hurt like hell; he touched the bandage again – it was wet. His hand came away red with his blood. He kept climbing as fast as he could. His instructions had made it clear where he would find his target where the signals had emanated from. Makarion's office was on the top floor. By the time he reached it he was breathing heavily, and the blood trickling down his leg was beginning to seep into his shoe.

The door was unlocked. Very carefully he eased it open. Makarion was standing with his back to him, staring out of the window down at the quay. On his desk was a small radio firing mechanism. Rousseau recognized it immediately; it was primitive but extremely effective. Not a sound broke the silence of the room.

Makarion glanced at his watch once more: it was almost time. He turned back to the desk, then stopped . . .

The Frenchman aimed the Beretta steadily at his chest. 'Move back, over there, against the wall.'

Makarion had no choice. He could not even reach the trigger before he was hit. Slowly he moved until his back was to the wall. Rousseau advanced across the room, covering the other man every step of the way. He got to the desk and, without ever moving his eyes from Makarion, he reached down and disconnected the trigger, then removed two high-powered batteries. He threw the mechanism to the floor and ground his heel into it, destroying it completely.

As he did so a huge explosion rocked the building, throwing him slightly off-balance on to his bad leg. The windows caved in from the blast wave, drowning his sharp cry of pain. Makarion threw himself across the room, crashing into the Frenchman as he tried to hold himself upright and get in a shot. They hit the floor together. Broken glass showered about their heads and thick, choking clouds of dust, shaken loose from the walls and ceiling, clouded the air around them.

They fought grimly, silently, as outside rockets and shells poured into the harbour. Makarion had his hand on the Frenchman's wrist. He smashed it brutally on the floor, cutting it on a piece of glass until Rousseau's hold on the weapon broke. At that moment Rousseau knew he was finished. He squirmed beneath the squat, heavy body of Makarion, trying to work himself loose – it was impossible.

Makarion remembered the bloodstained leg of the Frenchman as he had limped across the room. He drew back his own leg and dug his knee sharply into Rousseau's thigh. The pain was like a white-hot knife searing through his flesh. He screamed.

Makarion chopped his forearm down on the Frenchman's neck, choking off his cry. Rousseau could not force the arm from his throat. He struck out viciously with his free hand at the face above his head, hitting it time and time again. Blood spurted from Makarion's mouth, falling on to the Frenchman's face: still the arm on his throat did not move.

His strength was fading fast and the blows about Makarion's head were now weak. The arm pressed deeper down into his windpipe, cutting off the air.

Makarion felt the life go from the body beneath him as it convulsed once in death, then relaxed. He kept his arm in position for another minute, then rolled himself away, picking up the Beretta. Outside, the attack was still continuing. Their silent, bloody struggle had lasted a lifetime – but only a few minutes.

Makarion examined the remains of the bomb trigger mechanism – it was useless. He moved over to the window looking down at the quay. *Sea Victory* lay wreathed in smoke from the warehouse fire, but she was unscathed. He cursed savagely and whirled around, glaring at Rousseau's body. He fired four times – the silent, insignificant little plops of the weapon at odds with the horrific wounds they inflicted on the dead man.

He ran from the room and down the stairs two at a time –

there was still a way. He reached the ground floor and ran along the tiled passage, past Hatan's office, his feet crashing out a tattoo as the sound reverberated against the walls. His eyes were wild and he did not see the people he pushed through in the reception area. He threw back the door and ran out on to the dock road.

Forester was coming down the road towards him, supporting the American, hurrying towards *Sea Victory*. For an instant Makarion thought about killing him with the Beretta in his hand. Then he thrust the gun into his pocket and ran towards the Englishman, taking Kass's other arm and helping him to the boat. He wiped the blood from his face. Forester ignored it, assuming the injury had been caused by the heavy explosion. He was glad of Makarion's help.

Some of the refugees were panicking, trying to get ashore as the rockets hissed into the harbour around them. Forester saw one man staggering away from the boat carrying a heavy suitcase, trying to reach the shelter of the naval barracks. He didn't need to guess what was in the suitcase – probably all the wealth he possessed.

Kemp saw them first. He was standing beside the bridge, shooting as much tape as he could of the attack. He yelled to Henshaw, who was loosening the ropes forward. The Australian leapt ashore and helped to get Kass on board. The gangplank had already been pulled up on deck and they had to physically heave him over the side. Makarion and Forester quickly followed.

Rhys had come down from the wheelhouse to the stern deck. 'I was going to try and get her out to sea.'

Forester yelled at him above the roar of the explosions, 'Right, you take the stern lines. Henshaw, release forward. Let's get her out of here as fast as we can.'

A geyser of water spouted up over the decks, soaking them, emphasizing the point. Forester leapt for the ladder, shouting at Makarion, 'Take Kass into the saloon. Get Annabel to look after his leg.' He stopped, holding on to the rungs halfway up. He called to Rhys, 'Is she all right?'

Rhys was unravelling the stern lines. 'Yes, she's looking after the kids below – get the hell up there.'

Forester needed no further spur. He leapt up on to the upper deck and ran alongside the rail lines to the bridge. He plunged the starter, once, twice. She began to roar the second time. He glanced forward. Henshaw was clear. He ducked out of the doors and looked aft. Rhys waved him vigorously away. He wasted no further time: he threw the gears full throttle into reverse. The engines rose in crescendo, the screws biting hard at the shallow water, churning up the sediment and filth from the bottom, something Forester normally avoided. But today he had stronger priorities than the stench that began to pervade his nostrils.

The vessel started to pull back from her berth. Forester whirled the spokes of the wheel, dragging her stern first out into the main stream of the port exit. *Sea Victory* was forty feet from her original position when a rocket plunged into the spot she had occupied a moment before. The spout of water flooded the foredeck, spattering the lens of the video camera. Kemp swore, then realized it probably added to the effect. He did not stop taping, but held his vulnerable position close to the wheelhouse. Forester yelled at him to get under cover, but the Canadian was oblivious of everything except getting the action on tape. Below Kemp, on the foredeck, Armand crouched by the rail with a long sausage microphone poking out over the side, his recorder resting on the deck. Kemp panned right, taking in the dock area, the smashed upturned cab on the causeway and the half-sunk ambulance lying in the shallows. It was unreal.

All around them the combined weight of the assault was inflicting heavy destruction and loss of life – the noise was stupendous. Yet, as Forester struggled to save his ship and the lives of those on board, all that concerned Kemp and Armand was a recording of the event. It was brave, yet to Forester it made no sense. It seemed stupid, almost suicidal.

Rhys had gone below. He'd felt the deck timbers move beneath his feet when the second rocket exploded close to the hull. He heard the inrushing water before he saw it. The wooden hull had shifted slightly, trying to absorb the impact of the blast through the water. The leak had sprung around the exhaust outlet pipe, where the metal had remained immovable. The four bilge pumps were getting rid of some of it, but the water was rising – it would only be a matter of time unless something could be done.

Rhys clambered swiftly up on to the deck and ran to the wheelhouse companionway. He staggered inside, oil caking his hands and forehead where he had tried to keep the sweat from his eyes. The vessel was moving fast now, in reverse, back along the channel towards the main harbour. Forester didn't look at Rhys, all his attention fastened on getting her out without smashing into anything.

Rhys yelled above the roar of the engines, trying to make himself heard. 'We have a bad leak. The blast has shifted some of the timbers, we're taking water in by the exhaust pipe.'

A shell tore in overhead and instinctively Rhys ducked. Forester didn't move – the engineer doubted if he even heard it. The shell sucked the air from their lungs as it passed close overhead then plunged into a hotel near the water's edge. It seemed to rise in slow motion, like an opening flower. The walls collapsed outwards, the roof rising, then falling, before the whole structure fell in a huge cloud of red dust.

Rhys was staring mesmerized at the spectacle. Forester shouted at him, 'Can you fix it?'

Rhys tore his eyes from the clearing cloud of wreckage. 'I don't know, but I'm going to try – we have to cut the inflow down, or beach her.'

Forester weighed the odds, his mind racing. No way was he going to beach, certainly not here while they were still within range of the guns dug in on the mountainside. 'How much time before the bilges cannot cope?'

'A few minutes – five at most.'

'OK, get below, take Henshaw with you. Do what you can.'

Rhys nodded and ran from the wheelhouse.

The Commander had placed himself away from the armour, higher up the hillside where he could get a clearer view of the target area and direct the fire as accurately as possible.

The rocket-launchers were notoriously inaccurate. They blanketed a target, relying on weight of numbers to achieve a strike. Any directional skill was purely rudimentary. Which was why the back-up devised by Makarion was so vital. He could not understand why the bomb had

294

*failed to detonate once the attack had begun, and it was impossible to
make contact. There had been no answer to his frantic signals. He was
incensed at Makarion's failure, but there was nothing he could do about
that part of the operation. He concentrated his attention on the only
accurate weapon he had at his disposal – the gun mounted in the tank.*

*Several times he had observed rockets falling within feet of the vessel,
and once, at the beginning of the attack, the tank's weapon had almost
succeeded in destroying the ship. Now that it was under way it was
much more difficult. The range was changing constantly – he had to try
to guess where Sea Victory was going to be. Through his glasses he
watched the hotel collapse. It gave him a good guide as to the trajectory
of the shell. He rapidly gave instructions altering the range and angle,
trying to anticipate the vessel's position.*

*He checked his watch, timing the ship's progress through the channel
leading to the harbour. Time, distance and speed were crucial. Even if
the armour missed a direct hit, a strike within twenty-five feet should
be enough to cripple the wooden-hulled vessel.*

*One minute ticked slowly by. He now had the vital logistics. He fed
the information to his gun crew, working out an impact position for one
minute later. The tank's weapon was primed, aimed and ready to fire at
the position he'd given. The Commander watched the second hand tick
round. The gun crew waited for his command . . .*

Makarion had carried the American below to the main cabin
area, where Annabel was trying to calm Melissa and Mrs
Dawson's three young sons. He hadn't stayed with the women
– he wanted to be on deck; he needed to know if the Commander's barrage was going to succeed where his own operation
had failed. He raced back up to the stern deck, keeping as far
from the bridge as possible. If the ship was hit there would be
no chance of survival there.

He heard the shell scream overhead, felt the vacuum of its
passing, and watched, fascinated, as the hotel disintegrated on
the far bank of the channel. He wanted Sea Victory hit; he didn't
care if he survived or not. His chances of life were short anyway,
if this ship got away to sea again. His superiors did not take
kindly to failure and were quite ruthless when it came to
removing those who had not succeeded or were of no further
use.

He saw a pattern of rockets stitching a path into the dock area behind them, the spurts of water and thud of the explosions vibrating the hull beneath his feet. *Sea Victory* was almost in the clear. He started to move up to the wheelhouse.

The solution was now in his hands.

Forester scanned the docks on either side of the channel. It was rapidly widening as they approached the bend, prior to the harbour proper. There was room enough here for him to turn *Sea Victory*. Once out of reverse he could make better speed. It would also lessen the pressure on the exhaust outlet pipe.

Forester cursed savagely. He should have thought of that before.

At that precise moment the Commander ordered his gun crew to fire. Flames belched from the nozzle of the gun, propelling the shell from the barrel in a wide arc from the mountain to the narrow channel leading to the harbour.

Makarion reached the doorway of the wheelhouse as Forester started to spin the wheel around madly, at the same time adjusting the throttle controls of the engine. Makarion held on for dear life as the narrow-beamed vessel heeled over sharply, losing all forward momentum. The propellors stopped for an instant, then began to spin in the opposite direction, thrashing the grey water into a white foam. *Sea Victory* wallowed, stationary in the channel, caught between backward and forward movement.

The high-pitched whine of the approaching shell was louder than before. Makarion flung himself to the deck; Armand did the same. Only Jack Kemp and Forester, locked into their respective functions, denied their instincts.

The shell struck the middle of the harbour channel thirty feet off the port bow. The explosion caused a huge geyser of water and mud to spiral up from the channel, and the blast wave threw *Sea Victory* over to starboard, pitching Kemp across the deck. Only the rail saved him and his camera from sliding off the spray-soaked deck and into the channel.

Makarion lay in the doorway, his head between his arms,

waiting in an agony of suspense for the bomb he had placed to trigger itself as it was flung sharply from side to side – but it didn't.

Forester held tightly on to the wheel as the vessel heeled over. He heard crashes and the screams of terrified children below. He knew that all that had saved them was his dangerously reckless manoeuvre in mid stream. Another thirty feet and *Sea Victory* would have been a torn and bloody piece of wreckage sinking to the bottom. The bridge windows were clouded with spray and he switched on the circular wipers to give him some visibility. The screws were biting now and they were moving forward, increasing their speed all the time. The channel continued to broaden. Forester guided the vessel round the last bend, and then they were clear.

The harbour stretched out before them, dotted with craft of all shapes and sizes fleeing from the sudden onslaught. Off to starboard the Jounieh Yacht Club had emptied itself. The marina was deserted and a dark plume of smoke rose from behind the main building where a rocket had exploded.

Forester thrust the throttle as far forward as he could, pushing the vessel to its absolute limit. They had to get far enough away to do a complete check on the damage to the old ship. She was cracked and leaking, but she was still afloat; her passengers were shocked and frightened, but they were still alive. But it had been close. Forester didn't know how close.

Below decks it had been chaotic. After Makarion carried the American into the cabin, Mrs Dawson had retreated to the corner, her three children holding on to her. She was terrified. The sight of Kass's bloody wound reawakened the trauma of her husband's death.

Annabel was too busy to notice. Kass was holding Melissa on his knee while she examined his leg. She looked up at him. 'This needs stitching.'

He glanced at it briefly. 'I know. Can you do it?'

Annabel brushed her hair back from her face. She was sweating and it was not all due to the heat of the cabin. 'Yes I can, but it will be painful. I'm not sure if we have a local anaesthetic.'

Kass had none either. His bag had stayed in the hospital. 'Do it, otherwise it won't heal.'

Annabel stood up and went to the bathroom. She had to struggle through the solid packing cases containing the bullion. They were piled high, in and out of the bath. Finally she reached the medical cabinet. It was well stocked – there was a pain freezer that was used for knocks and strains. She took it with her.

Kass shook his head. 'Forget it – just sew up the wound. That stuff won't help.'

Annabel tried to get Melissa to sit with the Dawsons, but she wouldn't budge. She sat quietly on Kass's lap, her eyes wide and round with fear. Kass held her close to him, averting her eyes. 'Go ahead.'

Annabel cleaned the wound as best she could then, swallowing hard, she pulled the jagged edges together and carefully inserted the needle, trying desperately not to vomit. She wiped the blood away continuously, not looking up at the American. She knew if she saw his face she would have to stop.

Eventually it was done – and, in spite of herself, she felt a sense of achievement. The blood had stopped, apart from a little seepage, and it looked neat and clean. She clipped the fine thread and thrust the bloodstained bowl behind her. That should do.

Kass was drenched in sweat, his face pale and drawn. Slowly he unwrapped his arms from around the child and leaned forward. 'That's good – you bandage it now.' He felt *Sea Victory* yaw perilously to one side as Forester began to swing round in the channel. Kass held tightly on to Melissa and gripped the armchair to prevent himself being flung from it.

Annabel fell backwards – then a huge explosion, more violent than anything before, shook the hull. The effect below decks was spectacular and frightening: anything that could move, did. Glassware, crockery, furnishings vibrated as the old timbers groaned from the impact of the blast and the straining engines.

Mrs Dawson moaned with fear and one of the boys started to wail. Annabel picked herself up, crossed the cabin and put her arms around him. 'There now, don't cry – it will soon stop once we reach the harbour.'

Her words were as much for the mother as for the son. Annabel was terrified, too. Maybe they were safer from shrapnel and blast down here. But if *Sea Victory* were hit, she would sink quickly. Mentally she could see the water rushing in through the hole in the side of the ship, trapping them in this cabin. She closed her eyes, shutting out the nightmare. She patted the child on the back. 'It'll be all right, it'll be all right . . .'

Forester breathed more easily, guiding *Sea Victory* into the open harbour. Behind him, in the port area, dense clouds of smoke billowed upwards as the warehouse blazed.

Makarion grabbed the door jamb and hauled himself upright. There was nothing he could do at this moment, not until he could have the wheelhouse to himself for a while. 'You were lucky to get out.'

Forester didn't reply. He didn't feel lucky; he felt betrayed, used, and very exposed. He also felt responsible. It was his idea to come back – to take what he regarded as a legitimate risk. But nothing that had happened came under that category. *Sea Victory* had been made into a target, and that target had very nearly been hit. Yes, they had been lucky in that sense. Maybe the devil took care of his own.

The planes came in low, in close V-formation. They were almost at sea level to escape radar detection. The F14 Grumman Tomcats thundered and roared over *Sea Victory*, so close that Forester felt he could have reached up and touched them.

Six waves in all. By the time the last had skimmed over their radar antenna, the first were already firing their missiles into the mountainside. The earth was ripped and torn apart.

One after another, with deadly accuracy, the rockets unleashed themselves from below the wings of the aircraft and sped into the hillside, tossing the wrecked and blazing armour of the Strike Force aside. No one could live through that barrage; no one did. The pilots knew exactly where their targets were. They had been pinpointed since their arrival in the mountains over Jounieh early that morning. Only the politicians had held them up. Now the job was done – too late for those who had died on the hospital ship and for those killed ashore – but at least now the guns were silent. All that remained was the blackened earth, and more corpses for the graveyard.

Forester and the others stood by the rail in front of the wheelhouse and watched the American fighters slip away over the horizon, back to their carrier, as fast and as quickly as they had come.

Kass was gazing up at the mountain, watching a thin plume of smoke as it rose faintly into the air and disappeared. 'Well, that's that, I guess.'

Forester pulled a cigar from his shirt pocket and began to unwrap it. 'Better late than never, I suppose.'

He looked suddenly at Rhys. 'Hey, we haven't sunk yet – what did you do?'

Rhys grinned. 'Wrapped rubber sheeting round the exhaust pipe, then clamped it. That slowed it down, and it helps to be going forward rather than reverse.'

Forester sensed he was holding something back. 'But . . .?'

Rhys shrugged. 'But, I need a few hours to fix it so that we can make Larnaca.'

Forester clapped him on the back. 'Take as long as you like – we'll anchor right here. There's no way we are going back into Jounieh.'

He looked at Annabel. 'How are things below? Can you cope?'

She smiled, relieved to see him on top of things again. 'Yes . . . The Dawsons are in a bit of a state, as are some of the Lebanese women. Most of the men got off before we pulled out.' She looked around at the small group. 'Anyone fancy a drink?'

They all suddenly realized how thirsty they were.

'OK, I'll fix it. Meet me in the saloon in five minutes.'

Annabel left and Forester turned to Rhys. His efforts were now crucial if they were to get back to port. 'Is there anything you need? Can I help?'

Rhys declined. 'You're worse than useless in the engine room.' He looked at Henshaw. 'I'll need you, though.'

Forester walked with him to the companionway. 'Any idea how long?'

Rhys glanced at his watch. It was just 12.33. 'Five or six hours – we should be back under way again before dark.'

Rhys looked behind him at Makarion. 'Are we taking him back in?'

Forester shook his head. 'No.'

It was emphatic, and Rhys was relieved. He didn't question the decision. 'OK, I'll get to work now. Perhaps you could check out the rest of her. She took a pretty heavy knock when that last shell hit the water.'

Forester agreed. 'I'll do that – you worry about the leak.'

Forester went back into the wheelhouse. Kass was sitting by the chart table, Makarion staring through the bridge windows at the sea stretching out beyond the bay. 'When will you be completed, Captain?'

Forester eased down the throttle, then switched the engine off. 'This evening sometime, before sunset.'

Makarion nodded. That suited him. Dark would be better. This ship would just disappear off the map – another casualty of the war. He would wait.

THIRTY-ONE

Albert Hatan had still been trying to contact the Israeli gunboats when Makarion ran by outside his office. Another salvo of rockets exploded in the dock area and he abandoned his efforts. They were much too close for comfort. He took a key he always kept hanging from a hook inside one of his desk drawers. He then hurried to the front offices of Inter-Travel.

People were sheltering beneath counters and tables. A few more came rushing in from outside carrying suitcases – one he recognized as a passenger from *Sea Victory*.

With the key, he opened a heavy door at the rear of reception and switched on a light. Concrete steps led down to a basement that was equipped with blankets, food and water. It was a precaution most businessmen in Lebanon had taken since the civil war began. He called his staff, and then the other people in the shipping office, and stood by the top of the steps, ordering them down. Only when he was satisfied that the office was empty did he allow one of his staff to help him down the steps. There was no sign of Makarion, and Hatan's cashier, Kamal, confirmed that it was he who had run past Hatan's office, then out into the dock road. Hatan wrongly concluded that Makarion must have panicked.

As the attack continued he spoke to the passenger from *Sea Victory*, who told him that when he had left they had been trying to get the vessel out as quickly as possible. Hatan understood . . . It was the only sensible thing they could do. He hoped they had made it safely. Quite apart from his personal liking for both Annabel and Forester, if *Sea Victory* sank in the dock area, twenty-five million dollars in gold would be a tempting target for any one of the different militia – and the word would soon go round. In Lebanon it was unavoidable.

Quite abruptly, at about 12.30, the attack ceased. Hatan waited another five minutes to see if it would resume, then he led the way up the steps and back into the main building. As quickly as his old legs would carry him, he made his way to the front door and looked out over the berth *Sea Victory* had occupied. It was empty. Nor was there any sign of wreckage in the channel. Hatan breathed a sigh of relief. Perhaps they had managed to get away. He would try to contact them on the radio.

He went back to his office and sent Kamal to Makarion's room on the top floor to see if he had returned. He waited. Makarion was better than he at understanding the VHF radio and would be able to find the various wavebands that always confused him. It was not like Makarion to panic like that. He remembered he had once told him there was a shelter beneath the offices, but perhaps Makarion had forgotten. Hatan dismissed it. Few people behaved as you expected them to when real danger confronted them.

There was an urgent knock on his door and, before he could answer it, Kamal came bursting in. He was stuttering with fear and the old man spent some time calming him down and extracting the information. He forced a very reluctant cashier to accompany him up the staircase to Makarion's office. Even with his help it took some time and Hatan was shaking with exhaustion by the time he reached the door to the room.

Not surprisingly, Kamal refused to go in. It was in a shambles. Furniture had been smashed and overturned, and blood spattered the wall behind the desk. Hatan gazed a long time at Rousseau's crumpled body. The shots Makarion had pumped into him after his death had made him barely recognizable. The old man searched the room methodically, finding the broken pieces of the bomb trigger mechanism. It was impossible to know its purpose, and Hatan picked uncomprehendingly at the pieces. However, one thing was clear. The Frenchman who had arrived on the first voyage was dead, brutally killed and riddled with bullets, and Makarion had disappeared.

Hatan walked slowly out of the office. Kamal waited apprehensively by the top of the stairs. The old man held out his arm. 'Come, help me down.'

Sea Victory lay heaving in the swell of the bay, a sea anchor preventing her from drifting. While Rhys worked on the leak in the stern and Annabel prepared something for them to eat, Forester crawled about below, checking the timbers to see if the wooden vessel had sprung any more seams.

It was filthy work in the bilges, but it had to be done. He had armed himself with a powerful torch and, as far as he could tell, there were no major problems – at least, none he could spot from inside the hull. But she would have to go into dry dock for a complete examination before he could be sure. He cursed silently to himself. It put a block on their only source of income, right in the middle of the season. There would also be the costs of the docking.

He examined the pig-iron ballast to see if that had shifted when she had heeled over from the impact of the shell blast. There was no problem. He was relieved. At least they would not turn over when the first heavy wave hit them.

He heard Henshaw calling to him through the open trap. Forester yelled an acknowledgement and crawled back the way he had come. Henshaw peered down at his grimy face. 'It's the radio, Skipper. Inter-Travel – sounds like the old man.'

Forester wiped the sweat from his eyes, and clambered up the ladder. 'OK, I'll get it. There's nothing wrong down there, thank God.'

Henshaw gripped his arm and helped him up. 'Bloody good old boat.' He stamped the deck enthusiastically.

Forester grinned, his teeth gleaming from his oily, black face. 'Not too hard, Henshaw – the old thing might just decide to fall apart.'

Henshaw laughed. 'Not this one, Skipper.'

Forester made his way to the wheelhouse. The decks were hot under his feet. The sun was burnishing the fittings and bouncing off the deck. With no forward motion and no breeze to be picked up, most of the remaining Lebanese passengers were sheltering wherever they could find some shade. The ship rolled slowly up and down on the almost flat, calm sea, sweltering beneath the sun. The wheelhouse was like a sauna. Forester picked up the bakelite receiver – it was warm in his hands. 'Hello, this is *Sea Victory*. Over.'

Hatan's voice came in clear and strong. 'Hello, Forester. I'm glad you managed to get clear all right.'

Forester sighed. 'Yes, so am I. It was touch and go there for a while.'

'Are you coming back in?'

'No, I'm not. It would be stupid to risk it – anything might happen.'

Hatan's voice came back briskly. 'I agree, especially with your cargo, although the attack has ceased now.'

Forester smiled wryly to himself. 'Yes, we saw the planes going in. They were American, probably from a carrier. I wish they'd arrived a bit earlier.'

There was a silence from Hatan's end, just some static.

'Hello, Hatan, are you there? Over.'

'Yes, I'm sorry, Captain. I was thinking and I always forget you have no way of knowing that – I hate these machines.'

Forester was amused. 'Never mind, you do very well.'

'For an old man, you mean?' He continued, 'I have some news for you.'

Forester changed the handset round; his palm was getting sweaty. 'Go ahead.'

'That Frenchman who came with you on the first trip – I've checked his name against the manifest – Philippe Rousseau.'

'What about him?'

'He's dead!'

Forester was stunned. His first thought was that he had been killed in the attack. Jack and Armand had been looking for him . . . 'How? What happened?'

'Are you alone, Captain?'

Forester glanced around. Henshaw was standing in front of the bridge, on the forward sundeck. There was no one else. 'Yes, go ahead.'

'I found him in Makarion's office. He has been murdered – shot several times.'

Forester let his breath out slowly . . . Dear God. His mind had gone blank; he couldn't figure it out.

305

'Are you there, Captain?'

'In Makarion's office, you say?'

'That's right. There had been a fearful struggle –'

Forester interrupted. 'Makarion's here!'

He could feel Hatan's shocked surprise. 'On the boat?'

'Yes . . . Why would he want to kill Rousseau?'

'We don't know for sure it was him.'

Forester felt a surge of impatience at the old man's caution. 'Why else would he be trying to escape on my vessel?'

Hatan's voice changed. He spoke softly, warningly. 'If it *was* him, Captain, he is a dangerous man, whatever his motives. What will you do?'

Forester was thinking fast. If he turned round and headed back he would still face the same difficulties. Furthermore, Makarion might get desperate and try to stop them. 'I'll continue to Larnaca and inform the authorities there. You can confirm what has happened. He won't get past customs.'

Hatan thought about it. 'That seems to be the only sensible thing to do, but you must watch him.'

Forester smiled grimly. 'I won't take my eyes off him.' He changed tack: 'Have you managed to contact the Israeli gunboats yet?'

Hatan sighed deeply. 'No – nothing at all, but I'll keep trying.'

'OK. We're anchored in the harbour at the moment, carrying out some repairs. We expect to be under way before nightfall.'

'Thank you, Captain. I must go now, but I shall be by this transmitter all day. I'll come back to you if I manage to get the Israelis. I take it you'll continue in any case?'

'I have to. Thanks for your help, Hatan. Over and out.'

'Au revoir, Captain.'

The radio clicked and went dead. Slowly Forester replaced the handset. He stared contemplatively at it for a few moments, then called to Henshaw, 'Come below, I want to talk to you and Rhys.'

Henshaw stretched, enjoying the sunshine. Heat never seemed to affect him. 'Sure, Skipper.'

They both walked to the rear of the upper sundeck, then descended the companionway to the deck below. Climbing down the ladder to the engine room was like descending into

Hades. The temperature must have been around 120 Fahrenheit. Rhys was lying on his back, tightening a clamp. He didn't hear them until Forester called his name sharply.

He sat up, grinning at them. 'Didn't expect to see you down here.'

Forester held his nose – the smell of diesel oil was overpowering. 'How do you stand it?'

'Gets in the blood. Without it I'd probably get withdrawal symptoms.'

Forester gestured for both of them to come closer. He told them what Hatan had said.

Rhys looked dubious. 'Why the hell would he want to kill Rousseau?'

Forester had puzzled about that himself. 'I don't know.'

Henshaw reacted instinctively. 'I'll bet it's got something to do with this business of ours.'

Forester had been trying to make the connection. 'Maybe . . .' The pieces were all lying around, but he hadn't got time to put them together. 'Now, listen. I've not told any of the others. I don't want Annabel to have more problems on her plate. And if either Kemp or Armand knew about Rousseau's death, they might try to take care of Makarion themselves. So it's up to us.'

'You gonna lock him up now, Skipper?' As usual, Henshaw went straight for the sharp end.

'No, I'm not. He's probably armed and there is no need. We just wait till we get to Larnaca, then, once he is off the boat, I inform customs. Hatan will back me up.'

Rhys nodded. 'Seems best . . .'

Forester was still worried. Something nagged away inside him, but he couldn't think of a better way of handling the situation. 'I hope so. Meanwhile, stay loose. Don't tip him off, but keep your eyes open, all right?'

They both indicated their acceptance. It was the best they could do.

All afternoon Rhys sweated below, sealing the gaps between wrenched seams using wadding and pitch. Henshaw assisted as much as he could, but the responsibility rested firmly on

Rhys's shoulders. He accepted it uncomplainingly. It was work he understood and did well.

While he and Henshaw lost about twelve pounds of weight between them, in the saloon, Annabel plied the others with drinks as they basked the afternoon away. The sea remained empty. They seemed to be the only vessel inhabiting that part of the ocean. Once the ships fleeing from Jounieh had disappeared over the horizon, nothing disturbed the flat, glassy waters of the harbour. It was a strange afternoon, one that Forester would remember later as unreal, almost dreamlike.

Jack Kemp and Armand slouched by the bar most of the time, discussing the material they had shot. They were excited about it. They had accepted the necessity of returning to Cyprus, but were still worried about Rousseau.

Makarion dozed on one of the benches. Forester found his eyes drawn to him hypnotically, wondering what his real role was, where he fitted in. He was glad Makarion's eyes were closed, otherwise he didn't doubt he would have given himself away.

Kass and Annabel spent the rest of the afternoon endeavouring to recover Melissa's confidence. Annabel did not refer to Nazira. Tom had told her what had happened and she would dearly have liked to sympathize with Kass, but she knew this was neither the time nor the place. For the moment the American was blanking it out, while going through the motions with the child. That in itself was encouraging . . .

The sun began to dip quickly towards the horizon. *Sea Victory*'s shadow lengthened over the pale blue water, and a welcome breeze began to ruffle the curtains round the open windows. Forester went up to the wheelhouse. There was nothing for him to do, but he couldn't stand the sight of Makarion any longer. The man's utterly relaxed attitude unnerved him. If he had killed Rousseau he must have nerves of steel.

Forester paced the wheelhouse and glanced at his watch for the third time in five minutes. He stopped. From the saloon he heard a burst of cheering. He ran to the top of the companionway as Rhys began to climb it; he reached down and helped Rhys up the last few steps. The engineer was stripped to the waist, covered in a mixture of sweat, oil and pitch, but his face was triumphant. He grinned at Forester. 'It's done!'

Forester hugged him, heedless of the oil. He knew what it must have been like down in that hell hole all afternoon. He grabbed his brandy sour from the chart table and thrust it into Rhys's hand. 'Drink this, you deserve it. When we make port we'll crack open some champagne.'

Rhys shook his head, swallowing the tall drink in one gulp. 'No, thanks, a brandy sour is fine by me. Just let me take the wheel for a bit, Skipper. I need to feel some wind on my face.'

Forester studied him, knowing how claustrophobic the engine room must have been. This was as close as Rhys would ever get to admitting it had been tough. 'Sure, Rhys, help yourself – any time you like.'

Rhys raised his eyebrows. 'No time like the present.' He walked over to the wheel and held it for a moment, savouring the feel of it – finding comfort in its shape and texture. Then he reached over and pressed the starter. The engine roared into life immediately, settling down to a steady throb.

Forester yelled down to Henshaw to weigh the sea anchor. It rattled and banged its way upward until it nestled snugly alongside the bow – then Henshaw switched off the small electric motor that had raised it. He signalled to Forester. 'All clear, Skipper.'

Forester turned to Rhys. 'She's all yours.'

Rhys slowly pushed the throttle forward and *Sea Victory* began to gather way, pushing aside the water at her bows, increasing her momentum. The breeze ruffled Rhys's hair, blowing through the open doors of the wheelhouse. Rhys laughed – it was a release.

All on board felt the easing of tension – all except Makarion. He was wide awake. The strange, still, calm afternoon had gone. Night was creeping up from the east – soon it would be dark. Makarion waited for the dark.

Forester had sent Rhys down below for a well-earned rest. The white bow-wave of *Sea Victory* cut a phosphorous swathe through the glittering water, reflecting the glow from the ship's lights. Forester always had his ship well lit. He figured that it would be assumed he had nothing to hide. Except that tonight was different: he had twenty-five million dollars and a cold-blooded killer on board.

He turned quickly, sensing the presence of the figure standing in the doorway.

It was Makarion. 'I'm sorry, Captain, I didn't mean to startle you.'

Forester turned back to the wheel. 'I was thinking about something else,' he lied. 'My mind was miles away.'

Makarion came into the wheelhouse. 'Do you enjoy these night voyages?'

Forester gazed at Makarion's reflection in the big, curved window. 'They're different, quieter. You get a chance to think.'

Makarion leaned on the radar pedestal, the green glow lighting his face eerily from below. 'Yes, I suppose that's true – a time for reflection, contemplation.' He paused, studying Forester's profile. 'And what were you thinking about this afternoon, Captain?'

Forester looked at him, startled. 'What do you mean?'

Makarion smiled. 'I mean, after you left the bridge and joined the crew below – you came back to the saloon and you seemed to spend an awful long time studying me, Captain.'

Forester was dismissive. 'I don't know what you're talking about. I wasn't looking at you particularly.'

There was an acute silence in the wheelhouse, but for the sound of sea rushing by outside the open doors.

'I think you were, Captain. You see, I wasn't really asleep, and I was very conscious of your curious gaze.'

Forester pretended to ignore him, watching his reflection in the glass. 'You're imagining things, Makarion. I've got better things to do with my time than study you.'

Makarion straightened up, pulling the Beretta from his jacket pocket. 'Now, that's where you make your mistake – I'm probably one of the most interesting people you'll ever get a chance to study. So, if you have any questions, I suggest you ask them quickly.'

Forester stared at the gun. 'You must be crazy! I don't know what you're talking about.'

Makarion's voice hardened. 'Don't be stupid, Forester. I heard

310

the conversation you had on that thing with Hatan. I was just below the companionway. Incredible how sound carries on a boat when it's not under way.'

Forester didn't reply at first. His mind was racing, trying to work out what Makarion had in mind . . . He prompted him, 'Did you kill Rousseau?'

'Of course – if I hadn't, he would have killed me.'

Forester scoffed. 'Philippe? He wouldn't kill anybody; he was as gentle as a lamb.'

'I fear not, Captain. Your little lamb was a wolf in sheep's clothing. Rousseau worked for the Americans – probably CIA. I don't know, it doesn't matter now.'

He stared at Forester's disbelieving face, and suddenly felt a surge of anger. 'Look, who was it who first contacted you to charter this vessel into Jounieh? Rousseau! The Americans wanted this ship going in and out. Do you know who you had on board last time you came in from Larnaca?'

Forester stared straight ahead. 'Yes, I do – they were representatives of some of the militia.'

Makarion seemed pleased. 'Well, I'm glad you worked that out. But they were more than that. They were the *top* military/political groups, and the US was manipulating them.' He laughed. 'They were manipulating you too, Captain.'

Forester adjusted the wheel slightly, keeping her on course. 'Maybe so – but where do you fit into this? Why would Rousseau want to kill you if he worked for the Americans?'

'Because I'm the opposition. We do *not* want any cosy carving up of Lebanon between the various militia. Not till we control it.'

Forester reached for the pocket of his shirt. 'Do you mind if I have a smoke?'

'No reason why you should not enjoy a last cigar.'

Forester ignored the last bit and lit up, drawing in a long, soothing breath. It helped him to think. 'Is that why your colleagues up in the mountains tried to sink us this morning?'

Makarion glanced at the bulkhead clock. It was ten minutes to nine. 'That's right. As long as this boat is being used that way, it's a positive danger to our plans. So, you can blame the Americans for this, Captain.'

311

Forester shook his head. 'It doesn't make sense. Kass and I saw the Israeli armour dug in on the mountain this morning – that's why we were in such a hurry to get back.' He thought about it for a second, then continued, 'And why would the Israelis and the Americans be falling out over who controls the Lebanon? They're allies – yet those were US planes that went in there and blasted that armour. It just doesn't add up.'

Makarion was delighted – but he didn't allow the gun in his hand to waver for an instant. 'Yes, even the Americans will think they have knocked out an Israeli Strike Force. The Israelis will deny it, of course, which is what the US would expect. But the Americans will always be a little worried about their raid on the mountains above Jounieh – wondering when the Israelis will strike back, because they always do. That is their declared policy. Only the Israelis and ourselves will know the truth . . . and maybe you. At least for a few minutes before you die.'

Forester didn't say anything; there didn't seem to be much point. He was content to be an audience – to let the murderous bastard keep talking.

Makarion watched the Englishman, slightly amused. He was about to continue when he heard something. He stopped, listening. He could hear footsteps clattering up the companion-way from the deck below.

It was Annabel. She had spent most of the evening serving food. Everyone seemed to have developed an appetite. The food had all disappeared very quickly, gulped down with cold white wine. Rhys had dozed after eating – he was dog tired. Henshaw and Kemp had got into an argument about the respective merits of cricket and ice hockey. Neither Rhys nor Henshaw had noticed Makarion slip away.

Tom had told Annabel that he hoped to take the vessel all the way back to Larnaca, and she had prepared some chicken and hot coffee to keep him awake. As she came into the wheelhouse she saw that Makarion had a gun in his hand. He moved quickly away from the radar pedestal to get into a position where he could cover them both.

Forester's hands were clenched tight on the wheel. Through the reflection in the window he saw that just for an instant Makarion's gun was not on him. He had no time to turn and leap at him – he propelled himself backwards with all his strength. He heard the gun go off and felt the heat of the bullet singe his temple as he crashed into Makarion. They both sprawled on to the floor, Forester's head smashing into the leg of the chart table. He was dazed, struggling to get back to his feet – to get to close quarters. Makarion had held tightly on to the Beretta. He rolled like a cat and sprang up, levelling the gun at Forester, who was on his knees.

Annabel didn't hesitate. She flung the scalding hot coffee into his face. Makarion screamed with pain, staggering backwards into a corner, clawing with his free hand at his eyes. The pain seared and burned into his skull with unbelievable intensity. He bent over, cradling his face, moaning like a wounded animal. Through the blinding waves of agony he heard a sound as Forester staggered to his feet. He straightened up, suddenly remembering his enemy.

He could not see. Strange rippling waves of light, diffused and disorientating, caused him to sway. He stretched out a hand, feeling the wall of the cabin behind him. He brought the gun up sharply. Forester yelled a warning to Annabel and leapt towards her, throwing her to the floor. Makarion fired wildly in all directions, spraying the wheelhouse in an attempt to hit them. Forester rolled away from his wife, deliberately making a noise to draw the fire. Makarion used up another shot, missing him. He stood still, quiet, hardly breathing.

Makarion stopped, holding his head to one side, listening for the movement that would tell him where his target was. His senses were as sharp as a knife. Adrenalin pumped through his veins, responding to the danger, blanking out the pain in his eyes and face.

The engines of *Sea Victory* continued to pound relentlessly. The unattended wheel creaked as it swung around, answering to the shift in the rudder.

Makarion crouched in the corner, one arm stretched out in front of him like a sensor, his mouth open. His eyes were clenched shut, the burnt, reddened skin around the top of his face already beginning to blister.

Forester was on his feet. He looked at his wife, still lying on the floor, and put his finger to his lips. She did not move a

313

muscle. Neither of them knew how many more rounds were still in the magazine, but both of them realized that in this confined space they had little chance of not being hit if Makarion had the slightest idea of where they were.

Makarion heard people moving below. Someone was climbing the companionway. He screamed a warning, 'Stay back, stay out of here. I have a gun and I will kill both of them.' He fired a warning shot into the ceiling to lend authority to his threat.

Forester changed his position, the sound masked by the gun's explosion. He reached the table. All movement outside the wheelhouse had ceased. He always kept his revolver in the drawer. He knew he could not get it open without some noise, and then Makarion would have him. He reached up with infinite care for one of the chart cases.

Annabel watched him, terrified. But there was nothing she could do to help her husband: one sound and the gun would be on her. She watched it, fascinated, as it moved slowly around, the black hole of its muzzle like the eye of a cobra searching for its victim. She held her breath as it pointed in her direction. Makarion seemed to be looking at her, his face ghastly, his eyes clenched shut. She felt he sensed her presence. The gun steadied on her, the muzzle aimed directly between her eyes.

Forester threw the chart case into the far corner. It clattered to the deck and Makarion instantly swung the weapon away from Annabel and fired twice at the sound. The Englishman jerked the drawer open. It squeaked as it always did, but this time the noise seemed to thunder in his ears. Forester grabbed the gun as Makarion twisted round to face the sound he had heard, the Beretta in his hand firing as he turned.

Forester felt a tremendous blow in the side. It thrust him violently back against the table. Makarion was still firing, aiming blindly in his direction. Forester pulled the trigger twice and Makarion was carried back towards the wall. He crashed sideways into the corner of the wheelhouse, then slid to the floor, his legs splayed out in front of him.

Annabel moved first. She grabbed the gun in Makarion's hand – he felt her fingers gripping the weapon and tried to hold on to it, flailing weakly at her. Annabel was horrified: incredibly, he was still alive. Terror lent strength to her and she jerked the gun from his grasp and levelled it at him.

He sat there helpless, his face mutilated, his head moving strangely from side to side, as if he were trying to see. She could not bring herself to fire the weapon. She crawled backwards, getting as far away from him as she could. She felt her husband's legs behind her. He leaned down and helped her to her feet, holding her tightly to him.

Henshaw, who had moved swiftly to the other side of the ship and positioned himself beside the opposite door, charged in. He scanned the wheelhouse quickly, then knelt down by Makarion and searched him. There were no other weapons. He called to the others to come up. Slowly they all crowded into the wheelhouse.

Annabel could feel something warm on her hand. She drew back from Forester, seeing the blood for the first time. She turned and looked at David Kass, who was standing by the entrance to the bridge. She tried to keep the panic out of her voice. 'David, he's been wounded.'

Kass could see the stricken look in her eyes and was moving across the wheelhouse before she spoke.

Forester waved him away. 'I'm all right.' He gripped the American's arm tightly. 'Check him out, Kass, he was making threats. I don't know what he meant, but he intended to destroy this ship.'

Kass moved over to Makarion and knelt down beside him. He'd been hit twice – once in the upper chest, once in the stomach. He was bleeding profusely – it was hard to see what was keeping him alive. Kass looked up at Forester and Annabel and shook his head. 'He's dying, there's nothing I can do.'

Makarion moved. His hand gripped the American around the wrist, holding it relentlessly like a steel clamp. Makarion felt a surge of strength run through him – a grim pleasure suffused his body. He knew something they did not. He wanted to see their faces. He concentrated on trying to open his eyes. The lids seemed fastened together. Then there was some light, dim shadows, voices mumbling. He blinked and the shadows resolved themselves into figures, faces. He could see the American beside him, and Forester and Annabel . . . He smiled – it

315

was meant to be a smile. It was a ghastly parody, his face twisting with the effort, his eyes bulging from his face.

He stared at Kass. 'If I am to die, Doctor . . . so are you.' He paused, savouring his words. He focused his eyes on Forester. 'So are you, Captain, and your ship, and it will not be long for you to wait.'

He tried to laugh, then gagged as blood trickled from the side of his mouth. His eyes fastened on the bulkhead clock. 'Not long now,' he whispered. 'There is a weapon on your ship, Captain; it goes off soon.'

Forester pushed Annabel to one side and crouched down by the dying man. 'For Christ's sake, Makarion, there are women and children . . .' He stopped, Makarion's eyes mocked him.

'Look, we'll never come back, there is no need to destroy the ship. I've no intention of being used as a puppet . . .' He gripped Makarion's arm. 'It's my ship, I won't come back, I promise . . .'

Makarion's face set in a mask of bitter hatred. His eyes shone, then slowly emptied of life. Forester did not need to be told he was dead.

Kass unclamped the hand from round his wrist, pulling each finger back, one at a time, until he was free of his grasp. He stood up and pulled Forester into a chair, methodically ripping open his shirt and examining the wound in his side. Forester was lucky: the bullet had neatly creased through his flesh, between two ribs.

Annabel handed him some bandages from the medical cabinet. He smiled reassuringly at her. 'No problems . . .'

Forester swore. 'Not if that bastard was right.' He stared hard at Kass. 'It must be a bomb; we have to find it.'

Kass fastened the bandage. 'I know.' He patted the wound and Forester winced. 'Now you can look.'

Rhys shook his head hopelessly. 'It's no good, boss – there are a thousand places where he could hide a bomb on this ship.'

Forester stood up. 'Maybe, but he certainly didn't hide it below. You were in the stern and I was checking the hull. That leaves the cabin area and the saloon.'

'And here,' Annabel said.

Forester looked at her. 'That's right. And he came up here to tell me what was going to happen –'

316

Henshaw butted in. 'He was a bloody fanatic – he could have wanted to be certain of his own death.'

Forester agreed. 'That's right. The wheelhouse was deserted for a long time this afternoon.'

Annabel was remembering. 'He left the saloon at one point, just before you and Henshaw went down to talk to Rhys.'

Forester looked up at the VHF. 'After the call from Hatan . . .'

Rhys glanced swiftly round the wheelhouse. 'That must be when he did it, Skipper – it's got to be in here.'

Forester came to a decision. 'Right, I want everybody out of here except me and Rhys. Henshaw, you launch the life rafts and the boat. Get everyone into them as fast as you can.'

He strode over to the helm and switched off the engines. The sudden stillness after their constant and steady throb was chilling. It sharpened and emphasized their fears. Annabel put her arm around Forester's waist. 'I'm not going, I'm staying here with you.'

He gently disengaged himself. 'I have no time to argue. We have to find the bomb while you get the women and children into the boat. As soon as you are ready, signal to Rhys. I'm not hanging around – I'll join you, I promise.'

She looked into his eyes. She believed him, it made sense. 'All right, I'll call to Rhys when the boat is lowered.'

He nodded, looking at Henshaw. 'Get to it as fast as you can.'

Henshaw and Annabel left; Armand followed. The Canadian paused in the doorway. 'Is there anything I can do?'

Forester shook his head emphatically. 'Nothing. Rhys and I know this space better than anyone else. There's no time to look anywhere else. Just get them all on to those rafts and the boat as fast as you can.'

Kemp ducked through the doorway and disappeared.

The wheelhouse was empty now apart from Forester, Rhys and David Kass. And the dead body of Makarion. Forester looked at the American. 'Look, we're wasting time, will you just go . . .'

Kass declined. He reached into his pocket, pulling out a stethoscope. 'You forget, I'm a doctor and this might prove useful if there is a bomb ticking away in here. I can hear a lot better with this.'

317

Forester accepted that. 'Right, you check all the panelling, see if you can hear anything. I'll take the chart table and shelves. Rhys, see if you can spot anything round the wheel and the radar pedestal, and for God's sake don't jog anything.'

The bridge fell silent again. They worked intently, concentrating totally on what they were doing. Nothing disturbed them now, not even Makarion's open, dead eyes, watching them, mocking them. Forester found nothing in or near the chart table. He cleared the chart containers one by one, carefully removing each chart and examining the hollow interior – there was nothing, just charts. It was all as it should be; nothing had been disturbed.

It was Rhys who discovered the first clue. 'Skipper, come and look at this.'

Forester crossed quickly and knelt down beside him. Rhys pointed to the base of the radar pedestal. There was a wood panel at the back, which could be unscrewed to allow access to the main wiring. The dust that had collected on the deck behind the pedestal had been scraped back, and there was a scratch on the head of one of the screws. Forester moved Rhys back and lay down on the deck, pressing his head to the wood panelling. He could hear nothing. He got up on his knees and looked at Kass. 'You listen, see if there's anything.' He moved aside to allow the American in.

Kass adjusted the stethoscope to his ears and put the head to the panelling. He listened, then shook his head and tried the removable panel. This time the tick was loud and clear.

He removed the stethoscope from round his neck and handed it over. 'Listen.'

Forester took it, pushing the head against the panelling. 'That's it.' He stood up suddenly, flinging the stethoscope to Kass, moving across to the shelf behind the table. 'Right, both of you can go now. I'll deal with this.' He got the screwdriver and came back to the radar pedestal.

Kass and Rhys stood up, facing him. The American shook his head. 'There's no way that I'm leaving – not till we neutralize that thing in there, or we all get out.'

'I'm not debating this. That's an order and it applies to you as well, Rhys. Now will you get out!'

318

Kass looked at Rhys and spoke for both of them. 'Nope, you might need us. God knows what's behind that panel.'

Forester swore. There was nothing he could do. He knelt down by the pedestal and began to unscrew the panel. Kass and Rhys crouched either side of him, watching carefully. As the screw worked loose, Kass took it between his forefinger and thumb and undid it, while Forester worked on the next. There were four in all. When the last one came away, Forester and Rhys gently eased it back a fraction.

Kass spoke. 'Hold it. Let me have a look.' He peered inside – there were no wires attached to the panel. 'OK.'

They took it fully out and placed it on the deck.

Forester turned to Rhys. 'Get the torch – it's over there.' He pointed to just above the door. Rhys brought it back and handed it over. Forester squirmed partially around behind the pedestal and shone the torch inside.

There were two small digital clocks. One gave the present time, 2055 hours. The other had a red readout and was set at 2100 hours. They had five minutes.

Kass stared at him. He felt the sweat breaking out on his face. 'How long?'

Forester held up one hand, his fingers outstretched. 'It is set to go off at nine.'

Kass sat down on the deck, easing the pain in his leg. 'Do you know anything about these things?'

Forester looked at him for a long moment, judging his reply. He decided there was no point in lying. 'No – not a bloody thing.' He glanced at his engineer. 'Rhys?'

'No, boss – bombs aren't exactly up my alley, but I'll have a go, I've got wire-cutters in my box.'

'Get them, as fast as you can.'

Forester cursed himself as Rhys slid expertly down the companionway. 'I should have thought of that before.'

Kass disagreed. 'If you had sent him before we might not have got to the radar as quickly. What are you going to do?'

'There are several wires – different colours. I'm going to snap the lot.'

'You could blow us all up.'

Forester stood up, helping Kass to his feet. 'No, I will only blow me up. You're getting off now, if I have to throw you overboard myself.'

Kass could see he meant it. The longer they stood here arguing, the less chance they had of defusing the bomb. He held up his hands. 'OK, Captain, it's your boat.'

Forester nodded. 'Damn right it is.

Rhys came up the companionway two steps at a time. He had a complete tool box. He grabbed a small pair of wire-cutters and gave them to Forester. He was too out of breath to speak.

Forester took them. 'Right. Doctor Kass is going now. Help him down to the boat, Rhys – give me a yell as soon as everything is ready.'

Rhys was still trying to draw breath. He stared hard at Forester. 'You will come, boss?'

Forester nodded. 'I'll come.'

There was a brief moment of silence, then Kass turned abruptly to leave. As he did so a blinding white light suddenly enveloped the wheelhouse. Forester shaded his eyes, trying to see behind the dazzling beam of the searchlight that had them fixed in its beam – it was impossible. The radio crackled and burst into life. 'Hello, *Sea Victory*, this is Israeli naval ship. You will cease unloading your passengers and await further instructions.'

Forester froze for an instant, then moved fast to the handset. 'This is *Sea Victory*. I am the captain. Please listen carefully. There is an unexploded bomb in the wheelhouse. We have located it and are about to try to defuse it. My passengers and crew must continue to disembark. The bomb is set to detonate at 2100 hours' – he glanced at the clock – 'in almost three minutes. Can anyone advise?'

The VHF loudspeaker hummed, the static setting their nerves on edge. They sensed the disbelief in the silence that followed. The moment seemed to stretch agonizingly. In fact it lasted only a few seconds.

The voice came on again. This time the tone was completely different. The coldness had gone. It was calm, but human. Forester recognized the captain who had stopped them before. '*Sea Victory*, please describe exactly what the bomb looks like.'

Forester crawled down behind the pedestal once more and

320

shone the powerful torch inside, Rhys hung on to the handset until he was ready, then Forester took it from him. 'There appear to be several sticks of TNT and two digital clocks. One is recording the time as of now, the other is set at 2100 hours. There are several wires attached to the clocks.'

'What colours are the wires?'

'There are three. Red, blue and yellow.'

'Can you see where they are attached?'

Forester craned his neck, peering inside. 'The red one is connected to the TNT and runs directly to the clock.'

'Which clock?'

'The one with the fixed time.'

'And the others?'

'The blue one is connected between the two clocks, and the yellow one runs from the TNT to the moving digital.'

'What time does it say now?'

'2058, coming up to 59.'

There was another silence, then, 'All right, now listen carefully. Do not touch the red wire at all. Have you got that?'

'Yes . . . leave the red wire.'

'Right. Do not touch the yellow wire either.'

'OK, leave the yellow wire . . . You want me to cut the blue?'

'Yes, Captain, I do – you have no choice now. If the digital clock that is moving stops – you are safe. Otherwise you must jump for it.'

Forester's hands were sweating. He rubbed them on the front of his shirt. Then, very carefully, he inserted the cutters, gently easing the open mouth either side of the blue wire. He tightened his grip on the handles, bringing them slowly together. The cutting edges of the blades sliced easily through the blue wire, severing it.

The clock stopped. It read 2059 and thirty seconds.

The sweat dripped off Forester's face. He swallowed hard, trying to get the dryness from his throat. His voice cracked slightly. 'The clock has stopped,' he said into the handset.

He heard the Israeli let out a sigh of relief. 'Good – now, bend up the wires either side, so that they cannot possibly touch, and I suggest you leave the rest to us.'

Forester slid his hand inside the pedestal and picked up the deadly package. 'Not this time, Captain – I intend to get rid of this my own way.'

He put the handset down on the deck, then eased himself away from the radar scanner, holding the bomb. Kass held out a hand to help him up. Forester looked up at him, his face grim. Then he accepted the offer. Kass hauled him to his feet.

Forester walked out into the glare of the searchlight holding the bomb aloft. He threw it with all his strength as far as he could, forgetting the wound in his side. The clock dials reflected the glow from the searchlights, twisting in the air until the bomb hit the water. He ducked, expecting it to detonate, but nothing happened.

He went back to the wheelhouse, and picked up the handset, crashing it down into its holder. He looked at his engineer. 'Get below, Rhys, and tell Annabel the danger is over. I want everybody back on board as fast as possible, OK?'

'Right, Skipper.' He left.

Kass slumped down into the chair by the chart table. He felt drained, exhausted. 'What happens now?'

Forester wrapped his arms around the wheel, staring out at the circling gunboat. 'We leave as soon as everybody is back on board.'

Annabel hurried up the companionway, then paused in the doorway, looking at her husband. He turned and saw her. She crossed the deck quietly and put her arms around him, careful not to press against the wound in his side. He buried his face in her hair, trying not to think about the bomb – about what might have happened.

As soon as *Sea Victory* came under the eye of the searchlight, Kemp realized that he could use the camera. Both he and Armand had their equipment with them and the footage they had shot in Jounieh. If they were going to drift in a boat, then they intended to record it. Before they could board the lifeboat, they saw Forester throw the bomb mechanism overboard, then heard Rhys call down to Annabel that the danger was over.

Now they had the perfect opportunity to tape an Israeli blockade in action. The beam of the searchlight was playing

322

mostly over the bridge. Kemp gripped Armand by the wrist. 'Come on,' he whispered, 'let's get under cover.'

Armand looked at him oddly, surprised by the remark. 'What for?'

'We can shoot this from inside the saloon – they won't see us there.' He grinned. 'Besides, they are giving us all the light we need – it would be impolite to refuse.'

They faded from the stern deck and started to roll. They got almost everything – everything except the events unfolding inside the wheelhouse.

The radio came on again, jarring in their ears. '*Sea Victory*, you have on board a passenger called Makarion. We want him transferred to us for interrogation.'

Forester looked at the dead man in the corner. He disengaged himself from Annabel and picked up the handset. 'You can have him, Captain, and welcome.'

'What do you mean?'

'I mean that he is the bastard who planted the bomb – is he one of yours?'

Aaron Gould stared through his binoculars at the brightly lit wheelhouse of the British vessel. He could see everything except the body of Makarion – it was slumped below his eyeline. 'No, he is not – but we do know of him.'

'I'll bet you do . . .' Forester felt the anger spewing up inside him. Now the danger had passed, the reaction was setting in. He was sick of having been used as a sitting duck, first by the armour up in the hills, now by this cold-blooded bastard who had tried to blow them all apart. 'You'd better tell me who this man is, Captain, before I blow the evil sod's head off myself.'

Gould thought about it. He could send in his marines and forcibly take Makarion, but he knew the Englishman was at the end of his tether and in a dangerous mood. There was also the bullion. The Americans had made sure they knew about the twenty-five million dollars in gold. They knew that he knew, and there was no way round that: he had to give, in order to get.

He switched on the VHF. 'We monitored the transmission from your shipping agent in Jounieh.'

323

'Hatan?'

'Yes. We heard what was said about the Frenchman's death. We have known about Makarion for a long time. This is why I have been waiting here for you. Now we must take him.'

'Why?'

'He is an agent, Forester. He has been working for the Syrians in Jounieh. I can say no more.'

Forester stared at the dark shape of the gunboat, trying to see behind the white circle of light that pinned them like butterflies beneath its glare.

Could it be true? Was Makarion a Syrian? Is that what he had meant when he said only he and the Israelis would ever know the truth about who had launched the attack on Jounieh? It also explained why Rousseau had attempted to eliminate Makarion.

The pieces were falling into place. The jigsaw was complete.

But he didn't feel any better. He turned to Annabel. 'Is everybody on board now?'

'Yes. We had only managed to lower the boat before Rhys told us the danger was over.'

Forester studied her face, trying to see into her eyes and discover what she really felt. He put his hands on her shoulders, facing her. 'The danger's not over. That Israeli captain is not going to like it when he finds out Makarion *is* dead. He's bound to take us into Haifa for interrogation.' He paused, gripping her tightly. 'But I'm not going, not any more. I've had it. I'm going to make a run for it.' He stopped, thinking about it – weighing up the odds. 'They may try to sink us. I don't think so, not with the gold on board . . . they'll know about that. But it is a risk. I need to know what you think.'

Annabel stared at him. She didn't hesitate. 'What are we waiting for?'

Rhys had come back on to the bridge. He was standing quietly by the open door. Forester turned to him. 'All right. Rhys, come over here – don't do anything sudden, they'll be watching us. But when you get the signal I want you to start the engines and get the hell out of here as fast as she will go – got that?'

Rhys walked slowly over to the wheel and stared through the window. 'Ready when you are.'

324

Forester switched on the handset. 'Hello, Captain.'

'Yes, *Sea Victory*.'

'You want Makarion now?'

'That's right. I'll send an inflatable over.'

Forester turned towards the gunboat so that the Israeli captain could see his face. 'There's no need, I'll give him to you.'

He slammed the handset down and crossed quickly to Makarion's body, picking it up and flinging it over his shoulder. He staggered slightly as he felt the wound in his side. He walked the short distance to the rail outside the wheelhouse. The harsh circle of light held him in its centre, picking out the blood which was beginning to stain his shirt red. He was incensed, maddened by the growing realization of how he had been used – how the refugees he had been trying to help had been manipulated. He remembered the terrified screams of Mrs Dawson's children when the shell had exploded, almost sinking them; his wife's horrified face when she had tried to take the gun from the twitching, half-dead body of Makarion. His rage gave him strength. He lifted Makarion's body high above his head and screamed his defiance at the unseen, prowling gunboat behind the blinding light. 'You want him – here he is . . . take him!'

With the last of his strength he pitched Makarion into the dark waters below, then turned to Rhys. 'Now!' he yelled. 'Now!'

The engines roared into life, churning up the sea behind the vessel. Rhys spun the wheel, feeling for the steerage as it began to take hold.

The radio snapped on almost at once. '*Sea Victory*, come in please. You will return with us to Haifa.'

Forester picked up the handset, his anger and elation spent. 'This is *Sea Victory*. You have your Syrian. He nearly killed us all, I killed him.' He glanced around the bloody mess of the wheelhouse: Rhys at the helm; Kass still sitting in the chair, favouring the wound in his leg; his wife, her face drained of colour, watching him.

The VHF crackled emptily, waiting for his response. He switched on the handset. 'Hello, Israeli naval ship, are you there?'

Aaron Gould's voice echoed tinnily through the loudspeaker.

'Yes I'm here. Don't be stupid, Forester. You know what these ships are capable of. There is no point in trying to escape.'

Forester was exhausted. He'd had enough. 'I am not trying to escape. There are no terrorists on this ship, only their victims.' He stopped for a moment, gathering his thoughts. 'We have done nothing wrong. We have been shot at and bombed. We are tired, Captain, and we are going home . . . Shalom.' He switched off the handset.

Through the glasses Aaron Gould watched him walk over to the VHF and jerk out the socket. Now he was also deaf.

Wearily the Israeli captain put down the microphone. He had no choice any longer. The issue was stark and simple: either he let them go, or he sank their ship.

For the next three hours, as *Sea Victory* pounded through the night towards Cyprus, the Israeli gunboat continued to trail her, pinning her in its light, like a grey wolf of the sea – unvarying in its distance, constant in its menace.

Then, just after midnight, it began to slip further behind. The searchlight dimmed, then flicked off.

Forester went to the rail and listened, wondering if it was circling for an attack, waiting to pounce. But the powerful motors gradually faded, then disappeared altogether. There was nothing: the gunboat had gone.

He went back inside and put his arm around his wife. There was no jubilation, no cheers. They were all glad, just to be alive.

AUTHOR'S NOTE

For those of you who have come this far with the story there may still be a question mark. What is the real-life basis for the events described here?

Sea Victory exists. She is still plying the waters around Cyprus, and is still owned by the same man and wife upon whom *Ark* is based. I have known Nicolas Head a long time; he is a close and trusted friend. Back in the sixties, we wrote songs together – some of them were good. In the years since, we have drifted in and out of each other's company, but we have always tried to keep in touch.

Two years ago I read an article in the *Daily Mail*, describing his and Annabel's amazing escape, under fire, from Jounieh. I sent a telegram to him at the marina in Larnaca, warning him to take it easy. I know Nic. I knew he would try anything at least once.

He wrote back. It was a charming, quizzical and faintly self-mocking letter. One line best sums it up: 'Errol Flynn did this on the screen, why do I have to do it in real life?'

Later, I sailed with him and Annabel on *Sea Victory* and as we talked I became more and more fascinated by the events he described, the background and the context of the story. For already in my mind it was a story. He showed me his manuscript, which documented the dangers they had faced: the hardship, and the sheer bone-crushing weariness of attempting to rescue so many desperate people. This became the basis for *Ark*.

I read the ship's log, which was full of amazing testimonials. They ranged from refugees simply grateful for being alive, to nurses, politicians, diplomats and media people. All had sailed on the vessel through those momentous months. It was quite incredible.

It began for Nic and Annabel when they were approached in June 1982 by a group of French journalists seeking passage into Lebanon. The airport in Beirut was surrounded by the Israeli Army and had closed down. Nic agreed – he would. As they sailed into Lebanese waters they were stopped and nearly overturned by an Israeli gunboat, and only allowed to proceed to Jounieh because Rhys recognized the voice of the Israeli captain. They had met on the dock at Haifa when the vessel was under repair.

Jounieh was as I describe it: the cattle boat in the harbour was full of miserable and despairing Egyptians; the port was jammed with refugees seeking to escape from between the warring armies that surrounded the small coastal town.

It was at this point that the simple, one-off charter to carry in the television crew changed into something else. No one could ignore the plight of the refugees – least of all Nic and Annabel. And so they tried to get them out.

Many times they were stopped by the gunboats and turned back or escorted around the war zone with sick and frightened people packing *Sea Victory* to the gunnels, until the Israelis could reach a decision.

A woman went into labour on one of the voyages while the ship was wallowing at a standstill in heavy seas and the crew were being interrogated on board an Israeli gunboat. Eventually they were allowed to continue and, as the woman's labour pains increased, *Sea Victory* raced into Larnaca and an ambulance whisked the woman away. Forty minutes later she gave birth to a son.

There were dozens of incidents like that, and many fascinating characters that I have not included in the book. I regret that, but it was impossible to include them all: too many characters in a story, too many names and places to remember and the reader finds it difficult to keep track, loses sympathy. That is why I do not write a totally factual account. I need room to enable my imagination to deal creatively with the story and, in so doing, I believe in some ways I come closer to the essence of the truth than by giving a straight recounting of incident.

However, many of the characters in *Ark* clearly exist: in addition to Nic and Annabel, there was Rhys and the crew. The American doctor *did* journey to the Lebanon, as did the Palestinian freelance photographer. She did die in Beirut.

Samra Asaker is firmly based on a true incident, as were the Lebanese brother and sister. The dead soldiers resting on the graves of the British war cemetery, the twenty-five million dollars in gold bullion was in fact twenty-seven *tons* of gold. Worth, in 1982, more than 327 million dollars, yet it was only secured by a padlock . . . I could go on. But what matters is not pinning down how much is fiction and how much is fact, but whether I have managed to capture the whole spirit of the enterprise – how *Sea Victory*, in the course of 102 dangerous and exhausting voyages between Jounieh and Larnaca, evacuated 5,000 people from a bloody maelstrom, through a gunboat blockade that was broken time and time again.

Forty years on from its first encounter with danger during the Second World War, *Sea Victory* and her crew had their greatest triumph. That is worth recording.

Not Noah's, perhaps, but truly, an Ark.

JC
London
November 1984

LIST OF PASSENGERS

These are some of the diplomatic and media passengers who travelled on *Sea Victory* between June and September 1982:

9 June: Alain Louyot, *Le Point*
            Jean-Louis Marzoratti, *France-Soir*
            Daniel Cattellain, TV AZ
            Paul Chrzanowski, NBC News, Paris
            Jacques Robert, NBC News, Paris
            Laurent Maus, *Gamma*
            Oliver Mazelolle, RT Luxembourg
            Philip Ledru, Agence Sygma
            Georges Menager, *Paris Match*
17 June: M. Tierney, ABC Television
            John McKenzie, ABC News
            Don McCullin, *Sunday Times*, London
            Enrique X. Badello, Venezuelan Ambassador
18 June: William Irvine, US Embassy, Beirut
            Australian Commission
19 June: Stephen Hanrihan, *Toronto Star*
24 June: Andrew M. Haughton, Producer, '60 Minutes', 9
            Network, Australia
            Jane Weudt, 9 Network
            Michael Breen, 9 Network
            Peter Davies, 9 Network
10 July: Michael Rodin, Asst Canadian Military Attaché,
            Beirut
14 July: Valerie Ward, British Council, Beirut

17 July:	Bill Rigily, US Embassy, Athens
19 July:	James Jennings, Human Rights Campaign, Chicago
27 July:	Leonard Rodgers, Middle East Director, World Vision Int.
	Dave Gorton, British Embassy, Beirut
	Colin Crorkin, British Embassy, Beirut
28 July:	Graham Leach, BBC Middle East correspondent
	Jacques Hasday, Agence France Presse
29 July:	M. Turner, British Embassy, Beirut
	Peter Cornell, British Embassy, Beirut
	Peter Mayne, BBC Television News
1 August:	Edgar Wright, Major, US Army, US Embassy, Beirut
4 August:	John Thone, BBC Television News
5 August:	A. James, US Embassy, Beirut
	Dennis E. Palser, US Embassy, Beirut
11 August:	Terry Anderson, Associated Press
22 August:	R. U. Benson, *Daily Express*, London
	John Downing, *Daily Express* photographer, London
23 August:	Fritz van Vaag, Chairman RTS (Relief Transport Services), Red Cross
24 August:	Bob Basler, Reuters, New York
	Bob Pearson, Washington DC
26 August:	Dorothy Peck, US Embassy, Beirut
27 August:	Rod Coats, ABC Television cameraman, Australia
	Jack Cochrane, ABC Television News
	Gus Schuettler, Stars & Stripes, 61036, Riesheim, West Germany
28 August:	Malcolm H. Kerr, President, American University of Beirut
	Mike Dunk, ABC News
31 August:	Robert Walsh, Catholic Relief Services
5 September:	Nicholas Follows, CBS News
	Sean Robbit, CBS News
	Judah Passow, Network Photographers, USA

SHIP'S LOG, *SEA VICTORY*

The following are testimonials taken from the ship's log between June and September 1982:

9 June 1982: The gates of Lebanon were closed to us. Thanks for allowing us to go through the window. The Israeli gunboat was three times as fast, but three times as dangerous, and three times less pleasant.

> Alain Louyot, *Le Point*,
> Jean-Louis Marzoratti, *France-Soir*,
> Daniel Cattellain, TV AZ,
> Paul Chrzanowski, NBC News, Paris,
> Jacques Robert, NBC News, Paris,
> Laurent Maus, *Gamma*,
> Oliver Mazelolle, RT Luxembourg,
> Philip Ledru, Agence Sygma,
> Georges Menager, *Paris Match*

15 June 1982: A day to remember! Two triumphs. Escape from Lebanon, and freedom for the Falklands . . . If I had to be a refugee I couldn't have found a better refuge.

> Kay Orton, author

17 June 1982: Thank you for your *kindness*. I hope to see you on the return trip. I wish you well.

> Don McCullin, *Sunday Times*

18 June 1982: On behalf of myself and the US Government. Thank you for the fine assistance rendered by yourself and your truly dedicated crew.

> Bill Irvine, American Embassy, Beirut

18 June 1982: This is to record a sincere tribute to a dedicated owner, captain and crew, for a great service to people from many countries during a memorable journey marked by skill, cheerfulness and great help to all, from the babies to the grandparents. *Sea Victory* is living up to its name.

From Australia on cruise, thanks and best wishes.

Australian Commission for Community Relations

22 June 1982: Should admit this is a life-saver boat, let alone the comfort and good treatment we received which we were hungry for. Will never forget this trip as long as I live.

Thanks for all the nice crew and a big and million thanks to Annabel who has made this trip possible for me and my four children from the start.

Wadad El Mujtahed

7 July 1982: The next time there's a war I'll be waiting for you to take me back to sanity.

Many thanks,

Bob Adrian

7 July 1982: Thanks very much for returning me to civilization.

Eric Brom, British Embassy, Beirut

13 July 1982: What can I say, what can I write? All I can say thank God for meeting you. When we arrive to the boat I wasn't expecting to see lovely faces smiling for us, because as you know the sea is very difficult, to be respected. But because of you all we had to be calm and happy. This trip was the first one of my life and it was the best one, because I had to believe that friends are everything in life and better than money, they help when needed. They smile if you are happy, and they cry when you are sad. So many thanks to you and to God for the chance to meet you in the hardest point in the world, but you make it so easy in the end. I can say I like you.

Samin Wansa, Jedda Moda Hospital, Saudi Arabia

26/27 July 1982: Thank you for all those you have helped since 13 June who needed to leave Lebanon. Hundreds of people will remember *Sea Victory*, including us!

Leonard Rodgers, Mid-East Director, World Vision International

28 July 1982: Congratulations to the Heads and all the members of the crew of *Sea Victory* for keeping their heads while all around were losing theirs. A swift and noble exit from Jounieh harbour while under shellfire – carried out in the best Dunkirk spirit. A fine piece of British seamanship! Best wishes for an adventurous, but not too adventurous, future.

Graham Leach, BBC Middle East Correspondent

29 July 1982: What would the BBC do without *Sea Victory* and her crew? Looking forward to seeing you on the way back to Cyprus!

Peter Mayne, BBC Television News

1 or 2 August 1982: With many thanks for a fine trip from besieged Lebanon to Cyprus – Look forward to another under more peaceful circumstances.

Edgar Wright, Major, US Army, US Embassy, Beirut, Lebanon

4 August 1982: Many thanks for a safe 'escape' . . .

John Thone, BBC Television News

10 August 1982: Who can say 'tomorrow I shall . . .'? Nobody knows, or is allowed to be sure about the future. Hard work waits for us in Beirut. Hard hours, sad stories and maybe friends lost . . . But I'm sure of one thing. These last hours spent on *Sea Victory* are like a sweet kiss given by our lovely Captain Annabel.

From Jaire (French nurse of Médecins Sans Frontières)

11 August 1982: . . . Thanks for a peaceful trip. Just what I needed.

Terry Anderson, Associated Press

22 August 1982: Thank you for taking us from hell to heaven! . . .

Ross Benson, *Daily Express*, London

334

24 August 1982: I would've settled for anything to get me from Cyprus to Lebanon. Thanks for your gracious hospitality.

Bob Balser, Reuters, New York

28 August 1982: Many thanks for a delightful trip, which I hope to have the chance to repeat!

Malcolm H. Kerr, President, American University of Beirut*

*Malcolm H. Kerr was murdered in his university on 17 January 1984.